alien politics

alien politics

marxist state
theory retrieved

paul thomas

routledge
new york   london

Published in 1994 by

Routledge
29 West 35 Street
New York, NY 10001

Published in Great Britain by

Routledge
11 New Fetter Lane
London EC4P 4EE

Library of Congress Cataloging-in-Publication Data

Thomas, Paul, 1943–
    Alien politics : Marxist state theory retrieved / by Paul Thomas
      p. cm.
    Includes bibliographical references and index.
    ISBN 0-415-90869-8 (HB)—ISBN 0-415-90870-1 (PB)
    1. Marx, Karl, 1818–1883—Contributions in political science.
  I. Title.
JC233.M299T56 1994
320.5'315—dc20   93-41446
                                                          CIP

British Library Cataloguing-in-Publication Data also available.

This book is dedicated
to the memory of my parents,
Roy and Mona Thomas

CONTENTS

CONTENTS

PREFACE

Since the late 1960s, fierce but often turgid debates have raged among scholars about Marxist state theory. Participants in these debates were in some respects bitterly opposed. Yet they tended, by and large, to agree on one basic assumption: that the state, or the state as Marx thought of it, is class-determined or shaped by the play of class forces outside its boundaries. Disagreements duly proceeded about what this ruling class theory means. (It might mean, for instance, that the state is the instrument of the capitalist class, or that it is an agency structurally tied to ruling class interests or imperatives.) But the theory itself was, in the main, accepted—accepted, in my view, rather too readily and uncritically.

But what did its acceptance involve? It involved, in practice, the often impatient conflation or running-together of understandings of the state that are, in principle, separable: that of the state as being class-determined, and that of the state as an object, an instrument, a "finished thing" that is capable of being "seized" and turned to good account once it is seized by the right hands. Theorists—among them Marx himself, for a while, as well as Lenin—can be seen to have given vent to such impatience under the impress of revolutionary urgency.

But by now, such impatience can be seen to have invited dangerous illusions about what can be accomplished by seizing the state. Seizure of the state can be seen, for that matter, as a dangerous illusion in its own right. These illusions were played out to the bitter end in the erstwhile Soviet Union, and have done an enormous amount of damage elsewhere.

In what follows I hope to show that Marx, for his part, was not—or not always—prey to these damaging illusions. But my argument only begins as a Marxological one. It attempts to retrieve from the arguments of some later Marxist theorists (Gramsci, Poulantzas) as well as from Marx himself a theory of the state which is distinguishable from familiar and discredited ruling class theories. "Alien politics", as I term this alternative theory, is not just different from, and irreducible to, ruling class theory. It is also, if I am right, a much more viable and substantive theory of the state.

What, then, are its claims? Why *alien* politics? and why alien *politics*? Alienation in Marxist theory involves, first and foremost, loss, remoteness and enmity, and these need to be outlined in turn. Loss and remoteness refer us to the the distancing of common political concerns, their removal from the pattern of our individual lives, our day-to-day intimate reality. Their register is thus that of the separation of "public" from "private" spheres of existence in modern society. But their separation is to be regarded as inimical to the quality of our lives and not as a desideratum. Our public spheres are often regarded as "democratic". But "alien politics" invites us to view them as distant—as dialectical correlates of the *denial* of democracy in civil society, where our lives are most immediately led.

This enables us to gain sone purchase on the second part of our question: why alien *politics*? Because common action and democratic potential find no place in civil society, these are alienated and represented away from its orbit. Common action and collective concern, which in civil society are subsumed beneath self-assertion and the play of competing self-interests, are fused and concentrated at the level of the state, which arrogates them to itself. The state's claim to monopolize the concerns it terms "political" unduly restricts and formalizes them. But it should not be challenged along the lines that are now becoming common. It is often said these days that virtually everything in our lives—right down to our family relationships and our private desires—has suddenly become "political." There is something either complacent or desperate about such a belief. Voluntary common action needs to be reinstated within the civil society from which it has forcibly been excluded, and not assumed to somehow have remained there all along, in spite of its exclusion. Alien politics invites us, in other words, to take seriously Marx's distinction between "political" and "human" emancipation. The latter involves futurity, tasks, projects. It invites us to think of the communal and ethical shortcomings of civil society as things that need to be overcome, and not taken for granted or uncritically celebrated for the sake of their fissiparious "diversity."

All this is to say that alien politics involves, first and foremost, a genetic understanding of the state as it emerged historically alongside its no less modern counterpart, civil society. Neither term in the state-civil society polarity should be regarded as natural or "given." Nor indeed should the historically specific relationship between the two, which under early modern conditions took an altogether original, unprecedented and highly artificial turn. Marx in his better moments was sensitive to what this fundamental shift comported. It meant not the reduction of the state to civil society, but its counterposition to civil society. The distinction between state and civil society is a dualism that demands to be investigated dialectically—a distinction, that is to say, in which each term is dependent upon, autonomous from and in contradiction with the other. Because civil society is a discontinuous realm of private self-seeking in which agreement about the fundamentals of a shared, collective life cannot emerge, the state arrogates to itself all aspects of collective life that involve conscious, common deliberation and decision. The state comes to be seen, by Hegel and others, as the *ultima ratio* of politics. It seeks to monopolize politics. The state has been claiming the title of political monopolist from the moment of its emergence in early modernity right down to the present day. Such a claim, which today is a contested claim, could be advanced in the first place only in relation to the communal and ethical shortcomings of civil society, seen as the state's "other" or counterpart.

This point is more important than might initially be apparent. That the state's claim to monopolize the political is illegitimate is not in dispute here. But it matters greatly how we are to assess its illegitimacy. To say that everything in civil society or private life is promiscuously "political," as many people do today, is to ignore or overlook what is at stake in the separation of the state from civil society: the alienation of common or political concerns *away* from those of everyday life. This is the very leitmotif of alien politics. The alienated economic system of civil society is characterized, indeed defined, by its exclusion of common action and democratic potential. These are projected or represented outwards and upwards on to the level of the modern state. The state is an abstraction from civil society. The thoroughgoing denial of democracy in civil society, where the chief activities of daily life most immediately take place, is the ongoing, institutionalized counterpart to the concentration, distillation and fusion of all features of common action and collective concern within the state.

That the state is the dialectical correlate of the denial of democracy in civil society means that state and civil society do not relate in a zero-sum way. The state is *not* a function, instrument or "dependent variable" of civil society or of anything in civil society, whatever proponents of ruling-class theories of the state may think. Analysis of the state cannot be reduced to analysis of the economic and social. An important point about the counterposition of state to civil society was made by Anthony Giddens[1] but almost always passed over by other participants in debates about Marxist state theory. Capitalism separates control over persons (authority, the political) from control over allocative resources (productive forces, the economy). In this way, what is to count as "the political" is redefined and unduly narrowed. The political and the economic come to occupy different registers, neither of them reducible to the other. This means that there is no reason, *prima facie*, for the dominant economic class directly to exercise political power, which has been defined and restricted in such a way that it cannot encroach upon their control over society's allocative resources, a control which is the source of their wealth and of the state's revenues alike. This is not to advance the absurd claim that capitalists never exercise political power. Sometimes they do so and sometimes they do not. It is simply to say that they will be in control of social wealth (and state revenues) whether or not they occupy positions in the state. To put the same point another way, who wields political power and what form this power assumes can be matters of indifference to the capitalist class provided that the state does not "interfere" with its control of allocative resources in civil society.

Failure to countenance or think through this basic point has vitiated much Marxist state theory, and has generated enormous confusion. Much of this confusion can be cut through if we acknowledge that the counterposition of the state to civil society is categorical as well as dialectical. It refers to the existence of the modern state in the first instance. Its counterposition to civil society is there, in other words, in principle, regardless of the form the state takes, regardless of the ideologies and values of those who hold power in the state, and regardless of the extent of this power, or of the state's "reach" into civil society—provided only that this does not wrest away from the capitalist class its control over society's productive forces and labor power. And this is something the state almost never does.

This is to say that alien politics is above all else an expansive concept. It gives us a better explanation of the emergence of the modern state than ruling class theory ever saw fit to provide; and unlike ruling class theory, which today is out of its element, it still applies. Alien politics is no respecter of state forms, or of revolutions. It has a premonitory status that enables it to account for the failures of authoritarian communism. Alien politics can today serve as the basis of a critique both of capitalist states and their drawbacks *and* of those authoritarian state forms that happen to have grown up in the (misapplied) name of Marx. Now that the Berlin Wall is no longer there to obstruct our vision, we can see alien politics take on an overarching significance for our understanding of the modern state in all its various manifestations, communist as well as capitalist. More specifically, alien politics helps explain what ruling class theory would have great difficulty explaining—why, for instance, a boundlessly accomodating capitalism was reintroduced in such short order into the Soviet Union with Lenin's New Economic Policy (NEP), and why capitalism, as I write, is being almost vengefully reintroduced into China.

It should by now be evident that in mentioning his NEP we have not done with Lenin. Alien politics flies in the face of a Leninist interpretation of the state. But Leninism involves a fateful misinterpretation and misapplication of the Marxist theory of the state in two senses. First, Lenin's theory of the state superimposes some ideas from, or about, Marx's *Civil War in France* upon what Marx had written about the state for a *very* brief period in his career, that stretching from 1846 to 1850. The concentration of Marx's most rigid, dogmatic utterances about the state within the period of urgency surrounding the 1848 revolutionary wave is no coincidence, and Lenin's uncritical appropriation of these same utterances, under the impress of another period of revolutionary urgency and impatience, is no coincidence either. The immediate prospect of seizing state power evidently does not concentrate the mind wonderfully. Theoretical tasks seem to evaporate, recede and fade to black. As in a Lukácsian nightmare, the state automatically *becomes* a ruling class instrument that can be seized once its seizure looks imminent, and the proletariat no less automatically *becomes* a fully class-conscious agency capable by definition of doing the seizing. This at root is why Marx's writings of the 1846–50 period contain not just his most dogmatic utterances about the state, but also, as it were in the same breath, his most dogmatic utterances about class in general and the proletariat in particular. In short order, Marx in the *Eighteenth Brumaire* was to prove notably more flexible about state and class alike. But by then the damage was done. Marx, so to say, had provided Lenin with all the materials he might require with which to set the ruling class theory of the state in textual stone, and to transform it into dogma.

The second sense in which Lenin misappropriated Marx's theory of the state was no less fateful but, in the upshot, rather more ironical. Since there is no real theory of the transition to socialism in Marx's writings, Lenin used Marx's most dogmatic utterances to do the work of a theory of transition. The irony is that Lenin's arch enemy, the "renegade" Kautsky, was also guilty of using a (different) theory of the state to do the work of a (different) theory of transition. In this respect, at least, Lenin and Kautsky, the bitterest of foes, have rather more in common than either would have been comfortable believing. Nor do the ironies end here. Readers may be surprised to find me dealing with Kautsky, who in many respects is the theoretical dinosaur of legend, alongside Gramsci and Poulantzas. Yet Kautsky is vital to the argument of the latter part of his book. In it I argue that Eurocommunism came to grief, in large measure, because its theoreticians (who never admitted what they were doing) were bent upon implementing Kautsky's reformist program, which was regarded (wrongly) as a theory of transition. Eurocommunist theoreticians' pious invocations of Gramsci, to whom lip service was duly paid, hid their lack of attention to his ideas, which were about alien politics. Their refusal to invoke Kautsky, who was hardly ever mentioned by name, masked and concealed what was the programmatic application of his ideas, which do not begin to countenance alien politics.

It is arguable that had Eurocommunist stalwarts not marginalized the Gramsci they so busily flaunted, had they not shunted Poulantzas off to the margins of "left-Eurocommunism," Eurocommunism might have become something very different from the dead letter it did become. But to say that opportunities were missed for want of theoretical understanding is to say that alien politics *matters*. Gramsci and (the later) Poulantzas are the most astute and creative theorists of alien politics after Marx himself. They draw from Marx a theory of transition that is much more radical, much more thoroughgoing than a Leninist seizure of state power or a Kautskian parliamentary road to socialism. This theory helps us understand and contextualize Marx's principled opposition to putschism and revolutionary conspiratorialism, as well as his belief that only when "social force is no longer separated from [people] as political power" will "human emancipation" be complete.[2] Beyond this, Gramsci and Poulantzas as theorists of alien politics were aware, as Lenin and Kautsky were blithely unaware, that alienation cannot be overcome within the sphere of alienation. Alienation, in other words, cannot be overcome by one of its own terms, the state. "The political rule of the producer cannot co-exist with the perpetuation of his social slavery."[3] Revolutionary transition implies not just changes at the helm, at the level of the state. It implies root-and-branch transformation of the state *and* civil society alike, from top to bottom. Alienation can be solved, and transition effected, only if voluntary common action is reinstated and autonomous self-rule devolved within the social and economic realm from which alien politics—communist as well as capitalist—has forcibly excluded them. Only in this way can the re-alienation of alien politics be foreclosed once and for all—and for the very first time.

The historical record indicates the dangers of formulating or acting on a theory of transition that does not take alien politics into account. What needs to be remembered in assessing these dangers is that authoritarianism in its modern variants is alien politics run riot, as Marx's *Eighteenth Brumaire* presciently pointed out. This leads into a final prefatory point of some moment, and it is an ominous one indeed. It is striking, though little remarked, that Marx, Gramsci and Poulantzas, the three pre-eminent theorists of alien politics, all refined their understandings of the state in response to the onset of authoritarian regimes: Marx in response to the French Second Empire as well as to the Prussia of Frederick William IV; Gramsci in response to Italian fascism; and Poulantzas in response to the Greek colonels. Authoritarian regimes—which Marx and Gramsci, at least, were much more likely to encounter at first hand than democratic ones—have always played an important role in the recovery of democracy within the Marxist tradition. (An example that is barely touched on in this book, but which is consonant with its argument, is Rosa Luxemburg's reaction to Leninist authoritarianism.) To acknowledge this point is to underscore an important part of the argument this book proffers: that we need alien politics if we are to think seriously not just about capitalism and the state (which exist) but about socialism and democracy (which are unfinished business) too.

ACKNOWLEDGMENTS

This book germinated in my mind for some years, long enough for me to have accumulated a compendious list of intellectual debts. Most of these are in no way institutional. Even so, I must thank the American Council of Learned Societies, which generously awarded me a mini-grant just when I most needed it; the Committee on Research of the University of California, Berkeley, whose support was almost continuous; and my home department, the Political Science Department at Berkeley, which, particularly under the judicious chairmanship of David Collier, was unstinting.

On a more personal level, my heartfelt thanks to those friends and colleagues who read an earlier draft of the entire manuscript and whose comments helped me enormously in its revision: Hanna Pitkin, Michael Rogin, Martin Jay, Michael Th. Greven, Bertell Ollman and John Seery. It is my further pleasure to thank those friends and colleagues who planted ideas in my mind in the course of conversations without always realizing they had done so. Andrew Feenberg revealed to me some of the stakes of my own argument. Terrell Carver has constantly stimulated my thinking about Marx and Engels, and Michael Mosher about Hegel. I'd like to thank Gregg Kvistaad for getting me to think about the *Berufsverbot*, and Jonas Pontusson for getting me to think about Gramsci, Kautsky and Eurocommunism. Michael Rogin and Jerrold Siegel helped me think about Marx's *Eighteenth Brumaire*, and Neil Harding helped me (and so many others) think about Lenin. My thanks also to Cecelia Cancellaro at Routledge, Richard Ashcraft, Norman Jacobson, David Lloyd, Harold Mah, Eugene Maleska, Bhikhu Parekh, Carol Stack, Shannon Stimson, Jeremy Waldron, and to the unnamed readers to whom Cecelia Cancellaro and Naomi Schneider sent the manuscript in one of its earlier incarnations. I fear my subsequent revisions will not satisfy all those who read this earlier version. I want very much to thank them all the same.

In listing friends and colleagues who have helped me, often without knowing they were doing so, and who might be surprised to see their names listed here in view of past disagreements, I must insist on claiming sole responsibility for any drawbacks, omissions, flaws, solecisms or just plain mistakes in what follows. I am painfully aware that one of my greatest debts is to my most inspired teacher and toughest critic, who will, sadly, never read a book she did so much (directly and indirectly) to inspire and provoke. News reached me as I was working on this book of the sudden death, at far too early an age, of Judith N. ("Dita") Shklar. I owe her more than I shall ever be able to repay. This book is dedicated to the memory of my parents. If readers can also regard it as a tribute to Dita, a great spirit, this would be reward enough.

Paul Thomas
Berkeley, August 1993

INTRODUCTION:
WHAT PRICE THE STATE?

All of a sudden we seem to be living in a world, or at least an intellectual microclimate, in which everything without exception is being called "political"—the family is political, the personal is political, our economic transactions are political, our private desires are political, our very knowledge is political. Discussions about the "politics" of identity, gender and knowledge are going on all around us. Power itself, that indispensable offshoot of politics, seems now to have become hidden, disguised, internalized, diffused and dispersed through every nook and cranny of our lives. Power and politics appear to have less and less to do with institutions like the state, where they once were thought to reside, and more and more to do with their microfoundations within our day-to-day intimate reality.

In some ways this comparatively recent shift in thinking is salutary. It reminds us, at the very least, that "the political" and "the state" are not coterminous categories, and that state theory, my concern here, is not about to address, let alone solve, every question we may have about politics or power. The state is an aspect of our political lives. Sometimes it is the most important aspect of our political lives. But it has not always been so in the past (vain attempts to trace a conflict between "church" and "state" in the European Middle Ages notwithstanding) and it may not continue to be central in an uncertain future.

But has the supposed ubiquity of politics and power taken its place? Here I propose to sound a discordant note, in view of the danger that terms like "power" and "the political" will get stretched to the point of losing meaning. Can we not say that the state is political in a sense different from other institutions, practices and conceptualizations which have political effects? More pointedly, Hegel in 1820 distinguished family, civil society and the state as different, if complementary terms, signifying and characterizing different, if complementary aspects of our existence. Hegel's point was not that the family and civil society are spheres that have no political relevance or effects. It was that they are not themselves political in the sense that the state may be said to be political. If it makes sense today to speak of the state, along with some aspects of society, as being potentially subject to democratization (and I find myself in general agreement with Jean Cohen and Andrew Arato's argument in *Civil Society and Political Theory*[1] that these are or ought to be), it is not obvious that we can speak of all social institutions (the family, the stock exchange, the prison system) as being potentially subject to democratization in the same way.

This does not mean, however, that the state is the sole focus for democratization, or that democratization should be regarded as a fait accompli rather than what it is, unfinished business. The question that ought to be addressed in discussions of democratization or of the supposed ubiquity of the political is why politics and the state, which are not the same thing, were pushed so artificially close together in the first place. It may be possible today to identify a pattern of retreat within which spheres of everyday life, areas of meaningful existence or even sites of resistance themselves take on "political" dimensions. But if we do so we should specify what they are retreating from, what they are bent upon resisting. They are in considerable measure reacting to the state, which has illegitimately arrogated to itself the wherewithal to monopolize "the political." To investigate this issue thoroughly would take the present discussion too far afield. But my subject, Marxist state theory, has some bearing on it, for it was Marx, battling with the ghost of Hegel, who first indicated that capitalism changed the coordinates of state–society relationships in a decisive and fundamental way, and in the process of doing so, made of the state a new kind of reality, one that was able to present itself as being the singular focus of the political.

There has been a tendency in recent Marxist state theory to delineate and discuss at considerable length the concept of "the capitalist state." It might seem tempting at such a juncture to take "the state" at its own word, and see it as a, or *the* political institution, and capitalism as an economic system. On these grounds one could simply deny that a state's action on behalf of capitalism or capitalists makes it a capitalist state. But such a dismissal would be idle and peremptory. If we bear in mind the evident dangers involved in speaking blithely about "the" capitalist state, which is an abstraction, as opposed to those capitalist states that exist, there is no reason not to employ the concept, hybrid though it may be. For one thing, there is no sense in denying that states promote capitalism. Most states do so, particularly now. But different states promote capitalism in different ways and to different extents; and there are many different kinds, modes, and stages of capitalism that different states are bent upon promoting. But the promotion of capitalism is an insufficient criterion anyway. As I write, the People's Republic of China is vigorously promoting capitalism, but it would be absurd to call it a capitalist state for this or any other reason. What other features can be advanced, then, to justify my use of the category of the capitalist state? Many of them are historical as well as conceptual. Anthony Giddens has indicated "how closely connected the ascendency to power of the bourgeoisie was with the transformation of the absolutist state into the nation-state," and that, in keeping with this historical proximity, "the nation state and capitalism have close structural connections."[2] To fixate one's attention upon capitalism as a system of social and economic relations, as the universalization of exchange of labor and commodities, as Marxists often do, is to forget the historical fact that the emerging bourgeois class could further its economic ends in the first place only by grasping the reins of power of already-constituted state institutions within an already-constituted system of states. Bourgeois revolutions both expressed and furthered radical alterations in the nature of these state institutions. In so doing they consolidated the conditions for the emergence and expansion of capitalism. On the one hand, bourgeois revolutions were never international; on the other, the nation-state was never a mere epiphenomenon of capitalism, even though some Marxists thought of it as little else. Marx, I shall argue, was not—or not always—one of them.

But this is to anticipate. What needs indicating at the present juncture is that to be concerned with state theory is to be concerned in one way or another with the specificity of the political. All the same, it may be that the specificity, not perhaps of the political, but of the state, is being struck at these days by institutional rather than intellectual developments. The system of states appears to be undergoing major shifts, with the internationalization of capital and the spread of capitalist values into places that would have been considered highly unlikely just a few years ago. At the same time, kaleidoscopic, nationalist upsurges in the former Soviet Union and Central and Eastern Europe should at the very least remind us that we can no longer afford to take for granted the coincidence of "state" and "nation" in the once-convenient, late-nineteenth-century composite of the "nation-state," and that people these days are often likely to focus not on the state but on the nation as their primary, terrifyingly incommunicable mode of political identity. To assert the principle of national self-determination and the inviolability of established state boundaries is to risk, or even to provoke, Bosnian horrors. Further afield, and further back, the superimposition of state systems—which often did not work—on to Middle Eastern societies by colonialist powers has had the ultimate effect of stimulating religiously-inspired, fundamentalist reactions against failed, Western-instigated attempts at modernization. But we are faced today not just with nationalist or fundamentalist challenges to the state from below. At another level, states themselves are commonly engaged in redefining, if not themselves, then certainly their relations with other states: economic alliances, free trade zones, trade blocs and economic "communities" form much of our political vocabulary these days (even if what is called international or multinational organization is in fact multi-state).

In a world where concern with the "military-industrial complex" is giving way to concern about an economic recession either caused or influenced by this complex's demise, in a world where multinational corporations, private centers of power, can manipulate public centers of power like the state, and where the World Bank and the International Monetary Fund can dictate state policies that affect millions of lives, it is hard not to think that the line between the economic and the political is now being blurred, or redrawn. It is not too hard to picture a kind of pincer movement, with the state in between the pincers, squeezed from above by multinational developments, and from below by the fragmented "politics" of fundamentalism, ethnicity, national-ism, particularism and identity. It may even be true that "the gap between the level of state efficacy and world systematicity . . . helps to explain the extension of internal discipline in late modern states."[3]

Yet the extension of discipline in such states often proceeds at the behest of these states themselves. Looked at from another angle, that is, the pincer movement has in no obvious sense lessened the repressive and ideological functions of the state, or the extent of its reach into civil society. (Reaganism and Thatcherism, for instance, tightened state control while claiming to loosen it, as we shall see later in this book.) The centrality once routinely awarded to states as the repositor-ies of sovereignty and as foci for political obligation may be eroding, but states considered as repositories of power seem stubbornly to persist. To discuss surveillance without privileging the state as an agent of surveillance makes no sense at all. The conditions that made of the state a specifically modern phenomenon—including, if Andrew Feenberg is right, the principles of top-down surveillance and control from above that the bureaucratic state and the technostructure have shared throughout the capitalist era[4]—have not yet disappeared. Mod-ern techniques of surveillance may well be bringing the bureaucratic state and the technostructure closer together than ever before. We should remember throughout what follows that Marxism in its broad-est signification grew up in response to these developments, and was the first political movement and doctrine to do so.

States exist and operate in relation to capitalism and to capitalist civil society, however this term is defined or redefined. Hegel under-stood by "civil society" a realm that is institutionally separate from the state but not identified exclusively with the economy, or the "system of

5

Civil Society def.

needs" that it encompasses. Civil society's institutions form a kind of network or trellis of autonomous, self-organizing associations that order the economy into a degree of coherence. Its values are not those of the state, but need to be complemented by the more political and more integrative values enshrined by the state, values with which civil society must finally concur. State and civil society are countervailing powers or spheres. Neither can exist or operate without the existence and operation of the other. Jointly, they occupy a double register.

This book argues that the Hegel-Marx confrontation, which was about the relationship of civil society and the state, a confrontation which took place in the aftermath of the French Revolution, and as the Industrial Revolution was getting under way, helped set the terms of modern political discourse, terms with which we are not yet done. These terms—democracy, citizenship, labor, poverty, wealth—existed at the time of the Marx-Hegel confrontation in a tense, uneasy relationship, and still do. But it is a relationship, not a juxtaposition. To listen to colleagues in countries of the former Soviet Union, countries where the creation of the kind of civil society with which Hegel had some familiarity in 1820 is an urgent task and a live issue, is to be reminded of the interrelationship of these terms all over again. It is clear to some of our colleagues in the former Soviet Union that the "shock therapy" provided by hypercapitalism and the sudden irruption of "the market" is not about to sweep everything before it and provide magically for everything that is needed for social reproduction. The market is not about to produce civil society all on its own; to suppose otherwise is to resort to economic determinism redux. Twentieth-century welfare states, indeed, have existed for this very reason (however eroded they may have become by Reaganism and Thatcherism). People need and expect their states not just to bestow upon them civil and political rights that until recently were denied them. States are also there to take care of their citizens' social needs, their claims to entitlement and protection, which need not be a concern of the market. Hegel, who provoked Marx's ire by denying this last point, was nevertheless aware of the danger that civil society will deteriorate and implode if the private gain that animates it becomes uncoupled from public-spiritedness. There is a real danger of this in Russia, where

Hegel view of civil society?

only the state can punish crime and deprivatize the bureaucracy—
which are not mutually exclusive tasks at present.

Hegel, Marx's original interlocutor, might not have been too
surprised had he been able to witness recent developments closer to
home, in his native Germany—how rapidly the facile optimism with
which former West annexed former East Germany gave way to a
realization that, as Hegel had recognized, language and ethnic heritage
do not automatically unite a people. Assimilation of a completely
different political and social structure that had lasted longer than the
Third Reich or Weimar, is not going to happen automatically—not,
that is, without initiatives proceeding from the state.

The Hegelian confrontation of state and society, far from being
outdated or out of its element in such recent cases, still has much to
teach us about what to expect in Central and Eastern Europe. The
fewer the active vestiges of civil society in a particular country, the
harder reform, be it political, economic or both, will prove. This is
one of the reasons why, even if we are approaching the end of the era
of states, as some think, it ill behooves us not to understand how and
why it came into being in the first place, and how it managed to
maintain itself for as long as it has. It is my contention that the Hegel-
Marx confrontation on the state and civil society has proved and is
still proving itself paradigmatic.

David Easton observed in 1968 that "political science could emerge
as a discipline separate from the other social sciences because of the
impetus Marx had given to the idea of the difference between state
and civil society, an idea virtually unheard of before his time."[5] This
grants too much to Marx. It was Hegel's philosophical composition
of the state that was responsible for challenging the form and tonality
of all theoretical writing about the state, before or since. Easton's
observation in any case sits ill with another observation in the same
1968 encyclopaedia that "(i)t is impossible to offer a unified definition
of the state that would be satisfactory even to the majority of those
seriously concerned with the problem."[6] Much, presumably, hangs
on the the words "unified definition," since the lack of one is indeed
a problem—not least for Marx, as we shall see. Be this as it may, John
A. Hall, writing twenty-five years later, observes confidently enough

that the state, which requires a composite definition, can readily enough be given one. It is, first, a set of political institutions manned by its own, bureaucratic personnel. These institutions include institutions monopolizing the legitimate use of violence and coercion. These institutions are, second, in the center of a geographically bounded territory, a society or a country. The state looks inward to its own society, it swims within its own capitalist society, but is also a state alongside other states, which looks outward to other states, among which it must perforce operate. Its behavior in one arena may be explicable only with reference to the other. States are not unitary entities, sufficient unto themselves, but are defined, and define themselves relationally, within a matrix of other states. The state, third, monopolizes rule-making within its own territorial boundaries—not just coercive rules, but also the kind of norms and values that help create a common political culture among its citizenry. States, that is, seek to legitimate themselves, and this too is part of their definition. Statehood so characterized is, fourth, "often an aspiration rather than an actual achievement."[7]

Hall points to a revival of interest in the state—in its legitimation, its relative autonomy, its hegemony—among Western Marxist theorists as having helped prompt social scientists at large into "bringing the state back in" to their own analyses. Theda Skocpol observed in 1979 that "virtually all Marxists continue simply to assume that state forms and activities vary in correspondance with modes of production, and that state rulers cannot act against the basic interests of a dominant class . . . The result is that still hardly anyone questions this Marxist version of the enduring sociological proclivity to absorb the state into society."[8] Skocpol's observation certainly puts its finger on a basic difficulty, which will be addressed more fully in what follows. For the time being, let it be observed simply that it needs to be tempered not only by subsequent developments in Marxist state theory and in Marxology since 1979, but also by Kenneth Dyson's point that within Marxist state theory there was all along a tension between collapsing the state *within* civil society, as being but one of its aspects, as in ruling-class theory, and counterposing the state *to* civil society.[9] Society-based as opposed to state-based explanation does not in itself distinguish

Marxist state theory from liberal state theories. Both society-based Marxist state theory and liberal state theory run the risk of making the political sphere what it is not: a dependent epiphenomenon of the economic sphere. What does distinguish Marxist state theory is its character as a composite of differently weighted elements. Bertell Ollman usefully observes that the state in Marxist state theories is, variously, an instrument of the capitalist class; an objective structure of political functions that can have economic effects; an arena for class struggle; an illusory community arising out of alienated class relations; and (obscurely, but not meaninglessly) a "hegemonic political ideology."[10] While Ollman's further point is well taken—that each of these characterizations brings out something important about the state, but that any one of them taken singly will distort the nature of the state— he does not take the next, obvious step. This is to deny that these various characterizations (and distortions) were ever equally weighted and to indicate that, historically, it is the first of Ollman's characterizations, ruling-class theory, that has in effect displaced and stood in for all the others—to the detriment of Marxist state theory taken as a whole. Most readers of this book will have encountered the more or less familiar Marxist formulation telling us that the state is only the expression of ruling-class interests or is merely an organ of class domination. It is my contention that, if this were all that Marxist state theory amounted to, it would hardly be worth writing about. It is my further contention that ruling-class theory is not a characterization of Marxist state theory but a surrogate for it. Ruling-class theory, that is to say, has been the part taken for the whole for too long. The fact that it is far and away the best-known aspect of Marxist state theory is part of the problem with which this book tries to deal. Ruling-class theory has had its chance, and has long ruled the roost within Marxist state theory. But it has never worked very well, or explained very much. It fails at the level of significance.

This leads to a procedural point of some importance. A member of the editorial board which accepted this book for publication had relayed to me the suggestion that it be retitled "Saving Marx." Even though this would be the title of a more comprehensive book than this one, I should indicate, by way of putting my cards on the table, that I do indeed wish in some sense to "save" Marx. The question is from what, and for the sake of what. In large measure, Marx needs to be saved from the vagaries of Cold-War scholarship, the scholarship that proceeded from both sides of what was until recently considered the great divide. This tarnished Marx's reputation as a theorist, made his theories seem disreputable, and attempted to make him responsible for practical and theoretical developments in twentieth-century Marxism of which he could have known nothing.[11] Responsibility is of course not a simple issue. There are passages in Marx's writings that could be invoked, and were invoked, with a view to making him appear to sanction in advance moves, theoretical as well as practical, that in reality were made for immediate, political reasons. More specifically within the compass of my concerns here, Marx was capable of dogmatic utterances about the state. These utterances are there in the record, and were to prove mightily convenient to those future theoreticians and political actors who sought either to apply or to discredit them. I hope to show in what follows that these utterances, which almost always involve the idea that the state is, or is nothing but, the instrument of the ruling class, are by no means crucial to what Marx had to say about the state. On the one hand, ruling-class theory cannot be summarily ruled out of court, or assumed to be nonexistent. It must, in other words, be accounted for as well as rejected. The most I would concede, in its proper place, is that if ruling-class theory is to be used at all, it should be used as Nicos Poulantzas (who is discussed later in this book) uses it. If, as Poulantzas believes, the state is a complex, to be looked at relationally, then ruling-class theory is one possible aspect from which interconnections can be traced. This seems to me to be in keeping with Marx's own methodological injunctions in *The German Ideology* ("definite individuals who are productively active in a definite way enter into . . . defininite social and political relations. Empirical observation must in each separate instance bring out empirically . . . the connection of the social and political structure with production").[12] It does not follow from this that, all on its own, ruling-class theory constitutes a viable theory of the state. But to say that Marx had no real theory of the state because of the evident shortcomings of ruling-class theory would be a serious mistake. I propose to argue in what follows that there is in Marx's writings a theory of the state that is viable. It is viable not because of Marx's various dogmatic utterances but despite them. It has to be elicited, drawn out and retrieved from his writings, and not read into them. To say that this broader, more comprehensive theory is flawed by Marx's dogmatic pronunciamentos is to say that one of the people, and if I am right the most important person, from whom I wish to save Marx is Marx himself.

I make no apology for saying this. I do so in an attempt to distance my efforts to retrieve Marx's state theory from other attempts to figure out "what Marx really meant." These attempts are often undertaken in the apparent belief that Marx's texts hold secret meanings accessible only to the cognoscenti, and that if these texts are interpreted in the appropriate manner a pure, unsullied Marx would emerge, sufficent unto the day, whose words alone, suitably interpreted, will throw confusion to the winds once and for all. But there is no longer anything recondite or arcane about Marx's theory of what I am calling "alien politics." It was originally adumbrated in early writings that were slow to present themselves to scholars, but it is there in other writings that were more available too. In examining all these writings in the earlier part of this book I am advancing a Marxological argument. But not all the stakes involved in this argument are Marxological or even Marxist ones. In particular, I am not in search of some pristine, pure essence of Marx that others have unscrupulously muddied and sullied. What I find in his various writings that deal with the state is, to the contrary, complexity, ambivalence and equivocation. In what follows I attempt to delineate some of the ways in which a dogmatically ossified state theory emerged in the history of Marxism. This theory has done much to discredit itself and the Marxism for which it was all too frequently made to stand. But I am not doing this for the sake of exonerating Marx. I am doing it for the sake of retrieving something in his writings that is, or ought to be of interest to anyone, Marxist or non-Marxist, theorist or nontheorist, who is concerned with the state, something about which we all ought to be concerned. When he wrote about the state, Marx was in effect frequently at odds with himself, and it is precisely the gaps, lacunae and ambivalences in his arguments that make them significant. I am not trying to squeeze what Marx's texts say on to some procrustean bed of underlying consistency. I am trying to open out areas of tension within these texts where arguments fail to come together, and isolate nodal points where knots refuse to tie. In Marx's writings, as in others' writings, it is where arguments fail to hang together with perfect consistency that they become most provocative.

Anthony Giddens claims, quite rightly, that "one cannot pretend that Marx's references to the state are always internally consistent. . . . Marx's reasoning on the state [reflects] important elements of the ideas he was arguing against."[13] Putting to one side for the moment the question of Hegel's reflection in Marx's writings, we can say that Marx's ruling-class theory follows liberal state theory rather too closely in regarding the state as a secondary phenomenon which derives its character and drive from the impact of extrinsic social forces upon it. Both Marxian ruling-class theory and liberalism understand the state as being penetrated from without by groups or classes in civil society, in such a way that the state finally becomes reducible to the play of these outside social forces. Ruling-class theory, like liberal theory, collapses the state into civil society. But in so doing, it downplays what Marx also considered a constituent element of capitalist society, where the state is counterposed to civil society. In particular, ruling-class theory begs the question of whether there would have been a capitalist civil society without state action of the kind that encouraged its emergence.

It is clear from *The German Ideology* alone that a great many political preconditions have to obtain if capitalists are to extract surplus value and command labor power. Marx agrees that the basis of the private ownership of productive stock is what J.-B. Say said it was: positive law.[14] Marx was aware that the state was responsible for having assigned the labor market, the labor contract and other forms of exchange their "private" status. The state guaranteed the sanctity of the private realm just as this latter was arraying itself against traditional, premodern property relationships. It was the state that centralized political power and territorial control, undermining the residual effects of feudal remnants in society. If workers had to be legally freed to dispose of their ability to work as they choose, if they had to be forcibly dispossessed of their prior ownership of the means of production, state action was required for each development. This is to say that a state that is capable of freeing labor and of making possible its future expropriation is not just useful to capitalism; it is indispensible to and constitutive of capitalism.

I argue in what follows that Marx, in "settling accounts" with Hegel and the Young-Hegelians in the early 1840s produced a prototypical theory of the state that I call "alien politics." This theory is irreducible to and at odds with the ruling-class theory that was dealt out rather than elaborated for a brief period later in Marx's career. But as a theory of the state, alien politics is more viable than ruling-class theory. My point in trying to demonstrate this is not to revert to the tattered and shopworn debates of yesteryear about a young versus a mature Marx, and certainly not to privilege the former over the latter. What Marx said about the state crosscuts this distinction in an intriguing way. Marx's combat with Hegel, which was a political combat rather than the philosophical combat some have made of it, was deferred, not renounced. Marx never really dropped alien politics for ruling-class theory, as some have supposed. They always jostled about uneasily together in his writings. Nor did he trade in a ruling-class theory of the state for alien politics in later, post-1848 writings, even though it is alien politics, not ruling-class theory, that resurfaces in these later writings. As a result of this theoretical shortfall, economically reductive elements were given an artificial lease of life by Engels, Lenin, Kautsky and others. Soon, these elements came to prevail in, and almost to constitute, Marxist state theory. The "almost" is important here. It was left to later thinkers (Gramsci and Poulantzas) to put the pieces together and begin the task of retrieving alien politics.

What is at stake in recovering or retrieving alien politics from ruling-class theories of the state? In the last analysis the answer to this question is the single word, democratization. But to see how alien politics and ruling-class theory are related to democratization, we must stand back and take a broad view. The relationship between capitalism and democracy has long been a tense, uneasy and problematic one. The claim we sometimes hear advanced today, that liberalization of the economic realm necessarily involves democratization of the political realm (let alone the social realm), seems to me to be quite unproven. It appears to smack of economic determinism, and to be founded on spurious assumptions about the purchase of an abstract, fetishized notion of "freedom" as something capable in its own right of spreading from the economy into the political arena. Capitalism has long had a political theory appropriate to it, which in broad terms grew up alongside it. This theory is not democracy but liberalism.

The advent of the capitalist market economy was complemented by and dependent upon the formation of the liberal state, whose job, in C. B. Macpherson's words, was "to maintain and promote . . . liberal society, which was not necessarily a democratic or an equal society."[15] The bourgeoisie in its heroic period was not fighting for the replacement of one ruling class by another, a notion that is missing from the vocabulary they used at the time. They were fighting for a set of principles—the freeing of the market from feudal and autocratic residues, the rule of law, the career open to talents, and representative government. All these are eminently liberal principles. But only the last-named has any necessary connection with democracy. The nineteenth-century conjuring trick by which democracy, which in its origin had nothing to do with representation, became reconfigured as representative democracy cannot be my concern here, but the fact that representative government, at a pinch, proved not indispensable can and should be. In Prussia the opening of the capitalist market proceeded under reactionary auspices and had the effect of strengthening, not loosening, state autocracy. Even liberalism does not always fit the bill. On a broad view, capitalism, whatever its elective affinities with liberalism may be in principle, in practice appears compatible with all manner of nondemocratic state forms, from Chile to China. Capitalism may well be boundlessly accomodating to widely different forms of the modern state—provided only that the state concerned does what they all do, and preserves the conditions of the labor contract.

The capitalist labor contract, the sale of labor power, and alienated labor remained in being throughout all manner of subsequent political shifts, some of which extended the reach of the state into civil society. The transition from liberal to liberal-democratic state forms was one such shift, the growth of representative democracy another. In our own century we have witnessed the advent (and then the declension) of the welfare state and of the state understood in Keynesian terms as a benign instrument for the achievement of social reform and redistribution of wealth. We have also witnessed various experiments in "public ownership," the nationalization of certain aspects of what tended to be called, in a revealing phrase, the "commanding heights" of the economy. That all these twentieth-century experiments proved reversible in the event points up how limited, how restricted they were, and were meant to be, all along. Today, Western states no longer attempt to regulate crises for the sake of maintaining full employment. They no longer actively set out to enhance public welfare. They no longer award any kind of universalistic status to the interests of workers, which should remind us that these "interests" were intended all along to have been restricted within the nexus of wage labor, which was never itself challenged or even questioned. The most that Keynesianism conceded, though not for long, was that a higher level of wages would be not an impediment but a stimulus to economic growth. It was Marx, not Keynes, who asked us to imagine a world without wage labor, and it was wage labor that remained sacrosanct despite him. Similarly with what was called "public ownership." This in reality was state ownership of the kind that never challenged wage labor or involved democratization of conditions of work at the level of the workshop or factory. The state became an abstract collective capitalist, and things proceeded much as before. The state more generally, throughout all these successive developments, remained insulated from the economy, and politics, centred and focused on the state, remained alien from people's lives in society.

Of course, socialism and democracy have also long enjoyed an uneasy, tense relationship. The promise, which was once considerable and ennobling, of a sustained merger between the two, turned out to be in vain. But why did it fall short? In considerable measure, the graft failed to take because of the deflection of Marxism, socialism's dominant face, into dogmatic, nondemocratic and antidemocratic directions. These directions came not to seem off course, but to be the only course. But as I write, this course no longer exists. The end of the Cold War, the demise of the USSR, along with its "official" version of Marxism, presents Western Marxists with an enormous, unprecedented critical opportunity. What was once a rather occulted notion of alien politics, which is intimately connected with the democratic elements of Marx's political thinking, may at long last be able to come into its own. The *étatiste,* bureaucratic model of communism, built up at such immense cost in the USSR, can be isolated and criticized alongside a critical characterization of alien politics in our own societies. Such dual criticism is by no means a contradiction in terms, and may well be what the times demand. Alien politics as a strain in Marx's writings is now more helpful than ever before, because it suggests how both the now depassed Soviet state system and the troubled capitalist state system can be critically appraised with an eye toward democratic transformation from below.

When Marx wrote in 1843 that "in democracy the state . . . is the real universal" and that "the modern French have conceived it thus: in true democracy the political state disappears,"[16] he is certainly not thinking (*pace* J. L. Talmon) of the Jacobins. He is thinking of Rousseau. Democracy, much as Rousseau had understood it, has considerable purchase for Marx as the basis of a critique not just of capitalist society at large, but also of the various political forms of the state in which "man has only a legal existence," as the bearer of rights. The point in levelling such criticisms is to "transform society into a community of men to achieve their highest purposes—a democratic state."[17] The reach of democracy so understood goes beyond what is normally attributed to Marx. Commentaries have often more or less grudgingly admitted that, in established democracies like Britain and the United States of America, the workers in Marx's view might gain power by legal means, through the ballot box.

But this is a belief about the road to power, and not about the uses to which power or democratized social control might be put. I wish to insist that, in Marx's view, thoroughgoing institutional changes, and not just different versions of existing political institutions, are needed for the realization of democratic socialism, properly so-called. It is this other, broader meaning of democratization that was beginning to emerge in 1843, and was to find expression in Marx's later writings too. In the contrast Marx draws between the "rule of property" and the "rule of man," between the depoliticization alien politics involves and the repoliticization that "real, human emancipation" entails, what needs to be achieved is the extension of democratization to social relations, and not its projection upwards and outwards on to the level of the alien state. The extension of democracy is seen here as a task, a project, that awaits its attainment and not, as with some advocates of the idea that everything is political, a *fait accompli*. Democratization has to be seen as unfinished business.

Martin Jay observed in passing that "(w)hen discussing the bourgeois state . . . Marx had not interpreted it solely as the 'executive committee of the ruling class' but also as an adumbration, albeit distorted, of the reconciliation of social contradictions that the triumph of the proletariat was to bring about."[18] Putting aside for the moment the question of whether the triumph of the proletariat is going to bring about anything at all any longer, it does appear that the state, for its part, could in principle be both the executive committee of the ruling class and an adumbration in alien form of social reconciliation. The point remains, however likely or unlikely this may be, that it is the latter, not the former, that has democratic implications. Ruling-class theory is top-down. Its register is that of control, command, domination. It regards the state *prima facie* as an apparatus, a set of institutions to be manned, taken over, seized. These institutions vary only with the class makeup of those doing the seizing and the manning. What this means is that if, at a stretch, the state could be both class instrumentality and alien, the stretch would have to be very wide indeed, since the state is understood differently in either case. The ruling class definition of the state is different *in kind* from the alien politics definition. It involves a different notion of representation, the direct representation of class interests. The alien state goes beyond the attribution of interests to workers in virtue of their social positions, their place in the network of social relations. It represents in estranged form not the interests but the communal capacities of its citizenry. Here, it is a question of the indirect representation of needs, on the assumption that community is a human need denied by capitalism and by the state/civil society couplet that accompanies capitalism.

Ruling class theory, to reiterate, does not break with the principle of top-down surveillance and control from above. It occupies itself with a change in the personnel of those doing the controlling, with who is at the helm. It does not reconfigure the helm itself. Alien politics, by contrast, does reconfigure the helm. The dealienation of alien politics has democratic implications that go beyond the rule of or by the "immense majority" that Marx mentioned in the *Manifesto of the Communist Party*. These implications are not just numerical and quantitative. They involve what is to be a qualitative shift, one which would strike at the notion of politics as top-down control and coordination. While ruling-class theory does not counterpose the state to civil society so much as collapse the state into civil society, as one of its terms, expressions, functions or instruments, alien politics, far from deriving the political from the economic, far from remaining enmeshed within the state/civil society distinction, takes some critical distance on the distinction between state and civil society. Once the alien state is reintegrated into society, social control is extended and broadened, not concentrated and distilled at a single point. It means that people are in charge of their own creations—economic, aesthetic, political— and that direct control, not just of the state apparatus but of all the conditions of existence, is on the political agenda for the first time in human history.

I have no wish in what follows to derogate class analysis in general. Class relations, after all, enter into the very constitution, the very definition of the labor process in capitalism. The commodification of labor power, property and wealth is the *conditio sine qua non* of the process of accumulation that characterizes capitalism as a distinctive mode of production. Class struggle around wage labor and industrial discipline, along with the surveillance this involves, has long characterized capitalist industry. At the same time, class conflict at a political level has been a major means of transforming capitalist societies from within. The point remains, however, that, as a rule, class struggle and class conflict, so defined, have proceeded at different levels, along different paths which in the event intersected only rarely. This leads to a point of considerable importance. A defining characteristic of capitalist society that sets it apart from all other known forms of society is its way of decisively separating the political from the economic spheres. Anthony Giddens's useful, categorical distinction between two types of domination, authority, or command over persons, and allocation, or command over objects or material resources, helps us see what is at stake here. These two kinds of domination relate under capitalism in a wholly original way. Command over persons and command over resources are separate processes or spheres, falling into different hands, under capitalism. The power of the dominant class in capitalism is primarily rooted in its control over allocative resources, and not in control over persons in any direct or immediate sense. The capitalist class does not generally, and need not in principle, make up the personnel of the state, as earlier ruling classes, by and large, did. The business of the capitalist class, as of America in the adage, *is* business. It is not politics in any direct sense. Karl Kautsky's famous paradox, that under capitalism the ruling class does not rule, is, as far as it goes, quite correct (though what he does with it is another matter, as we shall see). Production is institutionally separate from politics, and (as in liberal political theories), is resistant to political control, which is always seen, *prima facie,* as outside "intervention." The factory sign Marx mentions in *Capital,* NO ADMISSION EXCEPT ON BUSINESS, carries talismanic force and applies as much to the state as to anything else.

It is because of its separation and institutional insulation from politics, or from political restraint, that production under capitalism, and only under capitalism, becomes the dynamo of social transformation in its own right. Only under capitalism does it have a right of its own in the required sense. The separation of the economic from the political sphere is based upon, and is implicit within, the capitalist labor contract. The labor contract converts allocative resources into authoritative resources at the level of the workplace. This derogates the political sphere in two senses, at two different levels which the contract is designed to keep apart. It first denies the worker any rights of participation in the authoritative apparatus of decision-making within the industrial enterprise, which is why to this day schemes for worker participation or for what the French used to call "autogestion" can so much as appear innovative or radical. But the labor contract has, and is meant to have, no such purchase at what comes to be known as the "political" level "properly" so-called, which is that of the state. The political is displaced upwards on to the level of the state, which may seem and is likely to be very distant from the shop floor. The labor contract derogates the political in the second sense of assigning specifically political rights, not to the worker as worker, but to the worker as citizen. Citizenship is categorically and institutionally separate from the authority system of the industrial enterprise. It has to do with the authority system of the state, which is not normally derived from command over allocative resources. The important point here is that relations between state and citizen come to be seen as political relations, and as the only significant political relations, whereas relations between labor and capital are regarded, in all seriousness, as being nonpolitical ones. Considerable effort is expended in keeping relations between labor and capital non-"political" in this sense. Industrial conflict is, in principle, insulated from party competition in the state, and the line in practice has been drawn, and adhered to, with some care. Industrial conflict is not supposed to turn "political," or to overlap local boundaries. Local picketing is permissible, but "flying pickets," supportive pickets from elsewhere who flew in the face of Margaret Thatcher, are not. Strikes over wages and conditions at particular plants are grudgingly absorbed by the system. But make a work stoppage "political," because more expansive, and the state will "intervene" with a vengeance, as in the case of the coal miners' strike in Thatcher's Britain—to give but one recent example from a galaxy of other ones.

There is something extraordinary about this topographical separation of the political from the economic, not least because we normally take it for granted. It is a specifically capitalist achievement of some magnitude. It would appear on the face of it a very skewed understanding of the term "political" that would render the transformation of labor into labor power a nonpolitical process. Yet to a remarkable extent this is how it has been regarded, at least by those who were not undergoing the suffering this transformation involved. The capitalist labor contract does not involve the appropriation of surplus products but the extraction of surplus *value,* an exploitative relationship that is hidden within the overall system of economic production and distribution. Because of it, wage labor comes to be, or to be regarded as, a purely economic transaction between employer and worker. The connections of mutual dependency between the two are themselves regarded as purely economic in character. Capitalist relations of production did not expand because of the bourgeoisie's monopoly of the means of violence or surveillance. To the contrary, the means of violence, if not of surveillance, were monopolized by the state in an orbit quite separate and distant from that occupied by class relations. Commitment to the liberal principle of "freedom of contract," which was at once part of a set of broader ideological claims to "liberty" for which the bourgeoisie, in its heroic period, fought, and also an established reality which the bourgeoisie sought to extend in economic organization, normally meant the extrusion of the sanctions of violence from the labor market. Once again, the sphere of private freedoms was institutionally distinguished from the sphere of public, political authority.

If the primary, constitutive contradiction of capitalist production is, as Marx thought, that between private appropriation and socialized production, what helps disguise or conceal the location of this contradiction is the domain allocated to "the political" vis-à-vis "the economic." The political, as we have seen, is supposed to concern itself only with the incorporation of the citizen, as regulated primarily by the franchise. Industrial conflict is kept out of politics, and politics is kept out of the workplace. This is not to say that the separation of spheres is absolute. The economic and the political are never separate in the sense of being detached or uncoupled one from the other. But they are insulated against each other in principle and at a basic institutional level. Each sphere is, so to say, relatively autonomous from, but dependent upon, what goes on in the other. One of the reasons why it does make sense to employ the category of the capitalist state is that the state has long been dependent upon the activities of capitalists, and on the accumulation of capital, which is after all the source of its own revenues. But if the state in this way operates within the boundaries of capitalist imperatives, these are imperatives that the state in its turn helps formulate and sustain, since it, not capitalism, does the taxing and amercement. The point remains that the state does not itself directly control an accumulation process upon which it perforce remains dependent. The structural basis of this distinguishing feature of capitalism is the insulation of the state from civil society and civil society, from the state. The (relative) autonomy of the state is one of the terms of this same insulation. This makes of the capitalist state a contradictory unity, in the sense of becoming a focus of the contradictory character of human social organization in the capitalist epoch. If private appropriation contradicts socialized production, the state depends upon and stands at the center of this contradiction. The instrumental relation to nature that is promoted by the rise of capitalism and propelled by the capitalist accumulation process becomes what Giddens calls the "fault-line"[19] of the capitalist state. And if the state, as in the Keynesian era, is to assume responsibility for the provision of community services, it can do so only on the basis of state revenues, which depend on the economic successes of capitalism.

This leads us into another level of contradiction, since the passage from the liberal to the liberal-democratic or welfare state was secured, historically, mainly through politically organized working-class pressure, pressure that was exerted in the first place because of the exigencies of wage labor and the capitalist wage contract. These are not exigencies the capitalist state is about to address, let alone rectify, for reasons already explained. And this in turn means that workers are going to remain alienated in the labor process to the extent that the capitalist state permits this, an extent that is bound to remain considerable. The state is unable, it lacks the agency, to do otherwise. The state faced with alienated labor is constrained not to countervail it because of the peculiarities of its own placement not within but vis-à-vis capitalist civil society. The state's inaction reinvigorates alienation in the labor process. But what is this alienation but another form of inaction that consists in not being able to do otherwise? Not being able to do otherwise or being structurally prevented from doing otherwise obviously strikes at human agency and freedom, for to be an agent, as opposed to an actor, means being able to act otherwise. Any person who is reduced to being an automatic part of a pre-given process whose operation owes nothing to the initiatives or purposes of that person is to that extent not a free agent. His or her freedom is derogated by top-down surveillance and control from above, because the self-monitoring of activity which the notion of free agency implies is forcibly denied.

Marx's own words in the *Grundrisse* are very much to the point here. Separate actions in society arise out of the conscious aims of individuals, but the outcome of these actions goes beyond the actors concerned. "[T]he totality of the process appears as an objective inter-connection arising directly from nature. To be sure, it arises out of the interaction of conscious individuals, but it does not reside in their consciousness, nor as a totality is it subsumed under them. Their own mutual collisions produce an alien social force that stands above them (and produces) their reciprocal efforts as a process and a power indepen-dent of them. . . . The social relation of individuals to each other as an autonomized force above the individuals—whether it is represented to be a national force, an accident, or in any form you like—is a necessary result of the fact that the starting point is not the free social individual."[20]

As we have seen, the institutional separation of politics from pro-duction, a distinguishing feature of capitalism, means that workers assume a political or public identity only as citizens, if at all; that the right to participate politically is at best unrelated to a person's position in the economic realm; and that a crimped, juridical understanding of equality does not admit of extension to the democratization of produc-tive relations. But all these unwelcome characteristics of alien politics constitute only one of its faces. The capitalist state is a contradictory, and not a purely negative, noxious or reprehensible phenomenon. This is to say that, seen from another angle, the separation of politics from production holds out a real promise. In Anthony Giddens's words, "the emergence of a 'public sphere' in the American and French Revolutions, predicated in principle upon universal rights and liberties of the whole . . . community, is as fundamental a disjunction in history as the commodification of labor and property to which Marx showed it to be fundamentally related." However assymmetrical to the class system of capitalism and the capitalist division of labor citizenship rights may be, they nevertheless opened up "new vistas of freedom and equality that Marxism itself seeks to radicalize."[21]

My contention here is that, just as the *Economic and Philosophic Manuscripts* of 1844 can and must inform our reading of Marx's later social and economic writings, so too can Marx's political writings of the same period, in the case of Marxist state theory. The emphasis in "On 'The Jewish Question' " and the "Critique of Hegels 'Philosophy of Right'," in particular, is on alien politics. Marx's reflections on the emergence of the modern state, which are traced out in these essays and elsewhere, have to them a resonance that is not met with in all of Marx's later writings. This disjuncture could pose a Marxological problem of a sort, if we wished, for instance, to assert the essential unity and integrity of Marx's *oeuvre* taken as a whole. This is not part of my brief here, though it has been elsewhere. Here, it is enough to assert that Marx may or may not have changed his mind about the state later on, after the early 1840s. He may have come to think that the kind of analysis given to the modern state as it emerged at the time of the American and French Revolutions had already served its purpose, and could thenceforward be shelved and put aside. There are difficulties with this view, some of which I have already dealt with in *Karl Marx and the Anarchists*[22] and others of which await their settlement in their due place, below. But for our immediate purposes the question can be settled, provisionally, along the following lines. To the extent that the later Marx did put aside his early reflections on the state, he was mistaken in doing so, since the line of inquiry opened up in these early essays is one that is eminently worth following through.

Marxist state theory, I am arguing, took a wrong turn; and whether or not this *détournement* is to be located in Marx's writings, it appears to have adversely affected the history of Marxism, not only as a method of social and political inquiry, but also, quite possibly, as a political movement. But even if Marxist state theory came to be constructed on the wrong foundations, I maintain that the right foundations were nevertheless implicit all along in Marx's earlier writings. In uncovering the arguments of these, I am endeavoring to reground Marxist state theory more firmly, and proposing to add to it as well as amend it into the bargain.

But none of the above is intended to deny the fact that my task in what follows has been made easier as well as more difficult by the work of my predecessors. Some, but by no means most, later Marxist theorists expressed views that were to be much closer to what I am calling "alien politics" than to the straightforward, and at times strident, "ruling-class" theory that *is* Marxist state theory in the eyes of all too many commentators and critics. There is something remarkable about this. I am concerned in what follows to salute such theorists, crucially, Antonio Gramsci, and (the later) Nicos Poulantzas, for the theoretical prescience of the contributions they have made. Even though the present, modest essay in retrieval owes much to their example, and even though I should be gratified if this book is regarded as being continuous with their arguments, it should be remembered that Gramsci, in particular, did not enjoy the ease of access to Marx's early writings that we today can enjoy more or less routinely. This, of course, makes his listening to what had become one of Marx's more muffled echoes all the more remarkable.

1

"THE STATE AS A
FINISHED THING"

Aristotle's well-known conviction that political participation has economic and social preconditions was cast into a new kind of relief by what was, at the time of Marx's earliest journalism, an original, unprecedented and hard-and-fast separation of the state from civil society. This separation signified the disjuncture of citizenship in the modern state, a hollow, formal mode of membership, from the life of the individual in civil society, a life which is irreducibly real, immediate and rent with divisions—divisions the state was supposed to reconcile. How did the state become detached in this way from civil society? Why did this disjuncture take place as it took place, or when it took place (and at no other time)? These were the questions Marx's earliest investigation of the modern state set out to investigate and answer. The issue as to whether or not the answers he gave are satisfactory is at one level less important than the fact that they were posed as questions in the first place. For these are questions that *matter*, and without posing them we are in no position to decide or even to discuss the question of the modern state's credentials, its claim to represent or embody the needs and aspirations of those people over whom it is set.

That Marx saw fit to pose these questions as questions, and to suggest an answer to them, is today often overlooked. Ironically, what has helped occlude from view Marx's early investigations of state and civil society is what has come down to us as Marxist state theory itself. Ask an educated person today what the main features of Marxist state theory are, and the reply will likely be that Marx believed that the state will "wither away" in the classless society of the future, and/ or that he entertained a "ruling-class" theory of the state, one that folded over into a notion of the "dictatorship of the proletariat." I have dealt elsewhere (and at length) with the point that these two prescriptions do not appear to sit together very comfortably.[1] Here, I propose to take a different tack, and direct my attention to the original questions which underlied these prescriptions, and to do so on the straightforward grounds that these questions remain important and unsettled—as well as on the more contentious grounds that the early Marx, seen either beyond or through later Marxist prescriptions, can help us resolve them.

This book argues that most Marxist state theory since Marx's death has allowed itself the luxury of going off on various unprofitable tangents, most of them having to do (directly or indirectly) with the purported "ruling-class" character of the capitalist state (or of the bourgeois state, which is often held to be the same thing). I argue, against this tendency, that a more theoretically fertile and suggestive approach to the problem of the modern state is the one outlined by Marx in his earlier writings, particularly (but by no means exclusively) in his 1843 essay "On 'The Jewish Question'." Elsewhere, I have argued that it is in effect an underlying motif of what Marx said about the state at any stage of his career.[2] My concerns here may be (and, I hope, will be) complementary to this earlier argument. They are nevertheless different from it. They are less concerned with questions of the textual consistency of Marx's *oeuvre*, as this stretches across the span of his forty years as a theorist, and more concerned with what are, in the last analysis, more than just Marxological questions; my concern is with the state and with how this is to be understood.

That this same concern was central to Marx too—at least in his writings of the early 1840s—has long been evident to scholars. The idea that the view of the state expressed in these early writings underlies much of what Marx was to write in subsequent years has gained a good deal of currency, particularly since the appearance of Shlomo Avineri's important book, *The Social and Political Thought of Karl Marx* in 1968.[3] Even so, it has in the meantime become clear (at least to me) that Avineri's very "philosophical" understanding of what the Marx-Hegel confrontation of these years comported is in some respects mistaken. Marx's reasons for doing battle with the shade of Hegel, it now seems to me, were political in the first instance and philosophical only by extension. To put the same point another way, Hegel, shorn for the purposes of argument of his philosophical scaffolding, can readily enough be seen as giving voice to a view of politics and of the state that neither begins nor ends with the *Philosophy of Right*. This is the view that politics is in the first instance the province of experts, of state bureaucrats whose political formation has the effect of freeing them from the contingency and "caprice" of "uninformed" public opinion, and of allowing as well as requiring them to engage, calmly and dispassionately, in rational decision-making about the public good. Conflict and interest are in this view relegated to their own arena, civil society, which is nonpolitical at the level of definition. *Beamtenpolitik* in all its various forms is statist in the specific sense that it stresses adherence to the norms of a pre-given hegemonic state, which is often in practice confounded with those of the particular government of the day. *Beamtenpolitik* emphasizes adherence both to a set of actions and to a form of consciousness. Actions and consciousness alike are defined as "political" from above, in accordance with a given idea of the state.

Hegel's *Philosophy of Right* gives classic expression to the idea that in *Beamtenpolitik* political subjectivity is from the outset state-oriented. The relations, interests and values animating individuals in civil society are accordingly delegitimized, since they can produce nothing more than "opinion," not knowledge, about matters political. This statist view of politics helps account for the fact that the state as a political construct has permeated German political discourse, and has done so down to this very day, much more thoroughly than that of other Western countries. Political parties in postwar West Germany, for instance, were commonly divided into *staatserhaltende* and *nichtstaatserhaltende* parties; political opposition was often, if not always, characterized as being inimical to the state, and not just as oppositional, as in the British conception of "loyal opposition." Similarly, the West German civil service was commonly regarded as being by definition *überparteilich*, a term meant to connote distance from—or, in the Hegelian lexicon, transcendence of—society's divisive play of interests and antagonisms. Leading schools of West German *Rechtslehre* held that the civil servant is the representative, or even the embodiment, not of society (as it were) represented upwards—as in nineteenth-century British characterizations of what was called "virtual representation"— but of a West German *Staatsidee* represented downwards. The West German bureaucrat, that is to say, was held to have the kind of relationship to the Federal Republic that was in no way dissimilar to, or for that matter undescended from, the relationship Marx pinpointed as obtaining between the bureaucrat in Hegel's system and the state. This statist conception at a very basic level occludes the citizen from the same kind—and not just the same degree—of political consideration enjoyed by the bureaucrat. A statist understanding of the bureaucrat folds over into a statist conception of the citizen too.

Given the resonance of such conceptions—which is by no means restricted to the Germany that long gave them a home—Hegel can be seen as having been anything but an isolated voice in the wilderness. Quite to the contrary, he gave expression to, and helped fortify and reinvigorate a view of politics and society that has remained constant, relevant and powerful in Germany until remarkably recently. The statist conception of politics as a professional activity in the first instance, an activity lodged and located in the state as a privileged and protected realm, separate from and insulated against civil society's clash and clamor of particularistic interests, and against its alleged potential for pluralistic stagnation—this characteristically but by no means exclusively Hegelian view survived, in its broadest outlines, into the German postwar economic miracle of our own times. (It may even have helped bring this "miracle" about.)

To see this helps us get a purchase on Marx's 1843 "Critique" of Hegel's *Philosophy of Right*, for this critique can be considered, at a very basic level, an expression of an alternative conception of what politics is, or should be, all about. It gives voice to an ascending theory of politics as opposed to the descending statist conception. More specifically, Marx takes issue with Hegel's high-handed, contemptuous dismissal of public opinion. Hegel's distrust of public opinion—which he wanted to render politically irrelevant, null and void—was profound. Accident and "caprice" can determine people's lives and opinions in civil society; the coordinating principles of the state, which are the polar opposites of accident and caprice, are therefore an embodiment of rationality. To Marx, it was the "therefore" that rankled; Hegel's perspective is inverted in the specific sense that he cannot so much as see that the state and the market effectively collude in making caprice and accident dominant throughout civil society in the first place. Marx's "Critique" can thus be seen to have had many later echoes. At one level, it is echoed whenever anyone opposes to statism a conception of politics as the representation of and struggle among variously defined social groupings or interests. What needs to be added, and what could be said to stifle these echoes, is of course that in Marx's hands one of these groupings, the proletariat understood as a class, came to have distinct precedence over any (or all) of the others; it is however not incidental to what follows in this book that Marx's characterization of the proletariat, and its centrality as what Avineri was to term the "universal class," did not come as a flash of blinding insight. It was a *process* that took place in stages. Nor is it incidental to the argument that follows that the writings my first chapters deal with are *early* writings which mark an early stage in Marx's itinerary. Otherwise put, the lack of a clearly formulated conception of the proletariat in these early writings by no means automatically operates to their detriment; the more clearly such a conception of the proletariat is formulated, the less useful and more troublesome it becomes. Its lack here is at one level a positive analytical advantage. On another level, however, it appears to pose problems. These can be resolved provisionally (and substantiated later on) along the following lines. Marx's early writings, those of the early 1840s, were criticisms, not expressions, of a dogmatic view of the state. However, they do, to their detriment, contain dogmatic views of class in general and of the proletariat or the poor in particular. It is thus possible to trace out a double movement of lines that intersect only later in Marx's career. Early on, an undogmatic understanding of the state was in certain respects stymied by a dogmatic view of class and of proletarian emancipation, to the point of later being dropped in favor of a correspondingly dogmatic set of formulations about the state. We can say then that dogmatic notions of class and emancipation dislodged nondogmatic state theory and rendered it in its turn dogmatic too. But this is not all there is to it. Marx's notions of class and emancipation were not always, and certainly not uniformly dogmatic. There is a long distance in this regard between Marx's "Critique" of 1843 and *The Eighteenth Brumaire of Louis Bonaparte* of 1852, which displays a much more nuanced, critical understanding of proletarian political subjectivity. The solution to our apparent dilemma lies in this very fact. If "class" over the span of these years moves from the dogmatic to the emancipatory, just as "state" moves during the same period from the emancipatory to the dogmatic, it is precisely at the point where these two lines intersect that we encounter Marx's most extreme, unsubstantiated formulations about the state in capitalist society, every one of which dates from a specific (and rather short) period in Marx's career, the period stretching from *The German Ideology* (1845 to 6) to the *Class Struggles in France* (where the phrase "dictatorship of the proletariat" first crops up) of 1850, and encompassing the *Manifesto of the Communist Party* (1848). It is important to recognize at the outset that the dogmatism of these years both abridged Marx's earlier speculations about the state (in some ways twisting these out of all recognition), *and* that it was effectively supplanted in its turn by the relative flexibility displayed by the *Brumaire*. What has been handed down to us as Marxian state theory, not to put too fine a point on it, was the product of a strictly limited period of his intellectual and political development; and it simply will not do any longer to take the part for the whole.

The issues dividing Marx from Hegel are more important for our present purposes, which are those of augmenting our understanding of the modern state, than the separate issues surrounding Marx's conception (or successive conceptions) of the proletariat. (These will, however, come together later on.) And the issues dividing Marx from Hegel, to reiterate, are not, as I write, issues that have passed from the face of the earth. To give but one relatively recent (and recently celebrated) example, opposition after 1972 to the West German "decree against radicals" or *Radikalenerlass* (known sometimes as the *Berufsverbot*) reconstructed or resuscitated the tensions that can readily enough be encountered in the Marx-Hegel confrontation that took place some fourteen decades earlier. These tensions spanned a conception of the state as a hegemonic, "given" structure or construct, on the one hand, and the political subjectivities not of bureaucrats but of citizens who are also members of civil society, on the other. Many of these latter, in the course of heated debates over the *Radikalenerlass*, articulated an unwillingness to live "under" a state structured or constructed along *Beamtenpolitik* lines—very much as Marx in 1843 had criticized Hegel's statist structuration.

Marx's challenge to Hegel's understanding of the state as the realm of "rational" politics, and of civil society as the site of politically negligible and dispensable "opinion," is, then, not at all a piece of arcane intellectual history of something now happily surpassed. To the contrary, it casts a long shadow. What is central to Marx's challenge, as we shall see, is the conviction that political subjectivity or agency can become tentative and attenuated for the citizens of modern states once it is restricted in principle within the bounds and confines of statism. The bifurcation of "politics" (of the kind that admits of being projected upwards onto the state machinery) and "society" (understood as civil society) entails the potential alienation of political subjectivity, a point to be investigated in more detail below.

What follows is important to an appreciation of Marx's understanding of bureaucracy (as opposed, for instance, to Max Weber's).

Marx rejects bureaucracy in considerable measure because he rejects *any* political institution that excludes individuals—some individuals, *any* individuals—on the basis of a set of "abstract" (that is, incomplete or partial) criteria or principles. The personnel of a modern bureaucracy—the Prussian being a prototype of the modern bureaucracy—is recruited and promoted according to criteria and values that are anything but politically innocuous. In particular, a bureaucracy that controls access to its own ranks on the basis of the political beliefs or convictions of aspirants is, in this view, illegitimate in principle. But an electorate made up only of "qualified" individuals, where the qualifications for the suffrage, be these educational, gender-based or racial, are set and drawn up by the state, is *prima facie* illegitimate for the same reason.

In the 1843 "Critique" Marx rejects on principle the idea of such qualifications for any kind of political activity or relevance; in "On 'The Jewish Question' " of the same year he stakes out a *more* radical position, rejecting in principle political participation itself in so far as this leads to a political realm alienated from its own roots in civil society. Such participation, participation "in abstraction," alienates itself from the very political subjectivity that is its own foundation. Marx's focus shifts away from a question of personnel (*who* is to be admitted into the bureaucracy, or by extension into those who are officially deemed to be politically relevant?) to what is a more fundamental question about the very existence of bodies like bureaucracies that exclude (some) people and loom large over what Marx terms people's "real development" in civil society.

To see how, for Marx, the critique of bureacracy and the critique of the modern state interpenetrated and folded back into each other from the very outset, we must look more closely at Marx's arguments in the "Critique" that are directed against Hegel's defense of bureaucracy. The purported "universality" of this *allgemeine Stand,* he argues, is not (as Hegel thought) expressed but belied by the written examinations an aspiring bureaucrat has to pass. The only kinds of knowledge that admit of being tested in this manner are skills, aptitudes or crafts, like shoemaking (Marx here reminds us of his training in Ancient Greek philosophy): "shoemaking is a skill without which one can be a good citizen of the state and a social human being; whereas the necessary 'political knowledge' is a requirement without which a person in the state lives outside the state, cut off from himself, in the air."[4] Hegel wants the "opinions and thoughts" of bureaucrats "first to pass a government test to prove that they are 'its' opinions and thoughts. For Hegel here stupidly speaks of the state as a finished thing"[5]; Hegel's state "is not content with 'a certain way of thinking as a mere possibility', it must count on it as a necessity."[6] The truth of the matter according to Marx is that any bureaucrat who becomes part of Hegel's state is forced to "desert" civil society. He "must step out of his civil society, disregard it, and withdraw from his whole organization into his individuality; for the sole existence he finds for his citizenship of the state is his sheer, blank individuality, since the existence of the state as executive is complete without him and his existence in civil society is complete without the state."[7] Entrance into the hallowed portals of state service is a "baptism" or a "transsubstantiation" of the realm of the profane into that of the sacred.[8] The individual bureaucrat is not about to effect this transfer unscathed or even intact, for what he gives up as the price of admission is his social essence. Hegel's bureaucratic aspirant must "effect a fundamental division within himself. As an actual citizen he finds himself in a twofold organization: the bureaucratic organization which is an external formal feature of the distant state, which does not touch him or his independent reality, and the social organization, the organization of civil society."[9] The only thing an aspiring civil servant can be tested on, in any case, is "state-knowledge," which is not practical knowledge but a set of hierarchical attitudes or dispositions. In a democracy no one would mistake bureaucratic skills for "state-knowledge," which would in changed form become something everyone would share. But since almost all Prussians in 1843 were precluded from exercizing any kind of political knowledge, they unintentionally compensated for its lack by inventing the fiction of the state as universal community. In this way the universality attributed to the state is simply "the affirmation of [people's] own estrangement" from community in their own daily lives.[10] How might the residual need for community be fulfilled? Marx at more than one point strikes a radical-democratic note:

In unrestricted suffrage . . . civil society actually raises itself for the first time to an abstraction of itself, to political existence as its true universal or essential existence. But the full achievement of this abstraction is at the same time the transcendence of this abstraction. Inasmuch as civil society actually establishes its true existence, it has thereby established its civil existence, its distinction from its political existence, as inessential. And with the one separated, the other, its opposite, collapses. Thus within the abstract political state the reform of voting is the demand for the dissolution of this state even as it is the demand for the dissolution of civil society.[11]

Marx would always in later years—other things being equal—maintain that the struggle for the franchise and the workers' movement should involve one another to the greatest extent practicable by given movements in given national settings at given times. And as Shlomo Avineri reminds us, Marx was constantly urging the workers' movement to seek out democratic rather than authoritarian allies, on the straightforward grounds that any future society would surely be stamped by its origins. In this sense, the above-quoted passage might seem to carry a certain proleptic resonance. Not too much should be made of this, however: what stands out about this passage is its extreme formalism. It is scarcely likely that a quantitative change (in the number of those eligible to cast ballots) could in and of itself produce the kind of qualitative change Marx is seeking. This very formalism became a problem later on for Kautsky and, by extension, for Eurocommunist state theory, as we shall see in my concluding chapter.

It is clear enough, however, who Marx was attacking in 1843. Paragraph 308 of Hegel's *Philosophy of Right* questions whether members of civil society should participate in political deliberations by proxy, through deputies or representatives, or through direct democracy of a Rousseauean kind. Hegel's answer to this rhetorical question—given that he is concerned to indicate, shrewdly, that Rousseau's participatory democracy presupposes something (community) it cannot of itself create (a message Marx himself might have taken rather more seriously)—is a foregone conclusion. He opts decisively for representation, on the grounds that arguments that everyone has a right to share directly in deliberating and deciding upon matters of common concern can be advanced only on the basis of an abstract conception of individuality, in which individuals are regarded without reference to their membership(s) of what is, after all, an articulated political and social totality.

Marx's response (this time) is shrewd. What Hegel fails to recognize is that his supposedly stark alternatives are in reality but variations on a single theme. They reduce themselves to a choice between a plurality and a totality of isolated, atomized individuals. Hegel's question lapses into a quantitative register, a mystified understanding of how the state relates to civil society in the first place. If you start from Hegel's own premise that the state is the realm of community and universality, merely to consider these values from a quantitative point of view makes no sense. (Marx is here providing, by extension, a critique of much—thankfully, not all—political science "reasoning" in our own century.) To do so would be to adopt a purely external perspective which occludes universality as a qualitative feature (or goal) of people's lives. Universality understood quantitatively would simply mean "the sum total of individuality" ("one individuality, many individualities, all individualities. One, many, all—none of these determinations changes the essence of the subject, individuality"). If individuality is seen instead as an "essential, spiritual, actual quality of the individual,"[12] people will be seen to relate one to another in ways other than that of simply being totted up. People will define themselves not as unrelated monads of the kind that can be aggregated, but as members of a community. The question then becomes not "all as individuals" but "individuals as all."

In Marx's view Hegel accepts the separation of individuals from universality because of his uncritical acceptance of the state's separation from civil society, which obliges him to deal with political participation abstractly and quantitatively. His question ("how should civil society participate in universality?") at once takes the abstraction of the state for granted and presumes the permanence of this same abstraction; in so doing, Hegel adopts an uncritical, dogmatic stance towards the given. He is seduced by the immediate and ensnared by the present. (In this way Hegel's celebrated aphorism that philosophy is "its own time apprehended in thought" admits of being turned back on Hegel himself.) It is crucial to Marx's argument at this juncture that mystified consciouness be accounted for as a social phenomenon as well as an intellectual shortcoming. Agreeing with Hegel that a particular view of civil society is "abstract" and "atomistic," Marx adds that:

> this point of view is abstract, but is is the abstraction of the political state as Hegel himself develops it. It is also atomistic, but this is the atomism of civil society itself. The "point of view" cannot be concrete when the object of that point of view is "abstract." The atomism into which civil society plunges in its political act results necessarily from the fact that the community, the communal essence within which the individual exists, is civil society separated from the state, or in other words that the political state is an abstraction from civil society.[13]

If "civil society is the unreality of political existence,"[14] the state is an expression of (and not, as Hegel would have it, the solution to) this same "unreality"; it is but one of its terms. Even so, Hegel proceeds blithely to accuse the partisans of *democracy* of thinking about the concept of state membership "abstractly":

> That the definition "being a member of the state" is an "abstract" definition is not however the fault of this [democratic] thinking but of Hegel's own line of argument and of actual modern conditions which presuppose the separation of actual life from political life and make the political quality into an abstract definition of actual state membership.[15]

Abstraction, so understood, is not, as with Feuerbach, merely a misguided mental process; it characterizes not just people's thinking but also their lives. People in civil society experience universality and rationality only as ideals or values that remain unreal, inoperative. Unity is, in other words, experienced in its lack—a lack registered by the existence of the modern state, separated categorically and in actuality from civil society. Marx, arguing against Hegel's claim that the democratic perspective "keeps civil and political life apart from each other and supends the latter so to speak in the air,"[16] insists to the contrary that "the notion does not keep civil and political life separate; it is merely *the representation of an actually existing separation*. That notion does not suspend political life in the air, rather political life is the *life in the air*, the ethereal region of civil society."[17] Marx, in making this point, proceeds from a position derived not just from Feuerbach but from Hegel himself, who had insisted that "the destiny [of individuals] is to lead a universal life."[18] To Marx, as to Hegel before him, universality is to be realized in the form of social institutions; universality that is only conceptualized is false, abstract, compensatory universality. For Hegel, the universality that is lacking in civil society is provided by the state, and by the fact that the state's estate, the bureaucracy, is a "universal" estate in the sense that its members belong to or connect with no other estate. They are members only of the state. Hegel here adopts the nineteenth-century liberal shibboleth of *la carrière ouverte aux talents*, as opposed to feudal, functional definitions of political office: anyone in principle is free to join the state service. Social background here is to count for nothing. Marx's rejoinder is once again a telling one: "In the bureaucracy the identity of state interest and particular private aim is established in such a way that the state interest becomes a particular private aim over against other private aims"; but "(i)n a true state, it is not a question of the possibility of every citizen devoting himself to the universal as a particular estate, but of the capability of the universal estate to really be universal, i.e. to be the estate of every citizen."[19] But if such a view were to be articulated in Prussia, the bureaucracy would regard it as inimical to its own existence. In this way "the actual purpose of the state appears to the bureaucracy as an objective hostile to the state,"[20] and "avowed political spirit [in civil society] as also political-mindedness" appears to the bureaucracy as "treason against its mystery." For "the bureaucracy is the imaginary state alongside the real state," whose consciousness must be viewed as a "secret, the mystery preserved within itself by the hierarchy and against the outside world by being a closed corporation."[21] Bureaucrats evidently inhabit and occupy the heights of an inverted world where the state has primacy over what is regarded throughout as a resolutely secondary civil society. This is the world of political illusion, mystification and superstition, what Marx calls a *république prêtre*, whose priests, the bureaucracy, are able to issue and broadcast false justifications of its existence and operations. As such, the bureaucracy represents the formalism or "scholasticism" of political life, which takes form for content and cause for effect, and which "solves" unreal problems while it avoids (and cannot even identify) genuine ones.[22] "State formalism" so conceived "constitutes itself as actual power and itself becomes its own material content . . . it goes without saying that the bureaucracy is a web of practical illusions, or the 'illusions of the state'." The bureaucracy takes itself to be the ultimate purpose of the state. "Hegel expounds no real content for his bureaucracy, but only some general features of its 'formal' organization: and indeed the bureaucracy is only the formalism of a content that lies outside itself."[23]

The term "estate" or *Stand* in Hegel's *Philosophy of Right* refers both to the legally recognized social group to which a given individual belongs and from which he derives much of his identity, and the role these groups play in relation to the state. Estates buckle the state to civil society; civil divisions have an explicit political significance. Estates also and at the same time are the locus of the rational or communal moment in civil society itself. They are in Erica Sherover-Marcuse's words "islands of universality in an otherwise atomistic, particularistic existence."[24] Estates provide their members with the only access to universality they can attain in the sphere of civil society; each estate will accordingly incorporate its own element of universality in its own way. That these ways will evidently differ from estate to estate gives an edge to the bureaucracy, which has universality "as the goal of its essential activity."

The "business estate," by way of explicit contrast, is "essentially oriented towards the particular."[25] It relates to universality indirectly through its connections with corporations (which are roughly equivalent to guilds). Only membership in a corporation confers membership in civil society for individuals who belong neither to the landed nobility (who are said to have a "natural"—by birthright—relation to the universal) nor to the bureaucracy, who are said to relate to it directly. This is to say that, for most people, to be a nonmember of a corporation is a condemnation to nullity. It is to be placed outside the pale, not just of the state, but also of civil society itself.

This gives us, and gave Marx, a vital clue to the character of the poor, of T. M. Knox's "rabble of paupers." These are defined not just by their poverty (people belonging to the "business estate" could also be poor, but they would be recognized and helped by other members of their estate). The poor are also unincorporated, thus unrecognized. It is for this very reason that their poverty renders them malcontent and rebellious. On Hegel's own showing, they have every reason to be malcontent and rebellious. Hegel here is nonetheless uncompromising. There is no honor in being poor: honor is civic honor. The unincorporated poor have no honor, no legal existence, because they belong to no legally recognized group in civil society. Hegel recognized that their labor nevertheless permits civil society to function, and that their poverty is by no means an accidental or incidental feature of its functioning. He even admits that that their immiseration is the other side of the coin of others' luxury.

All this was, as it were, too good a chance for Marx to miss. To say that the poor are nonmembers of civil society is *eo ipso* a condemnation of what they are nonmembers *of*. Any social order which denies recognition, membership or acknowledgment to persons who are perforce essential to its continued operation delegitimates itself in, by and through this very act. The problem, at rock bottom, is not at all what Hegel considered it to be. It is not that the poor threaten the stability of the system (though of course they do); it is the very existence of a social order that excludes them from membership and participation. Hegel's troubled depiction of the poor provided Marx with a critical opportunity. It is not hard to draw a connection between the "working men" of the *Manifesto of the Communist Party*, who "have no country," and to whom "law, morality and religion are . . . so many bourgeois prejudices, behind which lurk in ambush just as many bourgeois interests," and the poor as Hegel depicts them (even if Marx in 1848 was to part company from Hegel when he distinguished the proletariat, properly so-called, from the "passively rotting mass" who could become "the bribed tool of reactionary intrigue").[26]

But *was* the proletariat ever properly so-called? Marx's eventual identification of this group as *the* exclusive agency of social regeneration has proved troublesome ever since it was first formulated. Sherover-

Marcuse has ably traced out a tension between the dogmatic and the nondogmatic in Marx's early depictions of the proletariat.[27] Since these tensions are in some ways very similar to those that characterize the no less troubled evolution of Marx's theory of the state, and since in large measure they can be traced out in the same writings, those of the early 1840s, they need further analysis, not just because of Hegel's long shadow, but for a reason close to the central problematic of this book. The problem here can be put in a nutshell. If what Marx came up with, and handed down to us, is simply a rigid ruling-class theory of the state, we cannot ignore the genealogy of Marx's depictions of class in general or the proletarian class in particular. My contention is, of course, that there is much more to Marx's theory of the state than its ruling-class aspect. But this aspect is *there*, and must duly be accounted for in any balanced survey.

One way of getting a purchase on this problem is to recognize that tension between the critical and the dogmatic can be said to characterize not just Marx's understanding(s) of the proletariat but also Hegel's picture of the poor. These latter are outside the pale of a society their work (if they can find any) nevertheless upholds and sustains. But they are unacknowledged, they lack recognition, not because of what they do or do not do, but because of who they are. Recognition in the *Philosophy of Right* (though not in the celebrated "Master and Slave" set piece in Hegel's *Phenomenology of Spirit*) is *legal* recognition, through and through. The "rabble" are excluded from political significance *categorically*. Their activity (or its lack) is of no account, unless of course it should turn revolutionary. That this perception was Marx's very starting point almost goes without saying. In the fullness of time it blended into his perception that in modern society the poor and the poor alone could embody community, since they alone exhibit a need for community of the appropriate kind. But this perception itself admits of a dogmatic as well as a critical formulation, as we are about to see.

It has seldom been remarked that tension between the dogmatic and the critical can be seen even before Marx had effected the shift for which he is famous, between the poor and the proletariat. Marx's (very) early articles on the wood-theft laws deal with the customary rights of the rural poor in the Rhineland. Marx insists against Hegel that these, far from being excludable from society by philosophic fiat, are in reality the "elemental class" of society. The poor are the only group in civil society that is unaffected by the false values of civil society. They alone are undeceived, unconfused about what is really valuable about being human.

This is to say that the poor are able to perceive fundamental truths in an ontological as well as a moral sense. Unlike their antagonists, the Provincial Deputies sitting in the Rhineland Assembly, the poor do not confuse the essence of humanity with something inhuman; they do not "worship an alien material being"; they are not the victims of the fetishism which enslaves their political masters (and which survives as a concept into the first volume of *Capital*). The poor lack "a particular consciousness which is slavishly subordinate to this object (wood),"[28] which is all that the denizens of the Rhineland Assembly are able to bring to bear. Marx does not shrink from attributing to the poor a universal (because fundamental or "elemental") consciousness, deriving from their propertylessness. The poor own nothing but themselves; their property is their life, their freedom, their humanity and their citizenship. (Marx to all appearances—and we must remember that Marx's essays of the early 1840s were written under conditions of censorship—had not yet broken with the Hegelian idea of the state as a rational universal, and identifies the poor as better, if putative, citizens than their political adversaries.) These attributes are the "property" of all human beings *qua* human beings; Marx's poor are the "proprietors of freedom." The possession of private property, by contrast, distorts our sense of justice or compassion and warps our view of reality into the bargain. Marx's argument recalls that of Plato's *Republic*, but only up to a point. For Plato, lack of private property was a necessary condition for virtue, or for the adoption of a universalistic perspective. But by no stretch of the imagination can it be called a sufficient condition for these, in view of the severe educational regimen Plato's elite must perforce undergo. Propertylessness as such has a far greater purchase for Marx. It is the determining factor shaping the consciousness of the poor. Because these have only "universal property" in the sense outlined above, they can present universal claims; because their needs are "elemental," the poor exhibit universal concerns which cut through the self-interests of the propertied at their very root.

Hegel's discussion of poverty and the unincorporated poor was concerned above all else to indicate the disadvantages of belonging to no estate. The poor are characterized by lack. They lack the "advantages of society,"[29] advantages which (like the society that confers them) are not themselves in question. But for Marx they are very much in question—so much so that (in some ways untowardly) he makes a virtue out of necessity. The Hegelian nightmare, estatelessness, turns into a positive value in its own right. The benefits of being an outsider to civil society consist in being untouched, unscathed in one's moral character and consciousness by the play and ill effects of private interest.

Marx by now is claiming something that Plato could never have envisioned. The propertyless do not have to *do* anything to attain their universal consciousness. They already possess it by virtue of their social placement—even though (or precisely because) this placement is, in its turn, highly ambiguous (are the poor *in* civil society or *outside* it?). They possess universal consciousness simply by virtue of who they are and what they lack, private property. However unlikely this may seem—in light of Marx's later formulations, among other things—there seems to obtain an immediate connection between the social being of the poor and their consciousness. The "elemental" status of the dispossessed beneath and within human society, on the one hand, and their ability to see truth and act upon its dictates, on the other, are directly linked.

Marx is guilty here of dogmatically conflating two different registers, social placement and political action. Nowhere in these early essays does Marx so much as hint that the poor might have to struggle to develop a social instinct. They simply possess it by virtue of their status (or lack of it); they possess their values *a priori* by virtue of their place within the scheme of things. (Marx here, we might surmise, is attributing to one estate what much medieval political theory had attributed to all estates in society.) All the poor need to do, it would seem, is to *be*, not to become, what they are.

My point here is not to castigate Marx unduly for the dogmatism of an early position which he was later to surpass, once questions of revolutionary agency, which had not yet arisen, came to be on the agenda. My point is rather to question whether this dogmatism *ever* completely disappeared, even when the unincorporated poor had been displaced by the self-incorporating proletariat. How these latter were to organize themselves, and in pursuit of what, were after all to prove to be questions of some moment. At another level, I propose in what follows to investigate the hypothesis that a dogmatic position on the poor, which Marx, as we are about to see, inherited from the Jacobins as well as from Hegel, led Marx as well as later Marxists astray, away from the kind of theoretical speculation about the state his early writings exhibit, and towards the kind of dogmatic, ossified assertions about the state that are, at best distortions of its character. Just as we might expect, dogmatism about class and dogmatism about the state are likely to go hand in hand. The later history of Marxism is replete with examples of this pairing, as we are about to see; the question remains how far we can extend it back into the mother lode, Marx's thought itself.

Marx's notion of the virtues of poverty, as this is given expression in the "Debates," is not just anti-Hegelian; in a significant sense, it marks a pre-Hegelian lapse. Robespierre and Saint-Just had given voice to a formalistic conception of "the people" they had inherited from Rousseau. The people, which "always wills the good," became wedded to a determinate social group, the Parisian poor (or, more specifically, the *sans-culottes*), to whom moral, universalistic traits were duly attributed or ascribed.

Arguments that the poor are not corrupted by luxury, that they remain unseduced by the artificial, destructive pleasures of "society," that they are never motivated by private, nongeneral interests, that the only interests they do pursue are the essential, universal interests of humanity at large—all these are of distinctly Jacobin provenance. So, for that matter, is a particular way of glorifying poverty (and thus of insulting the poor by romanticizing them). The people, as Robespierre conceived of them, were the repository of natural virtue— Marx, too, uses the telling term "natural"— and were goodness incarnate in a social class. This "natural" virtue was to sustain the elusive revolutionary "Republic of Virtue," whose trustees the Jacobins took it upon themselves to become. This is to do what Marx was to do in the "Debates": to make the poor the touchstone and yardstick of the general state of society. Their situation is *eo ipso* a judgment on and condemnation of it; in this sense the poor are in Marx's required sense "elemental" to society at large.

Marx, in apparently adopting it, here actually falls behind the Jacobin position. The Jacobins, after all, fervently believed in educating the poor. Neither Robespierre nor Hegel assumed that the poor were somehow exempt from the heritage of despotism—which is why, in Robespierre's (and arguably in Rousseau's) case, true emancipation was to start only with the second generation, and why, in Hegel's case, the poor were simply irresponsible, not to be trusted. Whereas the Jacobins always believed that the poor were integral members of the society of the *ancien régime*, Marx, as we have seen, vacillates fatally on this very point. In light of this vacillation, his answer in his 1842 "Contribution to the Critique of Hegel's *Philosophy of Right*" to the rhetorical question—where "is the positive possibility of German emancipation?"—is well enough known, but still needs to be investigated. This "positive possibility" lies in "the formation of a class with radical chains, a class of civil society that is not a class of civil society, an estate that is the dissolution of all estates, a sphere [of society] that possesses a universal character as a result of its universal suffering."[30] But *how* does the proletariat possess "a universal character as a result of its universal suffering"? The suffering in question somehow has a redemptive quality; in yet another paradoxical formulation, it is the existence of the proletariat as "the complete loss of humanity" that awards it its mission, "the complete regeneration of humanity."[31] As in Matthew 20:16, the last shall be first; it shall be so, as in the "Debates," not because of the proletariat's activity, but because of its deprivation. Its very existence in deprivation establishes its historical mission, which in the first instance appears to involve a series of declamations, denunciations and pronunciamentos:

> By *proclaiming* the dissolution of the hitherto-existing world-order, the proletariat merely *declares* the secret of its own existence, for it is in fact the dissolution of this world order. By *demanding* the negation of private

property, the proletariat merely makes into a principle for society what society has already made into a principle for the proletariat, what, without its co-operation, is already incorporated in it as the negative result of society.[32]

Marx here conflates two different registers, the proletariat's place in the social order, which has indeed been attained "without its co-operation," and its consciousness, which cannot meaningfully be said to be attainable without a degree of cooperation. He avoids the problem of proletarian subjectivity altogether—and does so, to pile irony on irony, in the midst of an essay that busily claims that the impossibility of a minor, "political" revolution in Germany largely results from the fact that *other* social classes lack the subjective wherewithal for even a moderate struggle! The "universal" character of the proletariat is at this stage of Marx's elaboration a static, not a dynamic concept; I would argue, against Avineri, that in his substitution of the proletariat for Hegel's bureaucracy as society's "universal class" Marx here conflates two different registers, the proletariat's place in the social order, which has indeed been attained "without its co-operation" and its consciousness, which must involve at least a measure of "co-operation" on the proletariat's part. The substitution of proletariat as "universal class" for Hegel's bureaucracy as "universal estate" was, at least at the moment of its inception, a dogmatic move that was to have parlous effects on the elaboration not just of Marx's conception of class but also of the state. Like the poor in "Debates," the proletariat is said to "possess" a universal character by being what it is, rather than as a result of what it creates, produces or develops. Marx's position here is unduly foreshortened: revolutionary consciousness—which is absent from "Debates" but has been introduced into the "Contribution" as a desideratum—should not be regarded as a situational "given," but rather as a disposition the oppressed group in question strives to acquire through some form of activity or practice.

And practice—like theory—must be premonitory in character. Intentionality, agency and futurity need to be involved in any meaningful notion of revolutionary (or for that matter nonrevolutionary) subjectivity, as Marx only later (witness *The Eighteenth Brumaire*, to be dealt with in chapter three) became aware. It is arguable that Hegel's distrust of the people displays a greater understanding of the dynamics of oppression and even of what we now call the culture of poverty than Marx's formalistic romanticization of the proletariat in the "Contribution." The *Philosophy of Right*'s treatment of the French Revolution—which appears to have influenced Marx's in ways that await their specification in my next chapter—certainly reveals Hegel's understanding of the point that those who have been oppressed can turn the mistreatment they have received on others, and become oppressors in their turn. And it is Hegel, not Marx, who seems to be aware of the other side of this same coin, that the oppressed can become psychically complicit in their own oppression. But if Marx in his early confrontations with Hegel lapsed into a discernibly pre-Hegelian position, this should surprise only those who mistake the character of the Marx-Hegel confrontation. It is less surprising if we consider what this pre-Hegelian position was, and what it comported. We find Marx in 1843 wrestling with his earlier admiration for a French radical republicanism that seemed, after all, to come out rather well in comparison with lived political reality in the Germany of his day. And we find Marx between 1843 and 1845 criticizing, not extolling, the Jacobin notion of ancient community, virtue and equality as a "merely political" viewpoint, the adoption of which would do nothing to cure real, social ills, and might even prolong the suffering these entailed by claiming to be able to cure these ills by political means. Alan Gilbert's point that Marx throughout the 1840s was driven to reassess the French Revolution and its meaning in successive recapitulations[33] is well taken, even if Gilbert's understanding of the Jacobinism Marx was looking at is unduly foreshortened. (He understands the term proleptically as an embryonic expression of the idea of worker-peasant alliance, a misunderstanding—Jacobinism was an overwhelmingly urban phenomenon—that has the altogether salutary effect of obliging him to document, for the record, Marx's far from simplistic approach to the problems posed by various European peasantries.)

What needs to be remembered as we assess the French Revolution and its effects on Hegel and Marx, in the next chapter, is that the French Revolution had more than one face to present to those who—

like Marx, for a time—would wish to claim its inheritance. Claiming its inheritance has never been a simple matter. One distinct line stretching from the French Revolution extends, conspiratorially, from the *Cercle Social* of *enragés* (Hébert, Roux, Leclerc) through "Gracchus" Babeuf's *Conspiration des Egaux*, through Buonarroti, through Louis-Auguste Blanqui's revolutionary *sociétés* of the 1830s, right through to the League of the Just, Weitling and Communist League. This—along with Marx's celebration of the Silesian Weavers' Revolt of 1844 as the forerunner of an impending German revolution—should remind us that Marx has his place not just on a philosophical line extending from Hegel to Marx but also on a line stretching through successive, active revolutionaries whose communism was attracting workers during the 1830s and 1840s. Marx's position on this line, which became that of disputing conspiratorial or putschist notions of revolution (Weitling became, with others, an "alchemist of revolution") should not obscure the character of the line itself. It gave Marx a medium of existence and a forum from which his views could be broadcast.

2

MARX AND HEGEL: MEMORIES OF UNDERDEVELOPMENT

. . . The French Convention (1792 to 1795) is and remains the lighthouse of all revolutionary epochs. It inaugurated the revolution in that it removed all officials by decree.[1]

Community in its modern form—indeed human association itself, in most of its guises—is in Hegel's view both active and self-conscious. Hegel believed that morality can come to fruition only within politics, and that the state could be an integral, expressive unity. Law should reflect our moral dispositions if it is not to be an instance of pure coercion. Reason, for its part, is not to be regarded as a capacity of the dissociated individual but as something objective and historical, something that takes form in order and community. Community above all else is no longer given. It has to be constructed. Both state and civil society as Hegel and Marx understand the terms are constructs or human creations of the required kind. Moreover, the very being of a modern community resides in nothing that is extraneous to it. Such categories as God, religion, history, tradition, custom, language, race, blood ties—all these, regarded by most conservative thinkers as the mainstays of political legitimacy, were regarded by Hegel as "accidental" rather than central to community properly understood. Community in the modern sense of the term, then, is to be based on freedom from such extraneous determinations. Humanity, with Kant, had quite simply come of age. Modern community explicitly sets itself the task of determining its own being, its own identity. The political sphere is to be self-constituting, and the state, which is "elevated above the sphere of things that are made"[2] is to emerge as the basis, not an effect, of the individual's conscience and will. The self-affirming, self-defining modern subject is an agent, not an actor, released from feudal embeddedness and from all prior ties of dependence; the subject's autonomy can now at last become the politically generative principle, and human will the ground of right.

Self-constitution cannot, however, be absolute or unconditioned. It has its enabling conditions, and these should not be offended against or treated as though they were of no account. The Terror of the French Revolution was treated by Hegel and by Marx in remarkably similar terms, as an example of absolute, therefore misprised political self-constitution going beyond all reasonable historical bounds. Questions about how we should conduct ourselves always arise within a context of beliefs, habits and expectations. The French Revolution had blithely ignored (or attempted to abolish) these, with disastrous results. The outcome of such revolutionary presumption was a "maximum of frightfulness and terror."[3] Self-constitution, which is anything but deficient in principle, becomes deficient—and very dangerous—in practice if historical bounds are transgressed. The Terror is an example of a political illusion, or of an illusion about what politics can and cannot do. It shows what happens when you base politics directly on deficient principle. If political life is cut off, or cuts itself off from the conditions of its exercise, and if, within the orbit of this political life, an atmosphere develops in which nothing is regarded as nonpolitical (as was notoriously the case during the Terror) the illusion of absolute political self-constitution becomes palpable and enshrined. The cold, emotionless, calculating rationalism about human life and death that Hegel associated with Robespierre and Saint-Just chilled him to the marrow. The political sphere is, following the logic of this arid rationalism, abstracted away from all other spheres of human activity and treated as though it were absolutely self-sufficient and of boundless scope. The Terror pointed up, to Hegel and Marx alike, the lesson that if the political community is to determine its own being, and to constitute its own identity, it must do this within the context provided by history, language and tradition. This context cannot be created by political means, nor indeed can it be defined out of existence by political fiat, as the French Jacobins discovered to their (and others') cost. The former lesson impressed itself upon Hegel, the latter, seen as a specifically political illusion, upon Marx—a point to which I shall return.

Hegel's initial reaction to the French Revolution—that is, his reaction prior to the Terror—had been enthusiastic. The revolution, in his opinion had swept away a cobwebbed mass of antiquated, anachronistic institutions, and "had allowed the most advanced moral and political tendencies to assume concrete form."[4] Within France, the revolutionary upsurge abolished aristocratic privilege, ecclesiastical immunities and arbitrary royal authority, placing in their stead formal political equality and constitutional, representative government. It was, into the bargain, a revolution for export (or became one, after Brissot's curdling declamation). Beyond French boundaries, the revolution challenged the "remnants of feudal privilege and servitude, and helped establish rational legal codes, freedom of property and the person, and equal access to governmental service" (the last-named being a particularly live issue for Hegel's generation in Prussia, as John Edward Toews has demonstrated).[5]

These achievements help explain Hegel's apparently hyperbolic and overwritten reactions, of which the characterization of Napoleon as "the world-spirit on horseback" may be the best known. Hegel, indeed, did not shrink from adding to this an estimation of the significance of what the revolutionaries were bent upon: "Never since the sun had stood in the firmament and the planets revolved around him had it been perceived that man's existence centers in his head, i.e., in thought, inspired by which he builds up the world of reality." For our present purposes, what is most striking about Hegel's various, enthusiastic reactions to the French Revolution ("it was a superb sunrise")[6] is not that they linked it with the achievements of Kant in philosophy (though of course they did). It is that, in characterizing the revolution as the heroic consolidation of rational social and political forms, and as having replaced a decaying and obsolete political order with rational institutions, Hegel effectively coupled the revolution with modernity. The news from France presented the historical possibility of a radical transformation of the entire previous political constitution of reality. As Toews has pointed out, the news from France in the earlier stages of the revolution had a personal, generational resonance for Hegel and his contemporaries. All at once, the necessity of accomodation or resignation to the restricted horizons of their fathers' world dissolved; a generation of German intellectuals could now as never before identify their personal crises with the historical crisis of European politics and culture. To put the same point another way, the possibility of state service (which in Prussia included university teaching) as a way out of what has been termed a burgeoning "intellectual proletariat," on the one hand, and hopes for a collective historical transformation, on the other, were conjoined in an unprecedented, and dramatic manner.

Hegel, for his part, was years later to look back and describe the impact of the revolution as a "glorious mental dawn," a time when "a spiritual enthusiasm reverberated throughout the world" because of a general belief that "the reconciliation between the secular and the divine was now accomplished."[7] This widespread initial "spiritual enthusiasm" gradually disintegrated, as we have seen, once the revolution degenerated into war, dictatorship and the Terror, at which point it became a chilling moment of disillusioning truth; but even so, disappointment with the actual direction of historical developments during the mid-1790s did not lead members of Hegel's generation, and did not lead Hegel himself (however embittered he may have been, however betrayed he may have felt) to share in the general disillusionment of many of their contemporaries, and repudiate outright the eschatological hopes the revolution had, from the beginning, aroused. Hegel's generation absorbed the particular political impulse of the French Revolution into what they considered the more fundamental "revolution of the mind," to be sure; but this very absorption entailed the important insight that political liberation was a necessary part—a *sine qua non*, if not *the sine qua non*—of a more broadly cultural and philosophical transformation. Political revolution continued to be regarded as an instrument for the creation of a community of self-legislating moral subjects.

Hegel accordingly devoted much of his time from 1797 to 1801 to an investigation of political economy, history and constitutional theory. His interests were continually aroused by signs of political and social transformation, since these were signs that mankind was, at last liberating itself from the pre-Kantian tutelage of spurious authority, irrational myth and unquestioned dogma. Hegel was (to put it mildly) disinclined to resign himself to the necessity of a bifurcated world in which the philosophical ideals of autonomy, integrity and unity would remain eternally, and by definition, opposed to the social reality of fragmentation and particularized determination.[8] Even though Hegel's dissatisfaction in this regard was in the long run to overreach itself, and to find expression in the early writings of Marx, its more immediate resonance was in the pages of the *Philosophy of Right*. Hegel's central philosophical conviction in that work—which is that philosophic conception of the absolute can become the foundation of a new, cultural, political, and social order only if the stages or "moments" of its self-actualization in history are articulated—cannot occupy us here. Suffice it to say that this conviction is simply incomprehensible if we remove it from Hegel's prior dissatisfaction with the idea that philosophical ideals and social realities by definition have nothing to do with each other.

One of these philosophical stages or "moments" was, in any case, the modern state. It is important to what follows here that we acknowledge that Hegel understood the state as existing within the matrix of social as well as philosophical forces. What started life as the Romantic ideal of the identification of the individual and society needed to be comprehended as an instance of man's long struggle for mutual recognition. Other instances of the same struggle included the development of language, economic activity, social relations and political institutions. Hegel sought to systematize the meaning of the "concrete freedom" of "ethical life" under the conditions produced by the emancipation of the autonomous individual from the bonds of corporate privilege and hierarchical authority. In so doing Hegel showed an acute understanding of, and concern for, the tension between individual freedom as a principle and the impersonal necessity imposed on this principle as a result of the pursuit of individual private interests in modern, civil society.

This tension was to be resolved, as is well enough known, in and by the modern state. But how the state can accomplish this task cannot readily be understood unless we further characterize the tension between autonomy and fragmentation that, in Hegel's view, characterizes modern civil society. People in civil society encounter each other, or themselves through others, only indirectly, or not at all. Self-understanding (such as it is at this level) emphasizes the marginality of others in the conduct of everyday life. The intersection of private interests, aims and purposes serves some sort of public good, but does so indirectly and inadvertently. Rousseau, up to a point, was quite right; it is social, not solitary man who is alienated, but solitude, however tempting transcendental sojourns and autotelic flights may have been, is no solution to the problem of moral and cognitive fragmentation, but simply another expression of the same thing, as the plight of Hegel's Romantic contemporaries vouchsafed. The point remains that access to others, which is the preserve of the family and, at another level, the state in Hegel's triarchy, is denied at the level of civil society, where the fragmentation of human relationships is structural. We cannot connect at the level of economic life, because no agreeement on the fundamentals of political life can possibly emerge there. Rules governing property—its transfer, alienation, inheritance—do not demand moral agreement or assent. They remain external and formal, imposed from without. As economic actors we no not need to commit ourselves to these rules. We need simply observe them if the system is to function predictably.

Hegel's depiction of civil society is as much a portrayal of asocial sociability as Marx's more detailed characterization of industrial capitalism was later to provide—and for many of the same reasons. Hegel's civil society is disruptive, despiritualized. Its morally truncated inhabitants become equivalents one to another, as all distinguishing marks are systematically abstracted away from them. They come to occupy positions that could in principle be occupied by anyone else; Hegel—presciently enough, when we consider that modern civil society did not yet exist in Germany in any cut-and-dried manner—was pointing forward to the idea of a society of interchangeability. Hegel's depiction of civil society was and still remains devastating. It issues from the idea that the uninterrupted self-existence that is entailed in the quest for wealth fails, and must fail, the self. The self becomes unhinged; the dislocated, incoherent individual becomes incomprehensible even to him- or herself.

Civil society for these and other reasons remains incapable of solving the problems its own operation poses, problems that call for a political solution. These are nonetheless specifically modern problems which no premodern state form could have resolved. Under feudalism political privileges had in any case long been considered as private possessions; wealth and power had become coterminous. Hegel's big fear was that the feudal assimilation of wealth to power and power to wealth would recharge itself in the very different register of modernity—as it would, for instance, if the state were regarded as it was regarded by the Scottish "political economists" of Hegel's day as a mere umpire adjudicating economic claims. The state in this case would become not a political or moral agency, but an institutional device for regulating and defending property claims. The "political economists' " espousal of this view of the state indicates that Hegel's fear was by no means unfounded; and, as we shall see, what to Hegel would have been an unwarranted derogation or diminution of the political was to Marx a *fait accompli* to which Hegel's political theory offered no real solution. This is however to anticipate.

In Hegel's theory the state possessed the wherewithal to resolve the tensions animating civil society not despite but because of the changes wrought by the French Revolution. Hegel welcomed Napoleon's victories, even those won against Prussia, as triumphs of the principle of modern, rational politics over the irrational and obsolete political forms of the old regime, as we have seen. Germany, now that its turn had come, would be able to avoid the excesses of the French Revolution, because in Germany politics could and would be complemented (or so Hegel fondly believed) by a German spiritual autonomy that had already found expression in the Protestant tradition and in the philosophy of speculative idealism—each of which had passed the French by.[9] Regeneration was to take the form of a fusion of French politics with German religion and philosophy. But its institutional matrix was to be the state. Hegel placed overwhelming emphasis on the state proper, on its law, administration and constitutional structures, as the sphere within which the conflicts animating civil society were resolved, and the will of the individual could be integrated with the general will of the community.

The premise for the creation of a modern ethical community was to be an affirmation, not a denial, of the liberal individualism heralded by the French Enlightenment and expressed in the French Revolution. But this individualism was emphatically not to be its own justification. Similarly, Hegel up to a point supported free market relations, the sanctity of private property and equality before the law; but he believed in these, as Toews has reminded us, critically, "from the perspective of the educated professional stratum, the bourgeoisie of *Bildung* rather than *Besitz*."[10] The state was there in order not to supplant but to superintend the institutions of civil society, institutions whose operation was, in Marx's later opinion, to be given a new lease of life by the Hegelian state's inability to solve the problems it was supposed to solve. Indeed, whether any state could do what Hegel's state was supposed to do still remains an open question.

But if Hegel believed that the Germans had attained speculatively what the French had gained politically, so that the junction of the two could provide a politically fertile possibility, Marx for his part measured contemporary Germany *against* the French Revolution, and found it seriously wanting. Germans, in Marx's view, far from being in the vanguard, were quite simply "below the level of history." Germany, Marx states bluntly, is "an anachronism, a flagrant contradiction of generally accepted axioms."[11] German conditions were in

Marx's view so retrograde that even their outright abolition would not bring Germany up to date. Germans will quite simply never reach the present, in Marx's early view of them.[12] "If," Marx despaired, "I negate the German state of affairs in 1843, then, according to the French computation of things, I am hardly in the year 1789, and still less in the focus of the present."[13] What is interesting about Marx's position here is that he refutes the modernity of German politics, as Harold Mah has recently pointed out, by admitting, acknowledging and appealing to the modernity of German philosophy. He does not disagree with Hegel's belief that modernity had manifested itself in Germany through the medium of philosophy; he simply regards this disjuncture ("in politics the Germans thought what other nations did")[14] as proof of German backwardness. If "(w)e are the philosophical contemporaries of the present without being its historical contemporaries,"[15] as Marx summed up the situation, then this signals permanent disjuncture, and not at all Hegel's ultimate, and devoutly hoped for reconciliation.

Hegel's philosophy itself is the signal that modern politics appears, and can only appear, in Germany in speculative form. Marx, like Hegel himself, and like his closer contemporary Heinrich Heine, constructs a homology or parallelism between French politics and German thought. But, unlike Hegel or Heine, Marx does not do this in order to align the latter with the former. Marx accepts the uniqueness and singularity of German philosophical and cultural identity, and even gives this identity a decidedly modern character. But he does this not in order to predict the subsequent harmonization of "French" politics with "German" theorizing that Hegel and Heine in their different ways had predicted. Such convergence is, on the contrary, the least likely outcome. The modernity of German philosophy and culture is, in Marx's view, precisely what precludes the possibility of a modern German politics. Marx's fundamental, Feuerbachian point is that German philosophy compensates for an inadequate, deficient politics. Germany thus combines "the civilized shortcomings of the modern world . . . with the barbaric deficiencies of the *ancien régime*";[16] it shares "the restorations of modern nations" without sharing "their revolutions."[17] Thus, "Germany will one day find itself on the level of European decadence without ever having been on the level of European emancipation." Until that happy day, it will find itself marooned, stranded in a kind of historical limbo.[18]

The importance of Marx's early reflections on Germany in particular to his theory of the state in general is not just that the former mark a break from Hegel's beliefs. Neither is it just that it was on the basis of these reflections that Marx originally pinpointed the proletariat as the agency of revolutionary change in Germany, on the grounds that any agency of change in Germany must perforce owe nothing to German culture, politics, philosophy or society. (This latter point, which suggests rather ominously a kind of *politique du pire* according to which the more uprooted the proletariat, the better, raises a host of problems that cannot be dealt with here.) The importance of Marx's "German" reflections is also that their register, like Hegel's, is that of modernity and its characteristics. This very register has received insufficient attention in previous discussions of Marx's state theory. My contention is that, if Marx's theory of the state is looked at in the process of its formation, with respect, that is, to the historical context of its own elaboration, it will look richer and more relevant, more timely to our present-day concerns in the 1990s than other commentators have seen fit to make it seem.

What underlies all Marx's early speculation about the state is an insight of distinctly Hegelian provenance. This is that the distinction between state and civil society is a dualism that demands to be investigated dialectically. By dualism is meant a distinction in which each side or term is dependent upon, and in contradiction with the other. It is not just the state that is capable of trying to absolutize itself or extend itself beyond its own, finite, institutional boundaries. With the dissolution of feudal society, civil society, newly liberated, comes to appear to its champions as "natural," as indeed it still does to libertarian thinkers today. It comes to appear as what it is not because it lacks the determinations of rationality, reflexivity and universality which are said to characterize the state. Civil society as the state's counterpart appears as immediate, as lacking the mediations that characterize the state, and as "given." But civil society is in reality necessarily mediated, and not "given" at all. It is a product of the way in which feudalism was overcome.

One of the features of the concept of "political emancipation" elaborated by Marx in his 1843 essay "On 'The Jewish Question' " is that the political overthrow of the *ancien régime* released the economy from political determination from without. Because civil society was no longer politically determined, because it was to all appearances no longer determined by any rules or conventions external to its own, inner workings, it looked (to the early political economists, for example) as though a "natural" core of human activity, economic life, had been latent all along within the political and theological carapace of the feudal past, awaiting only its uncovering and liberation. Hegel and Marx were, in their different ways, highly critical of so providential an interpretation; and the more thoroughgoing of the two criticisms, Marx's, owed a great deal to Hegel's. "Political emancipation" from the feudal past was in the first instance only, or "purely" political—that is to say, one-sided and foreshortened. To begin with, "political emancipation" in short order becomes complicit in civil society's drive to remove whatever remained of feudal relations of production, relations which constrained and restricted productive activity instead of doing what comes "naturally" and encouraging its expansion. Political emancipation from feudalism accordingly produces a fundamental, and unprecedented dualism. In so far as "the political emancipators," as Marx calls them, conceive their task as being that of protecting civil society and safeguarding its members' interests, the state becomes a means to ends external to itself. By instrumentalizing itself in this way, the state contradicts its own grounding principle as a political community, and at the same time sanctions and legitimates the misrecognition, the blocked encounters among selves, that constitute, inform and fragment civil society.

The foundational claim of bourgeois revolutions is that of being able to speak in the name of "man," as in "the Rights of Man"—in the name, that is, of mankind in general, humanity *sans phrase*. Such claims are not meant to refer to people as producers and consumers, employers and employees, or as readers and writers. The claim to be able to speak in the name of "man" to the contrary, voices a demand for the transcendence of particular differences separating individuals one from another, and of the interests that are appropriate to this same separation. The state, once it is validated by the "rights of man," is there to generalize and to unify, to express not what divides us from one another but whatever it is that we continue to have in common.

It is, however, precisely the play of these "particular" differences that had called forth the state in its revamped form, and indeed had made the modern state necessary in the first place. To put the same point another way, the gridlock of particular interests, once these are given free play, constitutes the predicament that requires and invokes a political solution. Universal equivalence or common identity among people, the ideal underlying the articulation of the "rights of man," presupposes differences and distinctions among people living their lives in civil society, differences deeply rooted enough to have made universalistic claims of the required type necessary in the first place. To the extent that these differences matter to people in their everyday lives in civil society, their formal political identity or equivalence is likely to appear hollow and empty, in which case the state will, at the level of definition, be inadequate to its own, self-appointed task.

The difficulty here is not that the various avatars of "the rights of man" were blithely unaware of the problem they faced. It is, rather, that their efforts to confront and solve it are necessarily incoherent. The formal and "ideal" nature of the political claims the modern state advances on its own behalf requires that equivalence and identity among its its citizenry not be seen as a *fait accompli*. Hegel's argument in *The Philosophy of Right* had, according to Marx, indicated the danger that the modern, or even the Prussian, state, in having provided a complex system of institutions with which the individual subject could identify, had already allowed for critical reflection on the part of this subject on the institutions in question. If it is not a *fait accompli,* identity has to be seen as a potential category. But at another, even more intriguing level, the horizon formed by potential identity and integration necessarily becomes recessive and elusive. It never becomes possible to say we have finally reached it.

In the event, this paradox did not prevent what was to be a significant nineteenth-century development. Since the problem of equivalence or identity must necessarily precede and provoke its formalization, a developmental narrative must intervene in order to produce the formal identity or equivalence of citizens. This narrative had to do with the extension of the suffrage. Nineteenth-century political elites, having recoiled in horror from the excesses of the French Revolution and the direct, participatory democracy it was held to have enjoined, restricted political participation in two ways. They restricted it vertically, with respect to *who* was to be allowed to participate, and horizontally, with respect to *how much* participation was to be sanctioned. The latter question proved notoriously easier to settle than the former. Periodic voting in elections whose agenda, and whose very timing, was decided elsewhere was to mark the outer limit of political participation, no matter who was deemed "fit" to exercise the right to vote. Only then was "fitness" dutifully defined in such a way as to include, in their proper order, first workers and/or the propertyless, then (in our own century) women, and then (again in our own century) colonial peoples of color in their struggles for independence from their various "mother" countries.

These, however one evaluates them, are achievements, or deferrals of some magnitude. "On 'The Jewish Question' " is much more relevant to, and suggestive about these future developments than one might initially think. To see how and why this is the case we must, in the first instance, stand back and take our bearings. "On 'The Jewish Question' " proposes, at a very basic level, that the universalistic claims propounded by the modern state at the moment of its inception are claims advanced in a certain way for a certain purpose. It is on the basis of these claims that the modern state is said to be able to reconcile people, one with another, on the basis of their common humanity, their common status as human beings as such, their personhood *sans phrase*. Why did people need to be reconciled by political means? Because of the differences and distinctions setting them against each other in civil society. This means that claims advanced on behalf of the modern state are necessarily essentialist claims. It is argued that, beyond the differences exhibited within civil society, there lies some sort of human essence that transcends these differences, to which the state as a "universal" entity corresponds or can correspond.

This argument is at root Hegelian. Hegel's defense, as Shlomo Avineri and others have reminded us, is less of the Prussian state in particular as of the modern state in general.[19] What legitimates this latter category is, above all, its reconciliatory character. It is a "universal" entity in character and in purpose because it heals the wounds caused by the dissociative tendencies animating and fragmenting civil society. The Declaration of the Rights of Man and Citizen of 1789, coming as it did in the wake of the American Declaration of Independence and of the various American constitutions Marx was also concerned to anatomize in "On 'The Jewish Question'," supposes that citizenship in its modern form can reunite, can reunify, can recreate bonds among people who are dispersed across civil society. Citizenship reassembles, puts together again something that is always already rent asunder.

On the face of it, this solution seems more Rousseauean than Hegelian. Hegel, after all, had not extolled citizenship as a reintegrative agency in anything like the same way as Rousseau, and for that matter the French Revolution, had. Indeed, the complex, articulated, institutional structure outlined in Hegel's *Philosophy of Right* was in many ways explicitly designed to take the sting out of radical theories of participatory democracy like Rousseau's, and to indicate that such theories presuppose a commonality that they cannot of themselves create.

But if participatory democracy cannot provide the satisfactions its proponents, like Rousseau, thought it must provide, it is reasonable to extend Hegel's theory and propose that representative democracy, which Rousseau regarded as a contradiction in terms, is also unlikely to provide these. From the point of view Marx adopts in "On 'The Jewish Question'," the differences between representative and participatory democracy may not be enormous, since they share a belief in what Marx calls "the abstract nature of political man." Marx cites— or misquotes—Rousseau's chapter on the Legislator in the *Social Contract* as an example of this kind of abstraction. He does so as a means of ridiculing Rousseau's idea that a change in human nature would be required if political regeneration is to take place. In linking Rousseau with the theories of representative democracy that were propounded during the French and American Revolutions, theories Rousseau himself would surely have disparaged, Marx was stretching a point. But the point in question could be stretched still further, to cover Hegel. Marx was just as critical of Hegel's proffered solution to the problem of social and economic dislocation as he was of Rousseau's, or of those proffered during the French Revolution.

The complex articulation of Estates, Corporations, Monarchy and a bureaucracy based on that liberal passe-partout, *la carrière ouverte aux talents*, that Hegel outlines in *The Philosophy of Right* was in Marx's opinion an attempt at a medieval solution to a specifically modern problem. The dissociative tendencies that characterize civil society as Hegel portrays it are, after all, distinctively modern. They depend for their existence and persistence, as Hegel in his own way had recognized, upon a resolutely modern development, the growth of market relations and individualistically defined interests among human beings, and upon utilitarian justifications for these. These tendencies and justifications are unlikely to be countermanded by the extension of feudal monarchy, however streamlined it may have been in its presentation.

But monarchy is not the only aspect of feudalism that the French Revolution, in particular, had surpassed. What underlay feudal monarchy was a distinctive feature of medieval civilization, one that modernity could not possibly retrieve or resuscitate. In the Middle Ages a person's social status and political function were held to be inextricably, organically linked. To be a noble or a serf or a king was to occupy a position on a single ladder or scale. It was unclear where the political hierarchy ended and the socioeconomic hierarchy began, for hierarchy itself was supposed to be unitary. It was also held to involve personal characteristics. A noble was supposed not just to behave nobly, but to *be* noble; a serf was supposed to be servile, a churl churlish, a knave knavish. Such a system of justifications was, no doubt, shot through with wishful thinking; nobles, in all likelihood, did not, in practice, act nobly under all circumstances. The dominant presumption was nevertheless that they were *supposed* to act nobly, that to be of high birth implied elevated modes of conduct. The social, political, economic and personal were supposed to be mutually supporting categories. Your position in society, as in the Aristotelian political theory that was frequently used for justificatory purposes, was held to provide an accurate measure of where you ought to be in the God-given feudal hierarchy. Society during the Middle Ages had been made up accordingly of private spheres, each of which also had a public, political character. An estate was a social group that also wielded political power, in regulating its own affairs and in dealing with other groups in society.[20] Political and social life were cognate categories.

The contrast with modernity is explicit. Political power in modernity becomes concentrated, distilled, in a single, unitary body, the state. And the modern state, unlike its historical precursors, is monolithic, at least in the sense that it exists above and in opposition to the various private, material interests and impulses that make up civil society. In modern civil society itself, as Hegel to his credit had recognized, every one has a use, no one a place. Encounters among people are bound to remain blocked or indirect so long as society is made up of interchangeable slots into which anyone, in principle, could be fitted. The capitalist division of labor, as Marx was to recognize in *The German Ideology,* is unprecedented in the specific sense that the assignment of different tasks to different people need have nothing whatsoever to do with the skills, aptitudes, talents, gifts or inclinations of the individuals involved. Real, individual differences distinguishing one person from another are bracketed, put to one side. They do not cease to exist; they cease to matter. They do not count in the organization of labor and production. And they do not count at the political level either. The abstract equality involved in the modern notion of citizenship is what the word "abstract," in its Hegelian usage, implies: partial, incomplete, something that takes the part for the whole. Men, and not yet women, are said to be equal in their capacity as political beings the moment each and every one of them is enabled or permitted to cast a ballot.

What this conceals and, if we are to believe Marx, is designed to conceal, is the fact that in civil society people are going to be very unequal indeed, though not unequal in the feudal sense. To see this we must examine more closely the nature of the disaggregation and dispersion to which the modern state, as Marx sees it, corresponds. Modern civil society in effect reinvents human inequality. What comes to matter about a person, socially and economically speaking, is that person's *least* distinctive attribute, his or her capacity to expend labor power of the kind that is instantly and unproblematically measurable or quantifiable against that of anyone, or everyone else. What is distinctive about who a person is, or what a person does, is abstracted away. The modern state may be said to be "abstract" not in an identical but certainly in a corresponding sense. It, too, refers neither to people's real differences one from another, nor indeed to the occupational differences that are superimposed upon these differences without significantly expressing them. The modern state in effect "transcends" all these differences by simply ignoring them, by treating them as though they were of no account. But its "abstract" character does not end at this point. The state may be said to be "abstract" in the additional sense that what Marx calls its "illusory universality" attempts to compensate people for the real wrongs done to them in civil society. The state may also be said to be "abstract" because its "universality," however compensatory it may be, *is* "illusory." This means not that the state ceases to exist—its existence as it wages its wars and taxes its subjects is palpable—but that what it stands for, community, the public realm, is represented in an alien manner.

The public realm, so conceptualized, can only be defined against, or counterposed to the private—to which it is, in any case, said to be subordinate. Civil society, a network of resolutely private interests, operates systematically in such a way as to deny the possibility of any real community. The illusory, compensatory realm represented by the modern state is no more and can be no more than its surrogate or stand-in. The state's supposedly public character is correlative with the contours of people's real, private lives. As such, it is necessarily "abstract" in that it abstracts from people's individual and private characteristics and bases itself on what all people are said to share. What they share is at once bare-bones or residual *and* essentialist: some common human essence that is reflected and referred to by the modern state. But this essence is *itself* necessarily "abstract." "Humanity," so conceived, which is said to entitle people to political representation, bears no discernible relationship to who people are and what they do. The modern state, that is to say, marginalizes people's identities and exists only on the basis of this same marginalization. The time had not and has not yet come when we can afford to let that most convenient of abstractions, "the individual," be the measure of his or her own individuality.

This way of understanding the modern state in effect exposes the coordinates of the public-private distinction that liberal theory and practice have managed to map out and make hegemonic from Marx's day right down to our own. Liberalism proposes that the private is ultimately preeminent over the public, which is said to exist in the last analysis for the sake of the private. The private is defined and privileged against the political. This separation and this privileging have of course been challenged, but it is sobering to recognize that the most significant challenges were advanced at the points of juncture between feudalism and capitalism, just as the public-private split as we have learned to understand it first threatened to take hold. Rousseau, to give one prominent example, regarded the polarization of private and public as a real political threat, and was either strikingly original or utterly old-fashioned in attempting to reverse its terms. To Rousseau, it was public, not private life that was beleaguered and stood in need of protection, protection against the alluring siren songs of private interest, including those that proceeded from the family. Hegel, for his part, approached the private-public polarity rather differently. He redefined it in such a way that the family, a troublesome concept to Rousseau, became in the argument of *The Philosophy of Right* an officially sanctioned realm alongside civil society within the general area of private life. He also insisted that the private is the sphere of material necessity as well as the source of spontaneous, affective feelings and actions. To Hegel as to Rousseau, it was nevertheless the public realm, the arena of state action, that was privileged as the site of freedom.

What concerned Marx as a result of these prior developments was evidently not the weighting of terms within a pre-given public-private polarity, but what had happened with the onset of capitalist society to this polarity itself. What does the polarity mean? To what does it refer? To what needs, or interests, does it speak? And why did it arise when it arose, and not any earlier? In the first instance, the "splitting of man into public and private," Marx wrote in 1843, has the effect of dividing and debilitating both communal and individual existence, by setting them up against each other, as though they were zero-sum categories that could exist and operate only at each others' expense. In accordance with the double character of this loss, Marx famously looks forward to a time when "social force is no longer separated from [the individual] as political power,"[21] and argues that in the meantime bourgeois society will have redefined and reinforced the public-private split in an original manner. With the advent of modern, bourgeois society, "man" was no longer even considered to be a generic social being. People's powers were by the same token no longer apprehended as social powers. Their political existence, the realm, that is to say, of their social, collective and moral being, was alienated from the more immediate demands of their concrete material existence. Such alienation denotes, in the first instance, loss: the immense loss involved in the historical process that had instituted and was to sustain these changes. But alienation, here as elsewhere, must be seen not just as loss of control by the agent over what is alienated away, in this case the agent's political capacities, but also as enmity, and not just remoteness, on the part of what is alienated towards the agent.

That this is precisely what we find is best highlighted by using a by now familiar, but nonetheless telling contrast. As we have seen, during the Middle Ages "the classes of civil society and the political classes were identical because the organic principle of civil society was the principle of the state" at one and the same time. In medieval times, that is, "the political state in distinction from civil society was nothing but the representation of nationality." It is only the modern, bourgeois age that, by contrast, posited "the separation of civil society and political state as two different spheres, firmly opposed to each other."[22] Faced with this separation, a separation that is constitutive of the modern age, the escapism involved in appealing across the Middle Ages to ancient models, such appeals having been a resource for the French Revolutionaries and for Rousseau, and a temptation even for Hegel, can be seen as doubly misleading. In *The Holy Family* Marx accuses the French Revolutionaries of having strutted around the revolutionary stage in borrowed costume, having fatefully confused modern society with the classical city state in general or with Rome in particular. (The importance of this example of historical cross-dressing will become redoubled once we examine *The Eighteenth Brumaire of Louis Bonaparte*.) The specifically political illusion to which the French had fallen prey had been that of attempting to establish a version of "classical" political freedom in a context that no longer allowed for it, to establish ancient freedom in modern conditions. With the Greeks in particular, "civil society was a slave to political society." In modern, bourgeois society the opposite priorities pertain. In the Greek polis, no specifically or exclusively political sphere existed apart from the daily conduct of life and work. Public life, on the contrary, was the "real content" of individual life; the person who had no political status was the slave, an *Unmensch*. "In Greece the *res publica* was the real private concern, the real content of the citizen . . . and the private man was slave, i.e. the political state as political was the true and sole content of the citizen's life and will."[23]

In the Middle Ages, by contrast, the "private sphere" came to acquire political status in its own right. "Property, commerce, society, man (i.e., private man, the serf), were all political: the material content of the state was given by reason of its form; every private sphere had a political character or was a political sphere" directly. If property was paramount in feudal society it was so because its distribution and transmission were directly political matters. This means that the Middle Ages were characterized by a more integrated way of life in which "the life of the people" and "the life of the state" were congruent, and not mutually opposed. Yet this does not lead Marx to favor such integration, however able his anatomization of modern disintegration may have been. The congruence of "people" and "state" in the Middle Ages was made possible only because feudal societies were, by their very nature, fundamentally unfree. As Marx put it in a striking paradox, the medieval world was the "democracy of unfreedom, accomplished alienation."[24] As such, it furnishes no model for the future, just an unavailable antitype to the present.

On the one hand, "the old civil society [in the Middle Ages] had a directly political character; that is, the elements of civil life such as property, the family and types of occupation had been raised, in the form of lordship, caste and guilds, to being elements of political life."

But on the other hand, what Marx calls "political emancipation," coincident upon bourgeois revolution,

> released the political spirit, which had been broken, fragmented and lost, as it were, in the various culs-de-sac of feudal society. [Political emancipation] gathered up this scattered spirit, liberated it from its entanglement from civil life, and turned it into a sphere of the community, the general concern of the people independent of these particular elements of civil life. A particular activity and situation in life sank into a merely individual significance, no longer forming the general relation of the individual to the whole.[25]

Political emancipation, in other words, is "a reduction of man to [the status of] a member of civil society, to [that of] an egoistic independent individual on the one hand and to [that of] a citizen on the other."[26] The character of these wholly original categories and of the no less unprecedented relationship between them is of vital importance. It is by being an "egoistic independent individual" that one becomes a "citizen," and vice versa. The categories are dualistic: interdependent, mutually reinforcing—but no less contradictory for these reasons. Belonging to one of them entails needing to belong to the other; neither can be complete all on its own as a focus for association, and neither can be collapsed into its counterpart. "The abstraction of the state belongs to modern times because the abstraction of private life belongs to modern times." In consequence, "the abstract, reflected opposition" between civil or social and political life belongs only to modern times too; and "what distinguishes the modern state from those states in which a substantial unity between people and state obtained is . . . that the constitution itself has been formed into an actuality alongside the real life of the people."[27] The modern state, whatever its protestations on its own behalf, *cannot* reconcile divisions in society, divisions which are reproduced within the individuals who make up society, who are socioeconomic actors *and* citizens—since it is itself a term and product of these same divisions.

The modern state claims in effect to be both the site of reconciliation of one individual with others, and the agency by which such reconciliation is to be brought about. But the claim is incoherent. The modern state by its very nature lacks and must lack the wherewithal to effect any such reconciliation, since its very existence *qua* state preys upon the disintegration that made it necessary in the first place. If, as Hegel to his credit had recognized, the emergence of the modern state presupposes a radical and historically unprecedented separation of politics from society, it in no way follows from this separation that the modern state is able to liberate people from the parlous effects of predatory social agencies (private property, the division of labor, religion, money). All of these are, on the contrary, newly freed from, and unencumbered by, any semblance of political control. By its very nature, the modern state permits, and to a considerable extent must permit these predatory agencies, as well as other agencies that are more properly the province of the state itself, such as the police, the military, the bureaucracy, to flourish freely.

This point entails something that is directly pertinent to the essay by Bruno Bauer, "The Jewish Question," that had occasioned Marx's response. This is that the split between the citizen and the adherent of a particular religious faith is part of a much more fundamental schism. "The contradiction in which the adherent of a particular religion finds himself in relation to his citizenship is but one aspect of the universal secular contradiction between political state and civil society." If religion, no longer officially sanctioned or promulgated by the modern state, is displaced in such a way that it becomes a purely individual concern, this does not mean that the hold of religion on people who resort to it for reasons of their own is in any way lessened correspondingly. "Political emancipation" from religion, the emergence, in other words, of a state that prides itself on its "secular" character, leaves and must leave religion itself in existence. The state still needs religion, not this time to define its purposes by, but instead to define its purposes against. In this way, "the emancipation of the state from religion is not the emancipation of actual man from religion."[28] It is property that provides Marx, at this juncture, with his most immediate point of comparison. The abolition of property qualifications for the franchise does not, indeed cannot, abolish property. To the contrary, it presupposes the continued existence and significance of property, along with distinctions among people based upon the amount and type of property they hold. "Political emancipation" frees property from political restraint without at the same time freeing people from the restraint imposed by property and property relations in civil society. This point can be put more strongly. Once the degree and kind of property held is officially declared to be politically irrelevant, of no political account, it is property itself that becomes freed, responsible to nothing outside itself. Its newly oppressive, because newly unrestrained, nature becomes clearly exposed and keenly experienced by those persons who in their everyday lives bear the brunt of its free play. Property and religiosity are re-entrenched, not abolished, by the transition from medieval to modern state-forms. Any medieval state-form, using religion for its own purposes, obscures rather than expresses what are at root the human, not political, bases of religiosity. By contrast, the modern state that parades its lack of connection with any particular religious creed, the state that, as it were, professes its lack of profession of any particular set of religious beliefs, is not the abolition but the very consummation of religiosity. Its enunciation of its own secularism displaces religion from the orbit of government back into that of everyday life in civil society. The emancipation of the state from religion, much like its self-emancipation from property, does nothing for those who remain under the sway of religion and property. Religion, according to Marx, "only begins to exist in its true scope when the state declares it to be non-political and thus leaves it to itself."[29]

Marx, in making these claims, was concerned to identify a defining feature of the modern state. With the collapse of feudalism, a collapse that in Germany was far from complete, as Marx was all too well aware, civil society and the state become discontinuous in an unprecedented, radical way. Civil society and the property relations that animate it become wholly emancipated from all significant political restraint for the first time in history. This freedom, which is freedom of a very particular kind, appears on the social agenda for the very first time. Private life becomes independent of any consideration of the common good, or of public purpose. Political limitations on economic activity give way, and the market, newly sanctioned, becomes self-regulating. Emancipation from feudal, communal restrictions (the prohibition of usury, the abolition of guild regulations, sumptuary laws, censorship by ecclesistical fiat) has the effect of formally freeing civil society from state control.

The removal of political limitations on economic activity is decisive. It was signified most dramatically by, without being limited to, the Declaration of the Rights of Man and Citizen of 1789, which marked the emancipation of civil society from the purview of the state. Just as the state became "universal," out of the clutches of king, aristocracy and priesthood, proclamations of the "rights of man" recognized and acknowledged the citizenship of the individual *qua* individual, rich or poor, propertied or unpropertied, Jew or Christian. Citizenship thenceforward no longer depended on birth, rank, status or occupation. All such "accidental" characteristics or attributes were no longer to count politically. They were instead relegated to the level of purely individual concerns. This fundamental shift, Marx was concerned to point out, had political and social implications that may not have been immediately apparent, but which were nevertheless crucially important.

The emergence of bourgeois society that is signalled by the Declaration and other, similar documents bifurcates human existence in a fundamentally new way. Henceforward, "private" and "public" were no longer to be in any sense contiguous terms, as they had been in the past. In the Middle Ages, to take the most immediate example, the dominant persons in society had been, as we have seen, politically dominant at the same time, and by the same token. The privileges of the feudal, landowning aristocracy had organically linked the form of the state with the structure of society. Society had therefore had a "directly political character," albeit a resolutely unfree political character. But "political emancipation" detaches political significance from private condition in a radically original way. Citizenship and private life become discontinuous categories, mutually exclusive spheres of activity for the first time. The individual is now a worker, or a capitalist, or whatever, *and* a citizen. Vocation and political status are no longer linked together organically. Indeed, nothing links them together at all. Each is counterposed to the other. Occupational category and political status at best coexist uneasily alongside each other. This means that the best that can be hoped for is a kind of unstable equilibrium between the two, but since their respective imperatives are divergent in principle, one is entitled to wonder how frequently even this rather low-level hope is likely to find realization in practice.

The confrontation between these two newly counterposed areas of human existence has more than a purely conceptual existence. It is going to find expression within each individual as a rigid distinction between exclusive roles. The schism of state and society constantly reproduces itself within each individual, as in a distillate. Marx was to extend this particular and ominous outcome of "political emancipation" in *The German Ideology*:

> In the course of historical evolution, and precisely through the inevitable fact that within the division of labor social relations take on an independent existence, there appears a division within the life of each individual, in so far as it is personal and in so far as it is determined by some branch of labor and the conditions pertaining to it. (We do not mean . . . that, for example, the rentier, the capitalist, etc., cease to be persons: but their personality is conditioned and determined by quite definite class relationships and the division appears only in their opposition to another class and, for themselves, only when they go bankrupt.) In the [feudal] estate, this is as yet concealed; for instance, a nobleman always remains a nobleman, a commoner always a commoner, apart from his other relationships, a quality inseparable from their individuality. The division between the personal and the class individual, the accidental nature of the conditions of life for the individual, appears only with the emergence of the class, which is itself a product of the bourgeoisie.[30]

It is these newly "privatized" individuals who, denied any real participation in the conditions governing their existence, will seek solace or recompense. They seek this, as Feuerbach had famously pointed out, in a realm of universality, a realm separate from and counterposed to the limited sphere of the individual's mundane, finite existence. But with the onset of "political emancipation" this realm is no longer just religious. It is also, and more nearly, political. Marx awards the state in its modern form the consolatory functions once monopolized, according to Feuerbach, by religion. In the words of one striking passage:

> By its nature the perfected political state is man's species-life in opposition to his material life. All the presuppositions of this egoistic life remain in civil society outside the state but as qualities of civil society. Where the political state has achieved its full development man leads a double life, a heavenly as well as an earthly life, not only in thought or consciousness but also in reality. In the political community he regards himself as a communal being; but in civil society he is active as a private individual, treats other men as means, reduces himself to a means, and becomes the plaything of alien powers. The political state is as spiritual in relation to civil society as heaven is in relation to earth . . . In the state where he counts as a species-being, he is the imaginary member of an imaginary universality, divested of his real individual life and endowed with an unreal universality.[31]

The "unreal" universality of the citizen and the state are intrinsically connected. Taken together, they are coextensive in an ominous way. The remoteness and abstraction of political life, or what passes for political life, from ordinary, profane pursuits in civil society over which the state has relinquished control have distinct political consequences. Universality and communality remain part of people's lives in a "Feuerbachian"-compensatory fashion if their attainment, an attainment that speaks to a real and fundamental human need, is withheld or foreclosed in reality. The Feuerbachian insight that what people lack in fact they will attain, or devise, in fancy still applies but needs at this point to be refocused. If meaningful participation is withheld or denied, it turns abstract and fanciful, and thus newly appropriate to the fantasy world of citizenship. The state, simply put, becomes a sophisticated kind of religious fetish.

The separation of people's social nature into distinct, exclusive spheres of privacy and universality means that the latter ideal necessarily becomes fictitious. To say this is not simply to assert the comparatively trivial proposition that universality minus something is no longer universal. It is to underscore the historical point that that the state was first presented as "universal" at the very moment when the political was derogated, by the early "political economists," for example, as being in principle secondary to the more fundamental purposes of economic life. The state's "universality" was said to consist in its instrumental status as the "night watchman" holding the ring around the pursuit of privatistically defined interests. This means that political emancipation is by its very nature bound to have the effect of displacing and negating the very satisfactions and needs in whose name it justifies and must justify itself; Marx's comparison of the modern state with the rather older ideal of heaven is anything but a merely rhetorical trope.

At first glance, of course, it may seem that Marx in "On 'The Jewish Question'," an essay that was ostensibly a *pièce d'occasion* provoked by Bauer's statist opposition to Jewish emancipation, was simply concerned to invoke Feuerbach on religion against Bruno Bauer on religion. But Marx's awarding of religious or "heavenly" status to the modern, secular state in effect turns both arguments inside out. Bauer is, in short order, left high and dry. But Feuerbach, too, suffers a not dissimilar fate. The point here is not that Marx for a moment disparaged Feuerbach's characterization of religion as such. Quite to the contrary, his characterization of religion, as this was famously given expression as "the opium of the masses,"[32] is Feuerbachian through and through, to the point of reminding his readers that opiates in the modern age are commonly taken and not administered. The point is rather that Feuerbach's *idée maîtresse* of religion as comporting an imaginary compensation for wrongs suffered at a more "real," everyday level undergoes a sea change once it is extended to cover the state, and once the "real" level is stretched to cover modern civil society. Once this move is made, Feuerbach's notion of compensation is no longer properly Feuerbachian, and a point made about, and unduly restricted to religion has become a much more general capstone of "transformative criticism" at large. Such criticism has now become a method of social and political, and not just religious or psychological, analysis. Marx's point, that the modern state at its most apparently secular has become "heavenly," effects this change of register in an audacious, but not unfounded, manner. Heaven in relation to earth had, after all, long been regarded as what the Germans call a *Jenseits*, a "beyond," an otherworldly realm toward which we are intended to strive, and by which we are meant to set our sights. Heaven is an object of aspiration, the very summit of our endeavors, the goal, the *terminus ad quem* that alone gives aim and meaning to the vicissitudes of our earthly existence, and which alone makes our sufferings worth enduring.

Heaven is the ultimate in transcendence. It is changeless and harmonistic. It exists outside time and space. It is salvific and valedictory. And it is an object not of the apprehension we bring to bear on the everyday world we inhabit, but of contemplation. Heaven is sublime. It is a transcendent realm having immanent effects. It renders us passive and docile. Heaven is also, in Feuerbachian terms, a projection as well as an idealization. It moves, affects, impresses, refortifies those of us prepared to contemplate its mysteries. It gives us the strength to carry on. Which is to say that it is called forth by our *need* to carry on. Theodicy does not just acknowledge suffering; it *requires* suffering. Thanks to heaven, our capacity to master the conditions of our earthly existence is projected away from our earthly arena and assigned to superhuman forces that in turn impose the terms of their own significance. Only then is it up to us to interpret, internalize and make sense of heaven, and to adjust our actions here below accordingly. Heaven is, then, a text, not unlike a written constitution, as Marx was only too well aware.

What Hegel had put forward as the human need for the universal, corresponding to the communal side of human nature, or to what Marx, following Feuerbach, called "species-being," is under current conditions bound to remain elusive and unsatisfied. The proof of this is not so much religious as political. Once civil society was emancipated, freed from political restraint for the first time, property relations were enabled and encouraged to penetrate every crevice of the supposedly transcendent political realm. Yet the very fact that this realm, like heaven, is supposed to be transcendent, sets up a kind of vicious circle within the orbit of which people, because of their susceptibility to the vagaries of class and property relations within civil society, will, in their search for solace, award religious credentials to the state itself, no matter how secular this latter prides itself on being.

> The members of the political state are religious by virtue of the dualism between individual life and species-life, between the life of civil society and political life. They are religious inasmuch as they relate to their political life, which is beyond their real individuality as though it was their true life.[33]

What this means is that the state's abstract, idolatrous universality and economic laissez-faire are intrinsically linked. Political emancipation replaces the impact of personal power with the impersonal arbitrariness, the repressive anonymity of Adam Smith's "hidden hand." The illusion of liberty that the modern state creates and sustains is appropriate to the state's inability to liberate people from the disastrous effects of social forces to which it gives a free hand, and allows to flourish freely. The ideological expression and celebration of this state of affairs is the doctrine of the "rights of man" enunciated by the French and American Revolutions.

> None of the supposed rights of man go beyond the egoistic man, man as he is, man as a member of civil society: that is as an individual separated from the community, withdrawn into himself, wholly occupied with his private interest and acting in accordance with his private caprice. Man is far from being considered, in the rights of man, as a species-being: on the contrary, species-life itself, society, appears as a system that is external to the individual and as a limitation of his original independence. The only bond between men is natural necessity, need and private interest, the preservation of their property and their egoistic persons. . . . The political liberators reduce the political community to a mere means of preserving these so-called rights of man. . . . The citizen is said to be the servant of the egoistic man . . . the sphere in which man functions as a species-being is degraded below the sphere in which he functions as a political being . . . it is man as a bourgeois and not man as a citizen who is considered the true and authentic man.[34]

The "rights of man" refer to people as though they were self-contained, self-sufficient, self-motivated atoms closed to one another;

and this portrayal leads by extension to a social system close to the Hobbesian *bellum omnium contra omnes*.

> This is the liberty of man viewed as an isolated monad, withdrawn into himself . . . [it is] not based on the association of man with man but rather on the separation of man from man. . . . The practical application of the right of liberty is the right of private property . . . it lets every man find in every other man not the reality but the limitation of his own freedom.[35]

The "right of liberty" is, then, not based on the "connection" of human beings but on their separation.[36] But the concept of liberty enshrined by political emancipation regards the prevailing form of society as "natural," which is to presume that connections among human beings are *naturally* antagonistic. Liberty accordingly is defined only negatively, as freedom from interference, rather than positively, as freedom to or freedom for. In Marx's words, political emancipation emancipates civil society "from even the semblance of a universal content." In the Hegelian lexicon Marx is employing here, semblance or appearance [*Schein*] is one thing, illusion or *Täuschung* another. A *Schein* is an objective, if incomplete or abstract, manifestation of the rational and universal. This means that, in portraying the ideology and the reality of modern civil society as "atomistic," Marx was not claiming that people were in fact reduced to the status of atoms but that their behavior was in certain respects atomistic. To derive the former from the latter proposition would be to fall prey to the illusion of such theorists as Hobbes and Spinoza. Civil society was not, in Marx's view, the simple aggregate of human atoms, disconnected singulars unrelated to one another, that some British economists and utilitarians imagined, but a state of universal dependence of all on all.

> It is natural necessity, essential human properties, however alienated they may seem to be, and interest that hold together the members of civil society; civil, not political life is their real tie. It is therefore not the state that holds together the atoms of civil society, but the fact that they are atoms only in imagination, in the heaven of their fancy, but in reality beings tremendously different from atoms, in other words not divine

egoists but egoistic human beings. Only political superstition today imagines that social life must be held together by the state . . . [in] reality the state is held together by civil life.[37]

Marx's essay "On 'The Jewish Question' " was much more than a polemical *Streitschrift*, a mere riposte to the essay by Bruno Bauer that had provoked and occasioned it, even if it does turn the tables on Bauer's conviction that the Jews ought to give up practising the Jewish religion in order to enjoy the rights of citizenship; Bauer takes himself to be proposing a secular solution to a religious question, whereas in reality he is proposing a religious solution to a secular question. Marx extended the terms of the debate by incorporating into what was ostensibly an attack on Bauer a host of references—to Feuerbach, Hegel, Rousseau, the ideologues of the "rights of man," and others. Hegel, as well as Feuerbach, should be credited with having linked religion to human deprivation, with having refined the Enlightenment's view of religion as an agency that compensated, or tried to compensate, people for a social arena where their real lives were out of joint. Marx goes well beyond this kind of designation, however, in indicating that private, internalized religiosity signified a much more radical kind of alienation than did official, institutionalized religion. Indeed, Marx's terrain was by 1843 quite different from that of Feuerbach, for this and for other reasons. Marx conspicuously does not rest content, as Feuerbach had, with dramatically uncovering and exposing to the daylight the deficiency of religion as such, as though it were merely a hidden secret that would evaporate of its own accord once it was exposed to the atmosphere. Instead, he offers a historical analysis based on an analysis of people's nonreligious life; and in particular, he emphasises the part played in this nonreligious life by property relations. Feuerbach's notion of alienation, or what has been called his "transformative method," once it is extended in this way, from religion and contemplation to the broader register of politics and society, is no longer really Feuerbachian at all. Marx was concerned to shift the grounds of alienation, making it something that could not only be outlined but also solved, practically and socially; and it is of vital importance that we acknowledge at this juncture that Marx made this move by associating alienation in the first instance, not with production or the labor process, but with the state. My point here is not the obvious one that alien politics were as a matter of chronology elaborated before the notion of alienation in the labor process had been set out, in the *Economic and Political Manuscripts* of 1844. It is that the concept of "species-being," which is key to an understanding of Marx's argument in the *Manuscripts*, had in 1843 already been elaborated politically—as having to do with community in the first instance—as part of the elaboration of Marx's theory of "alien politics." The implications of this elaboration in "On 'The Jewish Question' " are programmatic:

> Only when the actual individual man takes back into himself the abstract citizen and in his everyday life, his individual work, and his individual relationships has become a species-being, only when he has recognized and organized his own powers (*forces propres*) as social powers so that social force is no longer separated from him as political force—only then is human emancipation complete.[38]

It is important at this juncture that we get a sense of what this category, "human emancipation," comports. At one level it can be seen as an extension of the logic of its counterpart, "political emancipation." If citizenship is, as Marx believed, a religious phenomenon, the fantasy of universality, then the reintegration of political powers to which Marx refers can be seen at this level as the realization of the fantasy of citizenship, as a genuine, thoroughgoing secularization of the spiritual world. But what form is this to take, and how is it to be brought about? Marx, to begin with, never believed that the state could be the agency or the instrument of its own reintegration. To put the same point another way, the state is an institutional expression of human alienation, and alienation cannot, by its very nature, be overcome within the sphere of alienation. This means that "human emancipation" in no way posits the mere substitution of some populist or Jacobin direct participatory democracy for a sham representative democracy. The problem goes rather deeper than this, since the modern state, whatever its constitutional form, far from being insulated against the claims of property and exchange, will in some way reflect or express the prevailing pattern of property relations. One does not have to reduce such expression or reflection to the level of one-to-one correspondance to see the force of Marx's point.

Alienation can be overcome only by an agency that does not reflect or embody property relations in anything like the same way. The animating principle of modern civil society, its *esprit général*, is private property; the proletariat is defined and given meaning by its property-lessness; it might appear to follow syllogistically (as it did to at least one Young-Hegelian theorist, Max Stirner), that the proletariat is therefore irrelevant to the functioning of modern society. Such a con-clusion would be manifestly absurd. The proletariat, we might surmise (though Marx himself vacillated dogmatically on this issue for a time), far from being in any way marginal to civil society, is its very basis; without this basis, civil society in its modern form could not and would not persist. Even so, the proletariat is, in a real sense, outside the exchange system its labor maintains, in that none of the benefits of this system percolate down or accrue to its members. Their poverty and hopelessness exclude them from these. Hegel's "system of needs" has in their case become distilled into a system of pure, raw need or neediness. Workers in modern civil society are by extension unable to satisfy any of their needs, even the most basic among them, without in effect doing what human beings at the most basic anthropological level have always done, that is create a new need along with the means for its satisfaction. This is the need for community, the very need otherwise foreclosed by the organization of modern civil society and projected, up and away, on to the level of the modern state.

But the identification of agency is not enough to characterize "human emancipation," which has to be seen also in its relation to its counterpart, "political emancipation." Once "human" has supplanted "political" emancipation, human control over the conditions of human existence is to be extended, not lessened—extended into the realm of a society that is at present regulated only by the impersonal forces of the market. With political emancipation there is no excess of political rule at all. Quite the contrary. The forces dominating civil society are not political or communal forces, but the impersonal forces of private property and the division of labor. Since the consequences of these unimpeded forces are inhuman and oppressive, what is required is the extension of rational, human control over them. This is to say that if, under such circumstances, citizenship is a fantasy, a dream, it is a fantasy that can and must be made real. Depoliticization can be supplanted by repoliticization. And if the human control modern civil society increasingly demands and denies is correspondingly projected upwards and outwards, on to the alien, fantastic level of the modern state, then humanity must bring back that which it has alienated away.

To see this is to become better able to characterize how political and human emancipation are categorically related. They are alternatives of a particular kind. Far from straightforwardly denying it, political emanciption *presages* "real, human emancipation." It blazes its trail, points the way forward—and parodies human emancipation in advance of its historical attainment. Citizenship in the alien state is a cruel joke on humanity, one which mocks the universality, the *Gemeinwesen*, the extension of real, social control humanity desperately and increasingly needs. It does this not by denying control outright, but by presenting it back to us in an alien, abstract form. Modern civil society claims to be able to put the material world at the disposal of humanity, yet at the same time and by the same token puts humanity at the disposal of the material process of production. In doing so, civil society removed many of the obstacles to the emergence of humanity as humanity could be, made up of many-sided individuals, and it is precisely because of this removal that citizenship could so much as *appear* as a purportedly universal category in the first place. Civil society, in this view of it, had more than one cutting edge to present. On the one hand its emergence and operation signalled the "real human emancipation" toward which it was tending, and which was presaged and in a way promised on the political level as citizenship and on the economic level by capitalism's own expansionist, universalizing tendencies. On the other hand, it made people the "plaything[s] of alien powers," powers that could not but stifle the "universal" side of human nature that Marx, and before him Hegel, had held so dear. Civil society, and the modernity for which it stands, creates the need as it denies the need for emancipation. It plays with mankind, apparently granting as it substantively withholds emancipation in any significant degree. While it supplies preconditions for the emergence of humanity as humanity could be, modern society is constrained to furnish these only in an alien and tantalizing form—that traced out by the modern state.

3

"THE SABER, THE COWL, THE MUSKET": MARX'S *BRUMAIRE*

I have argued that the confrontation between Marx and Hegel on the state raises a host of important issues, issues having to do with the genesis of Marx's state theory, with the origin as well as the credentials of the modern state itself, and with the relationship of the modern state as it emerged with the modern civil society that is its counterpart. I have argued further that these features, which on any reckoning are important features, of a distinctively Marxian state theory still need to be retrieved, to be brought out into the open. The irony is that one of the thickets from which these features need to be retrieved is what has come down to us as Marxist state theory itself, which has over the years become fetishized into a series of disputes owing little or nothing to the original confrontation with Hegel, or to the original issues around which this same confrontation took shape.

For all these reasons, my previous chapter necessarily took the form of an essay in retrieval. It proposed to retrieve the way in which Marx's state theory originated and took shape, and the terms according to which it ought, finally, to be judged. Plainly, neither of these tasks is yet close to completion; each of them needs further development. The former task involves the identification of what is at issue in Marx's state theory as it took shape historically, and it awaits completion in the present chapter. The latter task involves examination of theories of the state other than Marx's, and will be undertaken, in light of the present chapter, in subsequent ones.

My itinerary, then, will be from the Marxian to the Marxist—understanding the former as something still needing to be theoretically reconstructed and regrounded, and the latter as more of a convenient portmanteau term, an adjective that abridges a galaxy of claims and counterclaims about the capitalist state, than anything else. The Leninist interpretation of Marx's state theory was, notoriously, drawn in the other direction, from something that was called "Marxist" and was assumed in advance to therefore embody truth-value, to the "Marxian." Marx's texts, to the extent that these were made available, were methodically scoured for passages that would lend support to what was a political *position déjà prise*. In the process they became sacred texts of a sort: of the sort that admitted of being mined for the precious ores of documentation, and then of being duly consigned to the slag heap.

Marxism-Leninism interpreted Marxian state theory as having centered on a ruling-class theory that would, in one way or another, justify a revolutionary seizure of power, and which would do so more or less directly. Everything Marx had said about the state had perforce to be interpreted in the light of this political imperative, which was held to have needed Marx's textual justification, as it were, in advance. What this would mean with respect to what I have designated alien politics, or to what Marx himself termed "political emancipation," is that these would have to be seen as early, or even "immature," theoretical forays that are of value only in so far as they contain in advance or foreshadow Marx's "mature," seasoned theory of the state, which is, of course, the proto-Leninist one. My point here is not just that there is often an element of the purest intellectual skullduggery involved in attempts of this type (though of course there is); it is that, in a more immediate sense, Marxian state theory looks very different if its Leninist or Marxist-Leninist credentials are *not* privileged or assumed in advance to be hegemonic.

There is a further difficulty with the more or less straightforward ruling-class theory of the state that, once upon a time, proved so useful to Leninists, once they had extracted it from Marx's writings and set it up as something needing no further argument. This is that, as many commentators, to their credit, have noticed, it appears to sit ill with those passages in Marx's writings, passages which are by no means infrequent, where Marx points not to the subservience of the state to ruling-class demands and imperatives, but instead to the state's apparent independence from the social matrix that is, and is supposed to be, its foundation. The theoretical response to this incongruity generally took the form of wishing to preserve the primacy of the ruling-class theory, while acknowledging either that Marx never developed a definitive theory of the state, or that there is, alongside the ruling-class theory of the state, another theory of the state that stresses independence of, rather than one-for-one subservience to, ruling-class interests.[1]

What has come down to us as Marxian, and for that matter Marxist, state theory looks markedly different if we pointedly refrain from privileging its ruling-class aspect as a matter of course. My belief is that Marx's ability to pinpoint the state's independence from civil society derives much more nearly from his notions of "alien politics" and of "political emancipation" than it does from the ruling-class theory that is so often taken, by friend and foe alike, as an unquestioned and unquestionable datum. My presumption here is that to dislodge the ruling class from the central position it has long been made to occupy in Marxian state theory is not to weaken the theory, but to strengthen it by not disposing of but bracketing what is its weakest and most assailable feature. Marxian state theory, to put the same point another way, is enriched and not emasculated if it is not seen "automatically" through the lenses ruling-class notions have only too frequently provided.

Marxian state theory, to begin with, looks different, whether or not it looks better, if we pointedly refrain from laboriously trying as a matter of course to interpret everything else in it in the light of various strictures about the ruling-class character of political rule. Instances of the independence of the state from civil society no longer need creakingly to be brought into line with ruling-class notions as a *point d'appui*, and neither do the various instances of alien politics and political emancipation. There is, on the other hand, as I hope to show, no similar difficulty about bringing the independence of the state into line with alien politics, since it is my contention that the latter informed and influenced the former all along. The various more or less strident declamations about the ruling-class character of the state that pepper some of Marx's writings, declamations that really are there and which must be accounted for, operate more as summary, premature attempts to foreclose debate than as solid contributions to debates that have been raging from Marx's day right down to our own.

"Political conditions," says Marx, "are only the official expression of civil society." Such a characterization—no reader of Marx will be hard put to it to discover other, similar ones—admits of more than one interpretation. It is quite cognate, in the first instance, with "political emancipation," as outlined above; but it is also capable of being stretched into supporting a more rigid ruling-class theory of the state. Linkages in this latter instance could be effected readily enough by quoting various passages wrested from their context in *The German Ideology*. Example: "By the mere fact that it is a class and not an estate, the bourgeoisie is forced to organize itself no longer locally but nationally and to give a general form to its mean, average interest." This, "the form of organization the bourgeoisie necessarily adopts . . . for the mutual guarantee [of] its property and interest," is the state. Marx's most celebrated, and to my mind, overdrawn depictions of the state in the *Manifesto of the Communist Party* are at this point but a hop and a skip away: "political power is but the organized power of one class for oppressing another," and "the executive of the modern

state is but a committee for managing the affairs of the whole bourgeoisie."[2]

This view of the state, straightforward to the point of stridency,
is the one that passed over into Leninism and, again by virtue of its
easy compatibility with the notion of the "dictatorship of the proletariat," into twentieth-century Marxism at large. That, taken in itself, it
raises a host of problems (why just the *executive* of the modern state?
what *are* "the common affairs of the whole bourgeoisie," and how
likely is it that they will find some expression in the first place?)
has long been evident. The *Manifesto* was a call to arms written (on
commission) with a deadline, the supposed revolutionary *annus mirabilis* of 1848, in mind. It was intended, with no small flourish, to
guarantee the conditions of its own success as a revolutionary clarion
call. It was, in short, the kind of document in which overdrawn, pithy
phrases, phrases with a memorable tocsin ring to them, might have
been expected. The point here is not to deny the effectiveness of the
phrases in question; such a denial would be ridiculous if we consider
their undoubted power at the level of much later revolutionary propaganda, through which they rang like the tocsin they were supposed
to provide. It is simply to point up the character of the theoretical
accompaniment of this very effectiveness. In retrospect, it is hard to
believe the weight of interpretation that was to be hung on these rather
slender hooks. One has to look to the fate of certain, rather more
ambiguous, New Testament formulations over the long span of medieval political theory to find an analogue. But these later interpretations
of Marx's formulations are not—or not yet—our concern. To reiterate,
Marx's formulations themselves were, at best, distillations of the results of other, and rather more searching, examinations of the nature
and the role of the modern state. The main drawback at this remove
of the *Manifesto*'s drastic and sweeping characterizations of the state
is that, provocative though they may be, they tell us nothing about
the way in which bourgeois revolution and the emergence of modern
civil society had changed the nature, the very character of political
power.

Yet Marx by the year 1848 had discussed this momentous shift
at some considerable length, and was to continue to do so subse-

quently. The danger with Marx's more notorious slogans about the state is that if they are wrested out of context, and it is in the nature of a political slogan to be wrested out of context, they might suggest a crude and reductive conspiracy theory of the kind that Marx, in his more considered moments, did much to preclude:

> [If] the bourgeoisie politically, that is, through the agency of its state power, maintains "the injustice of the property relations," it does not create the latter which, conditioned by the modern division of labor, the modern form of exchange, competition, concentration, etc., does not proceed from the political rule of the bourgeoisie but, contrariwise, the political rule of the bourgeoisie proceeds from these modern relations of production, which are proclaimed by the bourgeois economists to be necessary and eternal laws.[3]

The notion of the state as an "engine of class despotism," then, does not exhaust what Marx had to say about the state. In its purest form, any rigidly ruling-class theory of the state presupposes the possibility of unalloyed class rule, along with the existence of an economic ruling class possessed of uniform common interests which it is capable of uniformly asserting. It should come as no surprise that the various examples of the bourgeoisie Marx encountered and analyzed seem not, according to his own admission, to have met so monolithic a set of requirements. The theory that the modern state is no more than the handmaiden or surrogate of the economic ruling class is, unsurprisingly enough, not borne out either in spirit or to the letter by any of Marx's more detailed historical investigations.

Three of these—*The Class Struggles in France, The Eighteenth Brumaire of Louis Bonaparte,* and *The Civil War in France*—deserve to be considered together, and will be here. The ruling-class theory of the state so stridently proclaimed rather than elaborated in the *Manifesto of the Communist Party* and elsewhere in no way prepares us for the flexibility and sophistication of these essays' treatments not just of that state but also of social class. The degree of internal cohesion, the type and extent of unity within a class, and with this the possibility of collective self-assertion by members of the class acting as members of it—all these are not treated as categorical postulates, but as open questions. Cohesion, unity and futurity vary, and vary considerably, from one class to another. Even so, Marx is not concerned with comparative statics. The articulation of the interests of one class, where indeed these are discernible, is going to affect the opportunities of other classes. Subdivisions within each class often make alliances across class lines possible and likely. The pattern, being both reflexive and articulated, is a complex one, and the question of the political representation of these various forces among, as well as within, classes makes it more complex still. The degree and kind of independence that may be exhibited by the political representatives of social forces is outlined and investigated by Marx according to the structure, contours and relationships of the class relationships that made up French society in the first half of the nineteenth century. More surprisingly, perhaps, what we encounter, in the upshot, is something for which no rigidly ruling-class theory could have prepared us: political power exercised not by an autonomous, unambiguous, unalloyed, internally united, bourgeois class, but on behalf of factions of a bourgeois class that is characterized by a severe lack of internal unity and autonomy.

The capitalist class in particular is divided into two factions, the finance capitalists and the industrialists, whose interests converge all too rarely. Different factions are politically dominant at different periods. The July Monarchy was a political expression of the interests of finance capital, "a joint-stock company for the exploitation of France's national wealth . . . [of which] Louis-Phillippe was the director. . . . Trade, industry, agriculture, shipping, the interests of the industrial bourgeoisie were bound to be continually endangered and prejudiced under this system."[4] After the 1848 Revolution, what Marx calls "the nameless realm of the Republic" became the only realm "in which both factions could maintain with equal power the common class interest without giving up their mutual rivalry . . . the bourgeois republic could not be anything but the perfected and clearly expressed rule of the whole bourgeois class."[5] Of what, however, did this "perfected and clearly expressed rule" consist? The internal divisions within the bourgeois class are such that "the nameless realm of the Republic" imploded. No sooner was this republic "perfected" than it summarily collapsed. It had been no more than the neutral territory on which the two factions of the French bourgeoisie, Legitimists and Orleanists, could dwell side by side with equality of rights. It was the unavoidable condition of their common rule, the sole form of state in which their general class interest subjected to itself at the same time both the claims of their particular factions and all the remaining classes of society.[6]

What Marx encountered and analyzed in France was not the united rule of an autonomous, united, well-defined and class-conscious bourgeoisie, but rather a factional politics that played itself out to the extent of letting the "grotesque mediocrity" of Louis Napoleon "play a hero's part," a factional politics within which Bonapartists, of whom there were remarkably few, at least initially, and bureaucrats, who were all too many, were enabled to hold the balance of power, even though (or precisely because) they represented in the last analysis none but themselves.

The state here is not so much a reflection of the forces in society as distinct, disjoined *from* society. Louis Bonaparte's *coup d'état* was "the victory of the executive . . . [by which the French nation] renounces all will of its own and submits to the power of an alien will, to authority"; "the struggle seems to be settled in such a way that all classes, equally impotent and equally mute, fall on their knees before the rifle butt." Marx goes on to say that "under the second Bonaparte . . . the state seemed to have made itself completely independent" of society; "bourgeois society, freed from political cares, attained a development unexpected even by itself."[7]

How does the state attain such an independent, powerful position? Situations of balance, of unstable equilibrium can obtain among classes, and factions of classes, in civil society. In such a stalemate, no single class, whatever its social predominance, can gain political dominance. To resolve this stalemate, the state itself steps in to redress the balance. Acting in its own right, the executive acts as moderator, umpire or *deus ex machina*. Classes, or factions, might then see the state itself, or its administrative apparatus in the case of a bureaucratized state like France, as a potential ally or protector. In countries like France, moreover, each successive ruling group has an interest in improving the power of the state apparatus, and in increasing the coercive potential at the disposal of the state. The personnel manning the administrative apparatus becomes an increasingly powerful faction having a vested interest in extending the scope of state action. Marx speaks of the "executive power with its enormous bureaucratic and military organization, with its ingenious state machinery embracing wide strata, with a host of officials numbering half a million" and refers to it famously as an "appalling parasitic body which enmeshes the body of French society like a net and chokes all its pores." His characterization is important enough to bear quoting at length:

> the exective power commands an army of officials numbering more than half a million individuals and which therefore constantly maintains an immense mass of interests and livelihoods in the most complete dependence; where the state enmeshes, controls, regulates, superintends, and tutors civil society from its most comprehensive manifestations of being to the private existence of individuals; where through the most extraordinary centralization this parasitic body acquires a ubiquity, an omniscience, a capacity for accelerated mobility and an elasticity which finds a counterpart only in the helpless dependence, in the loose shapelessness, of the actual body politic. . . .[8]

Several things about this passage are worthy of note. There is, first, Marx's evident distaste for totalizing, bureaucratic states, which leads one to wonder about what he would have made of those that were to be set up in his name the following century. There is, second, the fact that a strong, bureaucratic state is characterized as such, as well as condemned. This means, as Shlomo Avineri and others have indicated, that the notion that Marx, unlike, say, Weber, had no understanding of the importance of bureauracy in the modern world is quite mistaken. But, for our immediate purposes, the most striking feature of this passage, and passages like it, is that Marx's depiction in them of the state, of a state power that is "apparently soaring high above society," is one that recalls not the class-bound instrumentality outlined vaguely in the *Manifesto*, and met with (apparently) nowhere in real life. It recalls instead the alien universality and power desribed in "On 'The Jewish Question'," a universality that is "parasitic" on society in much the same way. Only in the latter, and not at all in the former view could the state be expected to "enmesh, control, regulate, superintend and tutor" civil society. Marx goes on to ask why the French National Assembly did not "simplify the administration of the state, reduce the army of officials . . . let civil society and public opinion create organs of their own, independent of the governmental power," as the Communards were later to do in 1871. His answer to his own question indicates that there is more than one way that the state can operate as the instrumentality of the ruling class.

> . . . it is precisely with the maintenance of that extensive state machine in its numerous ramifications that the material interests of the French bourgeoisie are interwoven in the closest fashion. Here it finds posts for its surplus population and makes up in the form of state salaries for what it cannot pocket in the form of profit, rents and honorariums. On the other hand, its political interests compelled it to increase daily the repressive measures and therefore the resources and the personnel of the state power, while at the same time it had to wage an uninterrupted war against public opinion and mistrustfully mutilate, cripple, the independent organs of the social movement where it did not succeed in amputating them entirely. Thus the French bourgeoisie was compelled by its class position to annihilate, on the one hand, the vital condition of all parliamentary power, and therefore, likewise, of its own, and to render irresistible, on the other hand, the executive power hostile to it.[9]

The paradox Marx is outlining sits ill with any rigid ruling-class theory of the state. On the one hand, "never did the bourgeoisie rule more absolutely"; on the other, Marx does not shrink from posing the question: of what does this purportedly absolute rule consist? Bourgeois rule expresses itself in a double bind having effects that are nothing short of fatal to bourgeois interests.

> The bourgeoisie confesses that its own interests dictate that it should be delivered from the consequences of its own rule; that in order to restore tranquillity in the country, its bourgeois parliament must, first of all, be given its quietus; that, in order to preserve its own social power intact, its political power must be broken; that the individual bourgeois can continue to exploit the other classes and to enjoy undisturbed property, family, religion and order only on condition that their class be condemned

along with the other classes to like political nullity; that in order to save its purse it must forfeit its crown, and the sword that is to safeguard it must at the same time be hung over its head like the sword of Damocles.[10]

France then, *escapes* the despotism of a class but only for the despotism of an individual. And Louis Bonaparte's *coup d'état* changes the role of the state, not permanently or irreversibly, but decisively. (The Second Empire was to prove anything but a transitory or short-lived phenomenon, after all.) At the moment of its inception, as Marx puts it, "as against civil society, the state machine has consolidated its position so thoroughly that the chief of the Society of December 10th [i.e. Louis Bonaparte] suffices for its head."[11] It has consolidated its position to the extent of appearing to be independent of any particular class, and of seeming superior to, set up against, society at large—as an instance, in fact, of alien politics. But Marx at this point adds an important qualification, insisting that "the state power is not suspended in mid-air. Bonaparte represents a class, and the most numerous class of French society at that, the small-holding peasants."[12] But what is the nature of this "representation," a term that appears to bristle with myriad meanings within the pages of the *Eighteenth Brumaire*? Over and above Louis Bonaparte's more or less straightforward bribes to other sections of French society (his offer of tranquillity to the bourgeoisie, and of a restoration of universal suffrage to the workers), bribes which in a certain sense cancel each other out, his own class basis is constituted by the peasantry. It is so constituted, however, only in a particular sense. Since they "cannot represent themselves" the French peasants "must be represented."[13] The organization of so inherently atomized a group as the peasantry has to proceed from outside and from above. The peasants' lack of cohesion makes them "incapable of enforcing their class interests in their own name whether through a parliament or a convention." They therefore require a representative who:

must at the same time appear as their master, as an authority over them, as an unlimited governmental power that protects them against the other classes and sends them rain and sunshine from above. The political influence of the small-holding peasants, therefore, finds its final expression in the executive power subordinating society to itself.[14]

Bonaparte, then, "represents" the peasantry in a very particular way. The peasants want, hope or expect that he will "represent" their interests. But they certainly lack the wherewithal to oblige him to do so. The Second Empire is anything but an instrument or even an expression of their will, if, indeed, they can be said to have a common will at all. This last point is crucial. It reminds us that the French peasantry are a social formation of a most unusual kind. They may in principle be capable of limiting to some extent the executive's freedom of action. But in practice it is doubtful whether such limitation would amount to very much, since the peasants themselves remain hopelessly disunited. One result is that Bonaparte sets himself "representative" tasks other than that of representing the peasantry:

> as the executive authority which has made itself an independent power, Bonaparte feels it his mission to safeguard "bourgeois order." But the strength of this bourgeois order lies in the middle class. He looks on himself, therefore, as the representative of the middle class and issues decrees in this sense. Nevertheless, he is somebody solely due to the fact that he has broken the political power of the middle class and daily breaks it anew.[15]

Nor is this all:

> as against the bourgeoisie, Bonaparte looks on himself at the same time as the representative of the peasants and of the people in general, who want to make the lower classes of the people happy within the frame of bourgeois society. . . . But, above all, Bonaparte looks on himself as the chief of the society of the 10th of December, as the representative of the *lumpenproletariat* to which he himself, his *entourage*, his government and his army belong.[16]

Small wonder, perhaps, that Marx, in among this apparently confusing welter of "representation" in its various guises (and "guises," as we shall see, is the right word to use here), stresses the "contradictory talk" of Louis Bonaparte and the "contradictions of his government, the confused groping about which seeks now to win, now to humiliate first one class and then another and arrays all of them uniformly against him." The point remains that the Bonapartist state's power of initiative remains largely unimpaired by the wishes and demands of any particular class or faction. This is not to say that Bonapartism on the other hand is in any way impartial or neutral as between contending classes. It claims and must claim to represent all of them and to transcend class divisions at large in the name of a more or less nebulous principle of national unity. It was nevertheless called into being and continued to exist for the sake of maintaining and strengthening the existing social order—one which is based, it goes without saying, on the domination of labor by capital. Marx, casting a retrospective, relieved glance back over the Second Empire, was later to characterize it as, above all, a transitional form: "it was the only form of government possible at a time when the bourgeoisie had already lost, and the working class had not yet acquired, the faculty of ruling the nation." It was, again,

at the same time the most prostitute and the ultimate form of the state power which nascent middle-class society had commenced to elaborate as a means of its own emancipation from feudalism, and which bourgeois society had finally transformed into a means for the enslavement of labor by capital.[17]

This seems unambiguous enough. Even so, Bonapartism, as Marx conceives of it, does have its ambiguities. "Bonaparte would like to appear as the patriarchal benefactor of all classes. But he cannot give to one class without taking from another." Nor is this all:

Driven by the contradictory demands of his situation and being at the same time, like a conjuror, under the necessity of keeping the public gaze upon himself . . . Bonaparte throws the entire bourgeois economy into confusion, violates every thing that seemed inviolable to the Revolution of 1848, makes some tolerant of revolution, others desirous of revolution, and produces actual anarchy in the name of order, while at the same time stripping its halo from the entire state machine, profaning it, and makes it at once loathsome and ridiculous.[18]

The imagery of masquerade that Marx employs in *The Eighteenth Brumaire* is much more important to an understanding of Marx's meaning than may be initially apparent. There are stage metaphors aplenty in *The Class Struggles in France*, metaphors of acting, action, command, the revolutionary "stage" that is seen from the boxes or the pit or the gallery. But all these have to do with display, whereas the register of the *Eighteenth Brumaire* has also to do with withdrawal and concealment, with charlatanry and pantomime, rather than with theater *per se*. To get some purchase on *The Eighteenth Brumaire*'s celebrated opening line, we must consider that the relationship of "tragedy" to "farce" is rather like that of artifice to artificiality. The former does not neccesarily imply cheap contrivance; the latter most certainly does. The French Revolution of 1789, Marx is not alone in remarking, was acted in borrowed, Roman robes ("when in Paris, do as the Romans do," as one contemporary wag put it). This both connects it with and severs it from the *Eighteenth Brumaire*, which was not just acted but acted *out* in borrowed robes. These robes serve not to expose but to cover, to conceal. There are some symbols that are enabling, that allow and encourage people to act; there are others that doom action in advance. Louis Bonaparte, who recycled the singularly ill-fitting robes of his uncle, shows us in effect that the same set of symbols, in different contexts, can have opposite effects. The first time around, borrowed Roman robes had had the effect of empowering people, enabling them to act decisively on the revolutionary stage. They even had this effect the second time around, in the "beautiful revolution" of 1848. But once the mantle is draped around the unseemly shoulders of Louis Bonaparte, it loses its force. Now the symbol, instead of encouraging action, forecloses it. Politics exists by a kind of proxy, at one remove, at least, from social reality. Louis Bonaparte, a political mountebank rather than a sorcerer or manipulator, serves as an extreme case, as a melodramatic reminder, if any were needed, that there are no purely political solutions to social problems, and that attempts to furnish these simply add political *to* social problems. But such accretion itself becomes mystified in its turn, not by the political drama itself but by the *kind* of playacting at which Louis Bonaparte proved so adept, or maladroit.

The world of Marx's *Eighteenth Brumaire* is in no way the world of the *Manifesto of the Communist Party* in which we were "compelled to face with sober senses" overwhelmingly objective developments taking place or unfolding before our very eyes. This world is replaced in short order (*The Eighteenth Brumaire* was written only some four years after the *Manifesto*) by a world inaccessible to our "sober senses," a world where illusions exert real force and are in fact the conditions on which action is based. Mere revelation, the work of *The Class Struggles in France* as well as of the *Manifesto*, will no longer fit the bill; social reality no longer unfolds before us in anything like the same sense. Our senses decieve us. The "old mole" whose "grubbing" all Europe will one day celebrate does its work blindly, underground, much as Democritus is said to have blinded himself in order to think better. Here it is not simply a question of the "ugly revolution" coming in the wake and as the nemesis of the "beautiful revolution." There is another, possibly even more ominous development that takes place alongside this one. Illusion succeeds reality, the nephew impersonates the uncle, enchantment follows disenchantment—a reversal of the *Manifesto*'s priorities as recently sketched so imaginatively by Marshall Berman.[19] In the *Brumaire*, "all that is solid melts into air," all over again, but this time in an utterly different sense. If the axis of *The Class Struggles in France* is that of class formation and demystification, corresponding to the "sober senses" appealed to in the *Manifesto*, that of the *Brumaire* is of class fragmentation and remystification. If Lamartine in *Class Struggles* is a masquerade concealing power, Bonaparte in the *Brumaire* is mountebank impotence that comes to embody power. The directness of the links between consciousness and action in the former work is broken in the latter. Who or what represents whom or what is no longer in any way clear. It is now impossible to give form to experience. There is no principle of organization, just a "confused groping about." The external world no longer carries any obvious meaning; we are faced instead with the inscrutability of images that are impenetrable to the underlying reality to which they are supposed to refer, or which they purport to represent. (As an aside, it is perhaps no coincidence that, by virtue of the complexity of its argument alone, the *Brumaire* calls to mind the no less ironically posed argument of "The Fetishism of Commodities" in *Capital*, vol. 1. In one of the great novels about 1848 (which happens to have been written rather later), Flaubert's *L'Education Sentimentale*, the protagonist—if protagonist is the word—Frédéric Moreau, breathes meaning into existence, at a time when symbols are all dead, by breathing life into fetishes. Coherence derives not just from consumption as an act, but from consumerism as a refuge, and even the revolution is something Moreau can contemplate like an *objet d'art*—as when he regards the iconoclastic mob as "sublime." Idolaters and iconoclasts have more in common than either group would feel comfortable believing.) What the events of 1848 to 1851 cast into doubt, for Flaubert as well as Marx, is "common sense," "common sense" perhaps in Tom Paine's sense of the term, which now, all at once, becomes a leitmotif of the revolutions of the eighteenth century, "the age of reason," as it was so aptly termed, not the nineteenth, which becomes the age of something else. The dislocation of consciousness that characterizes nineteenth-century revolutions, or *this* nineteenth-century revolution, at any rate, poses new tasks for the theorist, tasks for which no solution was set out in advance.

The vertiginous world of the *Eighteenth Brumaire* is one where our senses, even our sense of history, betray us. The world of the *Manifesto*, as Marshall Berman reminds us, was no less unsettling, but here the bourgeoisie at least think they know what they are doing so relentlessly, and meaning can, finally, be assigned to action by the theorist. There is, on the contrary, no basis in the *Brumaire* for the unification of private and public unless, of course, we are to regard the looting and plunder of *la douce France* by Bonaparte's entourage, the *lazzaroni* of the Society of the 10th December, as an enactment of the idea. This means that the bourgeoisie's world-shaping credentials, for which Marx had applauded it in the *Manifesto*, have given way, its accomplishments have receded. The achievements of the modern world are no longer being achieved, but abandoned, relinquished. They slip out of our grasp. These achievements include not only industry but also citizenship, which in France had been a kind of socially sanctioned escape clause ever since the Revolution of 1789, and which, like so much else, got lost in the confusion surrounding, and created by, the (shall we say) unprepossessing figure of Louis Bonaparte. We are dealing here, and not for the last time, with the realienation of alien politics, their realienation, in this instance, with a vengeance. Even so, it is a point of some considerable importance that if, in thinking about the Second Empire, we resort to the categories Marx had used in "On 'The Jewish Question'," the categories of "political" as opposed to "human emancipation," we will find that the Second Empire is in one important sense simply off the scale. It amounts to a reversion, a relapse of society to a point historically *prior* to that marked out by "political emancipation." Small wonder, perhaps, that Marx's disdain for "development, whose sole driving force is the calendar" is so evident in the *Brumaire*. Society is capable of spiralling backwards, as Marx's constant references to the saber, the cowl, the musket, and the like are meant to remind us. Not only does the past have the power to reemerge, no matter how ably it has been anatomized; in between the *Class Struggles in France* and *The Eighteenth Brumaire* Marx's confidence in what a ruthless unmasking can achieve suffered a decisive, if impermanent, setback. In the *Brumaire* the proletariat, which has only a shadowy existence, burrowing underground—the peasantry by contrast are etched in and configured much more firmly—is characterized by the *futurity* it embodies and comports. "Let the dead bury their dead." The past destroys itself, a process we watch happening in the *Class Struggles,* but the proletariat alone can slough off whatever borrowed robes it may once have assumed. For it alone needs to borrow or assume very little. The proletariat cannot, in other words, afford to delude itself, and in this it is, once again, so very different from a bourgeoisie that cannot afford *not* to delude itself if it is to be able to "act" at all. The bourgeoisie is compelled to strut around in borrowed robes, whether these fit or not. Its material and psychological dependence on the machinery of the state means that the bourgeoisie in effect has to deceive itself. Self-delusion becomes a constitutive part of its being. The question is of course that if the (French) bourgeoisie cannot rule united, how could the (French) proletariat be expected to do so in its wake? Disenchantment, taken in and of itself, neither emancipates nor guards itself against future, and retrogressive re-enchantment, as the argument of the *Eighteenth Brumaire* makes clear.

The question was answered not so much by Marx as for him, by the Communards of 1871. Marx's philippic on the Paris Commune, *The Civil War in France*, was to insist with all due forcefulness that "the direct antithesis to the [Second] Empire was the Commune," seen respectively as the "positive form" of "a Republic that was not only to supercede the monarchical form of class rule, but class rule itself," and as "the political form at last discovered under which to work out the economic emancipation of labor."[20] These are of course large claims, and Marx's reasons for advancing them, which take us to the heart of his state theory, need to be appraised with some care. They are not very difficult to uncover, and refer us back constantly not only to the earlier essays on French history but also, through these, to our old friends, "political" and "human" emancipation.

Bonapartism signifies, among other things, an attempt "to transform the purpose of the state into the purpose of bureaucracy and the purpose of bureaucracy into the purpose of the state,"[21] the very danger Marx had warned against a decade or so earlier, and indeed was to warn against later. In the *Class Struggles in France* the emphasis is on the instrumental and repressive character of the state. Its political character had changed:

> simultaneously with the economic changes in society. At the same pace at which the progress of modern industry developed, widened, intensified the class struggle between capital and labor, the state power assumed more and more the character of the national power of capital over labor, of a public force organized for public enslavement, of an engine of class despotism. After every revolution marking a progressive phase in the class struggle, the purely repressive character of the state stands out in bolder and bolder relief.[22]

"Bolder and bolder relief," is however, emphatically not the register of the *Eighteenth Brumaire*, as we have seen.

Bonapartism accordingly signified that:

> every common interest was immediately severed from society, counterposed to it as a higher, general interest, snatched from the activity of society's members themselves and made an object of government activity,

from a bridge, a schoolhouse and the communal property of a village
community to the railways, the national wealth and the national university
of France.[23]

These acts of expropriation had their conditions. Every previous
revolution, as Marx put it, had consolidated "the centralized state
power, with its ubiquitous organs of standing army, police, bureaucracy, clergy and judicature." All previous revolutions had "perfected
this [state] machine instead of smashing it. The parties that contended
in turn for domination regarded the possession of this huge state edifice
as the principal spoils of the victors." The pronounced shift in emphasis
on Marx's part, away from a rigidly ruling-class theory of the state,
and towards an emphasis on the power of the state apparatus itself,
helps explain Marx's insistence in 1871 that "the working class," for
its part, "cannot simply lay hold of the ready-made state machinery
and wield it for its own purposes,"[24] since this machinery is likely
under modern conditions to have purposes all of its own, and these
are unlikely to intersect and more likely to crosscut, or strike out, the
workers'.

The most positive feature of the Paris Commune, according to
The Civil War in France, Marx's 1871 address on it, was that it radically
deinsitutionalized political power, and in so doing repoliticized society
at large. "Public functions ceased to be the vital property of the tools
of the central government. Not only municipal administration, but
the whole initiative hitherto exercised by the State was laid into the
hands of the Commune." Society in this way seized hold of the conditions of its own existence, hitherto alienated away:

the unity of the nation was not to be broken, but, on the contrary, to
be organized by the Communal Constitution and to become a reality by
the destruction of the State power which claimed to be the embodiment
of that unity independent of, and superior to, the nation itself, of which
it was but a parasitic execresence. While the merely repressive organs of
the old governmental power were to be amputated, its legitimate functions
were to be wrested from an authority usurping pre-eminence over society
itself, and restored to the responsible organs of society.[25]

Marx's characterization of the "Communal Constitution" is all too clearly couched in terms, in the very idiom of "human" as opposed to "political" emancipation. "The Communal Constitution," says Marx, "would have restored to the social body all the forces hitherto absorbed by the state parasite feeding upon, and clogging the free movement of society. By this one act," he continues, "it would have initiated the regeneration of France." Marx's characterization of the attributes of the Commune is, accordingly, farreaching:

> It was a thoroughly expansive political form, while all previous forms of government had been emphatically repressive. Its true secret was this. It was essentially a working-class government, the product of the struggle of the producing class against the appropriating class, the political form at last discovered under which to work out the economic emancipation of labor.
>
> Except on this last condition, the Commune would have been an impossibility and a delusion. The political rule of the producer cannot coexist with the perpetuation of his social slavery. The Commune was therefore to serve as a lever for uprooting the economical foundations upon which rests the existence of classes, and therefore of class rule. With labor emancipated, every man becomes a working man, and productive labor ceases to be a class attribute.[26]

Marx's praise of the Commune, his insistence that it be seen as "the true representative of the all the healthier elements in French society" as well as "the bold champion of the emancipation," and, most markedly, as "the glorious harbinger of a new society," is nothing if not emphatic. It has seemed exaggerated as well as fulsome to some commentators. We now know of Marx's private reservations about the Commune's political pusillanimity, about its social composition and about the shortcomings in its ideology. ("The majority of the Commune was in no way socialist, nor could it be," Marx confided, not at all inaccurately, in the privacy of a later letter.) Marx was concerned throughout to distinguish between, on the one hand, what the Commune actually achieved—the practical measures it effected in the course of its woefully brief existence were indeed negligible, and the effects of its brutal suppression were to prove disastrous for the

European labor movement, as Marx was well aware—and, on the other hand, what the Commune *represented*. The draft manuscript of *The Civil War in France* defines the Commune as:

> the reabsorption of the state power by society as its own living forces instead of as forces controlling and subduing it, by the popular masses themselves forming their own force instead of the organized force of their suppression—the political form of their emancipation, instead of the artificial force (appropriated by their oppressors) . . . of society wielded for their oppression for their enemies.[27]

That this idiom carries over into the rather firmer syntax of the address Marx eventually delivered to the General Council of the First International, at some political cost to his own standing on it, should come as no surprise. It is very much the idiom of Marx's earlier writings on the French state, and, by extension, of his earlier writings on the state in general. The very concept of the bureaucratic state, which disfigures and distorts as well as reflects the society that gave it birth, signifies the separation between citizens and the means to their common action, the progressive extension of the sphere of alien regulation of life in society.

It is for this reason that Marx stresses the Commune's deinstitutionalization of political power to the extent that he does. This deinstitutionalization cuts through the usurpation and mystification of people's conscious control over the conditions of their lives. It is an act of reappropriation of what had been alienated away. It is this reappropriation that gives the Commune, for all its shortcomings, universal significance. The problem had been that of returning to society all the prerogatives usurped by the state so that socialized human beings, the subjects of their own existence rather than the objects worked upon by, and at the disposal of, alien powers, could freely associate together. People associated in this way would control the totality of their social lives and become "masters of their own movement."

Prior to the Commune this statement had to be written in the conditional tense. What awarded the Commune universal significance was its character as exemplar, as prolegomenon. Working people had demonstrated practically that they could take control of the conditions of their existence, and it is for the force of their example, above all else, that Marx applauds them in his address. What makes such action political, what makes it the prototype of the political action Marx had in mind for the working class, is its premonitory character. The proletariat had recaptured its own alienated social capacities. The Communards had sought not the consolidation of state power in different hands, but its root-and-branch destruction. Marx praised the Commune's popular, democratic, egalitarian character and heartily approved the way in which "not only municipal administration but the whole initiative hitherto exercised by the State was laid into the hands of the Commune." While the Communal form of government was to apply to even "the smallest country hamlet,"

> the unity of the nation was not to be broken, but, on the contrary, to be organized by the Communal Constitution and to become a reality. . . . Instead of deciding once in three or six years which member of the ruling class was to misrepresent the people in parliament, universal suffrage was to serve the people, constituted in Communes.[28]

Under the Communal Constitution, each delegate to the National Delegation in Paris was "to be at any time revocable and bound by the *mandat impératif* [formal instructions] of his constituents." Marx saw in the elected magistracy of the Commune a device that could undermine bureaucratic absolutism by rendering bureaucracy itself unnecessary. Basing itself autonomously on universal suffrage, the Commune approached the stage at which the distinction between the state and civil society would evaporate and disappear. Accordingly, Marx praised the Commune's elections and dismissals of public servants and the payment to these of workers' wages. This means that workers, by associating among themselves, could not only emerge from the fragmentation, the atomization, the isolation and homogenization imposed on them by capitalist society. They could also, more positively, forge new social bonds and create new, genuinely social needs among themselves. It is at this point that the arguments of "On

'The Jewish Question' " and *The Economic and Philosophic Manuscripts*
come together yet again. Marx's theory of alienation was never intended to be restricted to the dimensions of a critique of the organization of factory production on the shop floor in the machine age. It
was intended all along to have a resonance beyond the limits of the
assembly line; and much of this resonance is political as well as socioeconomic. As Marx put it in a letter of 1871, the political movement
of the working class

> has . . . as its final object the conquest of political power for this class,
> and this requires, of course, a previous organization of the working class
> developed up to a certain point, which itself arises from its economic
> struggles. But on the other hand, every movement in which the working
> class comes out as a class against the ruling class and tries to coerce them
> by pressure from without is a political movement. For instance, the
> attempt in a particular factory, or even in a particular trade, to force a
> shorter working day out of the individual capitalists by strikes etc., is a
> purely economic movement. The movement to force through an eight-
> hour *law*, etc., however, is a *political* movement. And in this way, out
> of the separate economic movements of the workers there grows up
> everywhere a *political* movement, that is to say the movement of the
> class, with the object of achieving its interests in a general form, in a form
> possessing generally, socially coercive force. Though these movements
> presuppose a certain degree of previous organization, they are in turn
> equally a means of developing this organization.[29]

[handwritten annotation] Political Movements develop out of the
economic Movements & concerns of the
working Class

4

THE STATE AS *TOPOS*: LENIN AND GRAMSCI

A useful way of taking stock and retracing briefly the steps of my earlier chapters is suggested by Hannah Arendt's ostensibly surprising observations that the theory of the young Marx "was firmly rooted in the institutions and theories of the ancients," particularly the Athenians, and that Marx's ideal of the best form of society is "as such . . . not utopian, but rather reproduces the political and social condition of . . . (ancient) Athens."[1] This latter claim should not be taken too literally. Arendt, unlike so many of her Cold-War contemporaries, was perfectly well aware that Marx had no wish to restore chattel slavery. Her claim is nonetheless suggestive and timely. We know that Marx as a young man was anything but exempt from what Eliza Marion Butler termed, in a fine book of the same title, "the tyranny of Greece over Germany."[2] Quite to the contrary, he freely admitted to wishing to restore ancient political freedoms. Marx wrote to Arnold Ruge in 1843 that:

> The feeling of self in man, freedom, will have to be awakened again in these [German] men. Only this feeling, which disappeared from the world with the Greeks, and with Christianity vanished into the blue mists of heaven, can again transform society into a community of men to achieve their highest purpose, a democratic state.[3]

Marx at this point was still a radical democrat, not a social revolutionary. But when he spoke of politics, he employed and juxtaposed what were in the first instance Greek categories: public and private realms. These to the Greeks constituted, respectively, the realm of active human freedom and the realm of animal, biological necessity. Marx was also following Greek tradition when he identified the public realm not only as the space for human freedom—that is, that of "the people acting for itself by itself"—but also, remarkably, as the space for "glorious deeds," "heroic resolve" and "greatness." It should not surprise us, in light of my previous chapter, that these phrases all occur in Marx's writings on the Paris Commune, for the Paris Commune was, as we have already seen, an "expansive political form" precisely of the required type.[4]

At first, Marx appears to have assumed that the restoration of ancient political freedoms could in some way be accomplished theoretically, that is by a thoroughgoing critique of religion and philosophy. It is only "once the otherworldly truth has disappeared" that "the truth of this world" could reestablish itself. But with the ensuing critique of politics which followed in the wake of his criticisms of religion and philosophy, Marx was quick to discover that it was much more difficult to turn the "slaves to heaven," as he once called the Germans, into the "stormers of heaven," as he termed the Communards in 1871,[5] than at first he imagined. The novel conditions of modern society had shifted the coordinates of political life decisively, dramatically and irreversibly, thus rendering any simple restoration or rerun of ancient politics out of the question.

In antiquity, the freedoms enjoyed by some had depended upon chattel slavery for others, so that socially necessary labor had been reduced to a subhuman sphere (the slave was an *Unmensch*), from which it had no influence on the practice of politics as freedom, except insofar as slavery provided political practice with one of its external enabling conditions. Modern society is based upon emancipated labor, which is the material condition for the egoistic interests of the bourgeoisie. With the formal emancipation of labor and the much more substantive emancipation of the bourgeoisie, enormous productive forces, "natural energies" put to human, or inhuman, use, were released into society. These forces swiftly proved to be beyond political control. They seemed to many people at the time to be obeying "natural" laws of their own. This changes the valency and the credentials of politics. Rather than eventuating in a realm of freedom superimposed upon enslaved labor, as it did in ancient Greece, politics becomes nothing but an expression or term of social division and conflict. It becomes one weapon among others in the struggle between classes that animates civil society. In particular, as we have seen, politics becomes a means of enhancing the particular egoisms of the bourgeoisie.

It is altogether possible, all the same, that Marx was still thinking in the spirit of the ancients when he declaimed that "nothing is more horrible than the logic of self-interest"[6] (the reader will recall the Platonic echoes in Marx's wood-theft articles in my first chapter). Be this as it may, modern capitalist society and its political forms constitute a severe form of regression. People who are potential universal beings are reduced to the particularistic status of animals, their lives determined by the rawest of physical needs. At the same time, modern state forms lack the wherewithal to control the forces that erupt elementally throughout civil society. Marx's turn from radical democracy to communism came about once he had convinced himself that freedom, still seen as public freedom, and not as the freedom to privacy so cherished by liberals, could be realized only as "human emanciption," a liberation far surpassing not only bourgeois notions of freedom but ancient Greek ones too.

We need at this point to ask in what sense bourgeois notions of freedom are to be surpassed. In the *Critique of the Gotha Program* Marx is quite explicit about this. He maintains not that the liberal-bourgeois values of liberty, equality and fraternity are imperfectly realized in capitalist society, and await their completion once it is surpassed, but that because they are values of a particular kind, abstractions which, as such, cannot comprehend or take account of individual differences or particular human needs, they should be dispensed with altogether. "The narrow horizon of bourgeois right," is to be, ought to be, must be "crossed in its entirety."[7] To contribute to one's community on the basis of one's ability, and to receive from that community on the basis not of one's "rights" but of one's needs, is a formula for justice in the distribution of society's resources that is altogether superior to the bourgeois principle of "equality," which has nothing in common with Marx's understanding of the term and is, in any case, nothing but a bourgeois right put in place in order to correct a bourgeois wrong. This, at root, is why Marx was in no way reluctant about disinterring and dusting off what was by 1875 an old socialist slogan— "From each according to his ability, to each according to his needs!"[8] It is clear that what Marx objected to in 1875 is exactly what he had objected to in 1843, faced as he then was with the liberal-bourgeois values enshrined in the French and American Revolutions: their abstract, formal character.

These principles treat real differences among people as though they were of no account, or as though they could simply be treated as wrinkles to be ironed out—and ironed out, what is worse, by political means, using the criteria of "rights." This procedure to Marx was inherently misleading and mystificatory. The entire register of freedom conceived of in the language of "rights" should be erased and replaced by another register which the language of rights effectively occludes: the register of needs and capacities. These are analytic categories whose logic is proved by their extension in history, as Rousseau had recognized. And as Rousseau had also recognized, modernity

signifies a fateful misapplication of these categories alongside an application of other categories that are in principle incapable of being extended in anything like the same way. The "rights of man," liberty,
equality, fraternity, are deficient in a particular way that Marx had
already pinpointed in 1843. Liberty is defined privatistically and negatively. Equality is at best the purely formal equality involved in the
periodic casting of ballots ("one man, one vote, one value"). It is
equality of the kind that evaporates the moment these votes are cast,
as Rousseau once again had indicated. This formal, abstract equality
is counterposed to actual political activity, whether this be widespead
and intense, as in the French Revolution, or narrow and alien, as when
politics becomes a distant spectacle, practiced only by specialists. It is
also counterposed to economic life which, under capitalism, is subject
not only to gross inequalities in income levels, but also to the depradations of a division of labor, in the factory or in society at large,
which expressly fails to respect real differences in individuals' talents
and aptitudes.

Small wonder, perhaps, that Marx cast his eyes back to an antiquity
when all such developments would have been inconceivable. The point
remains, however, that Marx was too good a student of Hegel to have
believed that ancient models could be prised out of their element and
slapped like labels onto modern society.[9] Bourgeois horizons are not
the only ones that need to be crossed. Ancient horizons are to be
eclipsed, too.

Only a force emanating from within society would be capable of
bringing forth so expansive, so unprecedented an idea of freedom, as
Marx at his least dogmatic was, perhaps painfully, aware. But even
as he articulates this idea of freedom, Marx is not averse to looking
back retrospectively. He still speaks, as we have seen, of communism
as "the restoration of man as a social, that is human being," or as the
"complete and conscious restoration of man to himself." What is to
be "restored" is nevertheless not ancient freedom, or is ancient freedom
but in a state of perfection no ancient theorist had ever dared imagine.
Specifically, communism as the universal public life of human beings
considered as "species-beings," the realization of the Greek idea of
human nature, would join together politics and philosophy once and

2

for all. This, too, had been a dream of the ancients. The Marxian promise, contained, that is, within the critical, emancipatory aspect of Marx's premonitory theorizing, is that of realizing it, making it come true. The ancients had the word; Marx, the word made flesh.

Short of such total human emancipation, political freedoms, seen in the more finite Greek sense, cannot be restored under modern conditions. They would lack a medium of existence. Unless private beings become universalized through their social experiences, unless the human species emerges as the universal public, unless, that is, the once merely philosophical ideal of an expansive human nature finally takes root, the political realm of "universal" existence will always be overwhelmed and stifled by the particularism of egoistic interests in civil society. Freedom will come, in the lexicon of the "Jewish Question," "when the real individual has absorbed the abstract citizen, and in his individual life has become a species-being." What is implied here, as we have seen, is a distinction between democracy as political, legal, and thus abstract and formal existence, on the one hand, and democracy as an aspect of a full, expansive human existence, on the other. Modern bourgeois political democracy, which creates a legal definition of citizenship and a "republic merely as a political constitution,"[10] while "real" life remains private life, merely attains the level of a formal or abstract democracy. Human emancipation means that "man treats himself as a universal and therefore free being." It is true, substantiated democracy because it is "the first true unity of the universal and the particular, i.e. private and public life."[11]

These are powerful, visionary arguments, which must in any balanced assessment of Marxian state theory be balanced against other, much more dogmatic and reductionist arguments, not all of which were produced by Marx's self-appointed successors. We shall never know whether Marx himself would have resuscitated them from their long slumber had he actually done what he proposed to do, on the very last page of the third volume of *Capital*, and given further attention to the modern state. But we are entitled to insist that they would have been, and to my mind still are, well worth the labor involved in resuscitating them. They point backwards, in the sense already outlined, and in their own right revive ancient and fundamental under-standings of what the practice of politics might involve, as Hannah Arendt reminds us. They certainly, for those, perhaps, who are inter-ested in augmenting or even defining the so-called "canon" of Western political theory, do much to reestablish Marx's standing and reputation as a political, and not just a social or economic, theorist. I shall argue that what I have termed Marx's theory of alien politics also points forward to our own political predicament in the present day, and that, in so doing, it attains a premonitory status having nothing to do with the various failures of what was, until recently, termed "actually existing" socialism and communism.

I shall broach this question in its proper place. In the meantime, the more immediate question that needs to be addressed has already been implied. If Marx might have resuscitated alien politics, but for whatever reason failed to do so, and if, as a result of his failure, the task has been left for others to perform, why is resuscitation, or disinterment, necessary in the first place? What, to put the same ques-tion another way, has been responsible for occulting it and hiding it from view all these years? The answer to these questions, if there is a single answer, is likely to be elusive and possibly even recessive, since it has to do with the oddly complex intellectual and institutional history of Marxism, along with the no less complex way these histories have interpenetrated within Marxism ever since we could first speak of Marxism. While this is not the place to try to penetrate these thickets, one observation about them is both apropos and indisputable. Alien politics failed to resound for so long largely because of what *did* come down to us as Marxist, or even Marxian state theory, which is in large measure a mélange of dogmatic, functionalist, instrumentalist and/or essentialist arguments that appear to owe nothing of any significance to alien politics at all. More than paradox is involved here. The alien-ation of alien politics, like all alienation, involves, at a very basic level, loss. What got lost was a theory about the modern state that may not solve every question there is to ask about it, but which is nevertheless much more substantive than what happened to replace it, and is for this reason alone well worth the effort of retrieval. Once it is retrieved, we can see that alien politics is not just of more substance than the crude ruling-class theories that effectively displaced it. Alien politics is also irreducible to any of these theories, as we are about to see.

Marx's important essays on nineteenth-century French politics, essays whose centerpiece is *The Eighteenth Brumaire of Louis Bonaparte*, are, by contrast, in no way incompatible with alien politics in anything like the same way. Marx, particularly in the *Eighteenth Brumaire*, resists easy temptations to which he had succumbed elsewhere. He moves away not just from the crude instrumentalism involved in depicting the state (or its "executive") as "but a committee for managing the common affairs of the whole bourgeoisie"; he also moves away from seeing the state as a monolithic, if bounded, entity. It has often been noticed that the state in the *Brumaire* is independent rather than monolithic, and that as a result it has seemed difficult to "reconcile" this state with the straightforward instrument of class rule encountered elsewhere. (It should be clear by now that I regard the question of the "reconciliation" of these as a *question mal posée*.) It has less often been noticed that the state in the *Brumaire* does not appear as a unitary, or even an *identifiable* object, entity or thing at all. It does not, in other words, appear in the guise of the kind of "object-state" that has fixed boundaries and a stable internal organization that would enable it to carry out or fulfill its externally determined "function." But this is what the state turns into in all too much subsequent Marxist state theory.

The characterization of the state in these instrumental as well as functionalist terms has bedevilled Marxist state theory ever since its inception. Functionalism of a specific kind and instrumentalism of a particular kind have, in effect, conspired together in what has come down to us as Marxist state theory. Jointly, they have muddied the waters. The "object-state," a concept I have derived by extension from Poulantzas's notion of the "state-subject," can take many forms. It has often proved difficult to characterize with any precision what the functions of the state, conceived of as "object-state," actually are in any given instance. It has proved no less difficult to explain the attributes of the state, seen as "object-state." It is unsurprising that heated disputes have broken out over such necessarily contentious issues.

What underlies all these various disputes, however, are a couple of underlying, and mutually sustaining core assumptions on which all parties could agree, and agree rather too readily. There is, to begin with, the assumption that the state has some externally defined or determined role to play or function to perform, however this role or function is characterized, and this, in effect, determines what the state itself finally *is*. (The underlying belief here is teleological in the Aristotelian sense: to know what something is, we must know what it is *for*. This belief has nothing to do with the state and is of no help in understanding the state.) The second assumption follows from, and has appeared to reinforce, the first. This is that the state is an identifiable agency that can be judged or measured by how well or how badly its own objective institutions, structures and processes fulfill the state's externally determined function. The function in question can vary in character. It could be, for instance, the accumulation of capital, the girding of bourgeois loins, the smiting of proletarians hip and thigh, or any combination of these. This variability does not affect the overall character of the argument. This assumption may be as unashamedly instrumentalist and functionalist as the previous one. But it is also, into the bargain, an assumption that both reifies the state, making of it something objective and tangible, and falsely universalizes it, making of it an abstraction, "the" state, that serves or can serve to obscure, instead of clarifying, the multiple interpenetrations between any known state and any known civil society. Specific configurations among and within state forms will then perforce be disregarded, even though they may be precisely what needs to be explained. Marx himself in effect provides a cue here, insisting, in the *Critique of the Gotha Program,* that there is no such thing as "the" present-day state, because existing state forms vary so much from country to country. They may have in common the quality of all being bourgeois state-forms; but this would mean that the category "bourgeois state" is an abstraction which in itself explains very little.

In what follows I shall pay comparatively little attention to the question of how and why the "object-state" displaced "alien politics" from what ought to have been its central position in Marxist state theory. I refrain from examining these questions not because they are necessarily complicated and contentious (though, of course, they are) but because they can serve to distract us from what is fundamentally at issue: the *effects* of the displacement in question. Even so, it is part of my argument that these same effects can be observed within Marxist state theory, as this has come down to us. It is also part of my argument that Marxist state theory has come down to us in an unduly attenuated form largely because of this same displacement. This book is in large measure a recuperation, an attempt to set the record straight. If I had to identify a single candidate responsible for having twisted it out of all recognition in the first place, the figure who snaps into focus would be Lenin, the very person who is, not at all coincidentally, responsible above all others for having formulated and set his seal upon the same notion of the "object-state" that has bedevilled so much subsequent speculation and practice. That Lenin may have had good reasons of his own, in the summer of 1917, for situating the state topographically, as a "site" and as an entity that admitted of being "taken," or "smashed" is a point that need not concern us here. What should concern us is the theoretical legacy of so fundamental a misunderstanding. It has had effects, not all of them theoretical ones, that are little short of devastating.

Lenin's *The State and Revolution,* to be sure, did not emerge out of nowhere. Engels wrote to Eduard Bernstein the year after Marx's death that "it is precisely the democratic republic that is the logical form of bourgeois rule . . . the last form of bourgeois rule, that in which it goes to pieces."[12] This rather incoherent formulation appears to be at odds with what Marx had said about democratic republics. Small wonder, perhaps, that Engels's most recent biographer concludes that "[a]s a politician Engels's work was severely circumscribed by the strategy he inherited from the politics of revolutionary constitutionalism."[13] The same could certainly not be said for Lenin. Even so, Engels's statement could have cued Lenin's *The State and Revolution,* which argues, quite similarly, that since the democratic republic is the best possible "shell" for capitalism, no change of personnel, institutions or parties at the level of the state apparatus can shake the political hold of capitalism. It is at this point that Lenin's well-known voluntaristic theory of the party insinuates itself into the argument. The basic drawback of Leninism considered as a theory of the state was indicated some time ago by Otto Kirchheimer. Lenin's theory of the state is in large measure supplanted by his theory of the party. Lenin, of course, claimed Marx's seal of approval for both theories, but in neither case is the claim warranted. That Lenin was acting opportunistically, in a situation Marx signally failed to forsee, let alone predict, did not pass unnoticed at the time. Even in the instance of the most significant point of contact between Marx's theory of the state and Lenin's, the notion of the dictatorship of the proletariat, Rosa Luxemburg, who was arguably Lenin's ablest antagonist in the years of the Second International, was quick to see the difference between what Marx had meant by the concept and the uses to which Lenin bid fair to put it. She insisted, in terms close to those that Dan and Martov were levelling at the same time, that proletarian dictatorship, as Marx had envisaged, is defined by the way it *applies* democracy, and not by the way it abolishes democracy.[14] Luxemburg's acumen did not in the event dislodge the latter, Leninist characterization from its dominant position. This was not because of Lenin's own theoretical acumen, but because of historical developments in Russia. But for these, *The State and Revolution* might have remained a mere *pièce de circonstance*, and not the hegemonic formulation of Marxist state theory it perforce, and regettably, became. *The State and Revolution* was at the time of its inception the product of what Kirchheimer terms "the brief but historically decisive period in between Russia's bourgeois and communist revolutions. Consequently it could not as yet embody the practical experiences of the Russian October Revolution; it is of especial interest becuse it reflects Lenin's conception of the proletarian state independently of its realization under Russian conditions. Within Soviet literature," Kirchheimer continues, "this work is considered the direct continuation of Marx's teachings on proletarian dictatorship."[15]

The State and Revolution is, however, nothing of the sort. So distant is Lenin's reductionist account from almost anything Marx had said that it has led some commentators, commentators who are rightly anxious to sever Marx from Marxism-Leninism, to protest too much and deny that Marx was serious about the concept of proletarian dictatorship in the first place. Shlomo Avineri is a case in point. He maintains that Marx "does not use the term more than two or three (sic) times in his life, and then in what is basically a private communication."[16] Avineri is stretching a point here. Marx in fact used the term eleven times. Moreover, his anarchist interlocutors in the First International, who were terrified of proletarian dictatorship, would have taken some convincing of its unimportance. We have only to look at what these "basically private communications" *were* to see how disingenuous Avineri's claim is.[17] One was Marx's letter to Joseph Weydermeyer (5 March 1852), in the course of which he describes "the dictatorship of the proletariat" as one of his three unique discoveries. The other purportedly "private" communication was nothing less than the *Critique of the Gotha Program*, which Marx never intended to be private (the leadership of the SPD sat on it for political reasons). Avineri is not really on much safer ground when he makes much of the fact that Marx does not use the phrase "dictatorship of the proletariat" in the *Manifesto of the Communist Party* (he first used it, for the record, in *The Class Struggles in France*). This probably means only that Marx had not yet come up with the phrase. The *Manifesto* certainly paraphrases its content and bearing accurately enough: the proletariat is to be "raise(d) to the position of ruling class," it is to be "organized as the ruling class." This will amount to its "political supremacy" and enable it to make "despotic inroads on the right of property." Avineri himself admits[18] that the "ten regulations" duly itemized as constituting jointly the *sine qua non* of the transition to communism all "involve the wielding of state power" programmatically. Avineri's belief that (Marxian) socialism is in practice what capitalism is *in potentia* effectively pushes the two kinds of society too close together—the "narrow horizon of bourgeois right," let us remember, is to be "crossed in its entirety," an admonition that does not appear to enjoin gradualism.

Avineri's protestation is mistaken because there is no real difficulty involved in distinguishing Marx's notion of proletarian dictatorship from Lenin's. Luxemburg's well-known admonition that Lenin's notion of the dictatorship of the proletariat could turn, with frightening ease, into the practice of dictatorship *over* the proletariat, the last thing Marx ever had in mind, was based upon her appreciation of this point. Dictatorship to Marx, forever the classicist, carried not so much its later, twentieth-century connotation of despotism and authoritarianism but its Roman meaning: an emergency, transitional assumption of power for a limited period and for the sake of carrying through determinate tasks that were to be specified in advance. This is not at all what Lenin had in mind. He was of course able to back-reference what were largely organizational imperatives by invoking phrases drawn from the available writings of Marx and Engels, but such invocations were necessarily tendentious and almost incantatory. Marx and Engels were not invoked in a spirit of calm, scholarly objectivity; concepts and phrases were torn from their contexts and made to carry talismanic force under the impress of events.

Closer examination of *The State and Revolution* reveals, moreover, that Engels is mined for slogans rather more thoroughly than Marx. There is nothing particularly surprising about this, since Engels's thought on matters political is in crucial respects at variance with Marx's, as I have indicated elsewhere. Briefly put, the crude and rather bare-bones notion of "the withering away of the state," which was useful to Lenin for a while, is Engels's notion, not Marx's (Marx never used it). More substantively, but no less problematically, Engels's rather Saint-Simonian notion that once the characteristics of the bourgeois state are extinguished, the functions of government are to be reduced to their technical components, so that "the government of men" is replaced—as this unfortunate slogan would have it—by "the administration of things," was also to prove useful to Lenin, not least because, in implying that the technicalities in question were open and accessible to everyone, it fitted in well with Lenin's odd notion of the "democratic." (All this is as though Marx's reflections on the bureaucracy as "universal estate" in 1843, and for that matter as though the *Eighteenth Brumaire*, had never been written.) What it came, in short order, to run up against was, of course, what Kirchheimer nicely characterizes as "the preconceived structure of the subject of the revolution, the proletarian party."[19] As Kirchheimer points out, "any thought of direct democracy is excluded in Lenin's theory of the party . . . (which) is dominated by the familiar concept of the necessarily conspiratorial nature of a hierarchical group of professional revolutionaries, of the 'Jacobins attached to the organization of class-conscious workers'. This is the thesis of the need for a heteronomous discipline not based on existing mass consciousness, and this is the famous doctrine that led to the splitting of the Russian workers' movement . . . (which) Lenin derived . . . from special exigiencies under Russian absolutism."[20]

Even though Marx had had no love for the exigiencies of Tsarism, and even though Luxemburg must have known this, she was not slow, as we have seen, in registering a sharp rebuke to Lenin at this very juncture. Again in Kirchheimer's well-judged words, "she regarded the sharp marking off of an organized party nucleus from the surrounding revolutionary environment as an attempt to transfer Blanquist principles of organization onto the social democratic movement of the working masses. According to her, social democracy is not only *connected* with the organization of the working class, it is the workers' *own* movement."[21] Accordingly, Luxemburg sharply criticized the mechanical transfer of capitalist factory discipline to the autonomous discipline of the working class, a transference that emerged much more clearly after the revolution than it had in Lenin's theoretical credo of 1902, *What is to be Done?* Against this Luxemburg, as is well enough known, emphasized "spontaneity," a troublesome notion that cannot occupy us here. It does however entail a proposition that carries over into the thought of Gramsci. This is that the function of the party is to synthesize, and not, as with Lenin, to *form*, the will of the masses. Gramsci, as we shall see, needed to retrieve this view from virtual oblivion largely because it was buried by the weight of Soviet developments. With the civil war, the structure of the Soviet state came practically to coincide with that of the Communist Party, which meant that the Soviets became empty husks, and Leninism itself an unequivocally authoritarian theory of the party, and with this an authoritarian and specifically non-Marxian theory of the state, whose theoretical avatar *The State and Revolution* came to be.

Discussing (and calumniating) *The State and Revolution*, A. J. Polan claims that "Lenin incorporated into his politics the theory of the commune-state as elaborated by Marx, without additions and without omissions."[22] He claims no less breathlessly that the "Soviet state that emerged after 1917 bore the stamp of *The State and Revolution* in all its subsequent phases, before *and* after the Bolsheviks secured the monopoly of power, before *and* after the decline of the soviets, before *and* after the rise of Stalin."[23] These are exaggerated claims that assign too much weight to one slender text, and as such must be rejected. But they should not be allowed to carry down in their wake Polan's underlying belief about "[t]win paradoxes of the collapse of Marx's theory of agency." These are "mass parties that, fundamentally, do not believe that the masses have any role to play in their own liberation; and tiny collectivities that ground themselves in mass self-emancipation but remain desperately devoid of mass support."[24] But even this last point, which is well-taken, is of limited application to *The State and Revolution*, which, as Polan is well aware, scarcely mentions the party. Instead, it fixates on the state.

Polan, in his determination not see *The State and Revolution* as an anomaly, for this or for any other reason, has here, despite himself, raised an important point. It is often supposed that the Bolsheviks seized power with a ready-made conception of the dictatorship of the proletariat, taken down from the Marxian peg and dusted off for the occasion. This supposition is untrue, for at least two reasons. The first is that, as we have seen, Lenin interpreted Marx's *The Civil War in France,* (which was, we should recall, a philippic commemorating a failed revolutionary uprising, and not at all a programmatic tocsin call to arms) and interpreted it in a very particular manner. In this he was no doubt cued, but by Engels, not Marx. Neil Harding observes what is in fact an example of a pattern that has had dire results in the history of Marxism. It is, says Harding:

> very telling that Marx himself carefully and consistently avoided identifying the Commune as a form of the dictatorship of the proletariat. So long as Marx was alive, Engels too was similarly careful. Only in 1891, long after Marx's death, did Engels in his Introduction to [a new edition of] Marx's *Civil War in France* identify the Commune as a, or *the*, form of the dictatorship of the proletariat.[25]

Engels, here as elsewhere, has a lot to answer for.

The other reason why Lenin, in writing *The State and Revolution* and, for that matter, in seizing power in 1917, was not applying a concept of proletarian dictatorship that had some prior theoretical existence is that there was no felt need to do so. The ready-made theory of dictatorship of the proletariat, which was Lenin's, not Marx's, in the upshot, had no immediate purchase in 1917. The idea that it must have had some purchase in light of subsequent developments awards Lenin too much and too little at the same time. We know that the fusion of the party and the state was to take place after 1917. We know, too, the form that fusion was to take: tight centralization, hierarchical subordination of lower administrative bodies to higher ones, rigid division of labor and authoritative allocation of function. But what we cannot legitimately infer from these future developments is that the Bolsheviks *began* by transferring the organizational model of the party onto the state, and then proceeded to impose the composite on society. In Neil Harding's words, such transferral and imposition was "certainly not the way in which the Bolsheviks justified the revolutionary seizure of power, nor does it reflect their intentions during the first nine months in power. During this period the dictatorship of the proletariat was seldom alluded to, and the theme of democratic centralism, as applied to state institutions, did not surface until the early 1920s. It is little noticed how implacably anti-statist was the motivation and justification for the Bolshevik Revolution."[26]

What helps us understand the implacable antistatism Lenin shared with a great many others at the time is not so much *The State and Revolution*, but *Imperialism, The Highest Stage of Capitalism*. By late 1916 Lenin had become convinced that capitalism was in its death throes. The war, he thought, was a manifestation of the worldwide contradictions of international finance capital, which had visited ruin, famine and devastation upon central and eastern Europe. In Lenin's own words, "The imperialist war has immensely accelerated and intensified the process of transformation of monopoly capitalism into state monopoly capitalism. The monstrous oppression of the working people by the state, which is merging more and more with the all-powerful capitalist associations, is becoming increasingly monstrous. The advanced countries are becoming military convict prisons for the workers."[27] The state and the mode of production had become linked. Neil Harding characterizes their juncture ably.

> It was, after all, the state that sustained the armies, navies, armaments, industries and administrative bureaucracies so vital for colonial expansion and the protection of exported capital. It was the imperialist state that created tariff barriers so that monopoly prices could be protected, the state that imposed the direct and especially the regressive indirect taxes to furnish the national debt, which, in its turn afforded lucrative outlets for finance capital. It was the state, in short, that guaranteed the reproduction of the mode of production of finance capitalism. It had therefore imperatively to be controlled by the magnates of finance capitalism, and so, in Lenin's view, it was. The state itself now became a terrain of plunder for the monopolists, a vehicle for organizing national production and, increasingly, a cudgel to put down opposition and criticism, especially that voiced by the socialist parties.[28]

There are at least two implications of this picture of total depravity. The first is that the only possible relationship between people and state, in Lenin's view, was one of bitter, no-holds-barred conflict. The state existed only to maintain the monopoly of power and wealth held by the privileged, and was consequently a machine of "monstrous oppression."[29] Lenin's unformulated concept of "Lloyd-Georgism"[30] was meant to refer to the insidious impact of the kind of social reform the more conciliatory state managers were prepared to dole out in carefully measured quantities, the better to forestall complete social disintegration; this, to Lenin, meant that the bourgeois state had become the core of the process whereby the organs of the proletariat were delivered up to imperialist politics[31]; "they were actually nationalised by this *imperialist* state . . . they transformed themselves into labor departments of the military machine."[32] (This helps explain the otherwise puzzlingly intense Bolshevik opposition to reform.) The other implication of the state's new-found presence in civil society was no less ominous. The historical originality of the imperialist state formation was that it now dictated the form of development of the productive forces, rather than they it. Bukharin went so far as to "hit on the heresy of the superstructure's determining the base"[33]: "the state power . . . sucks in all areas of production; it not only embraces the general conditions of the productive process; the state becomes more and more a direct exploiter, which organizes and directs production as a collective capitalist." The state emerges as "the New Leviathan, beside which the fantasy of Thomas Hobbes seems but a child's plaything." It aims at "absorbing within the domain of state regulation every one and everything."[34]

Add to all this the belief shared by Lenin and Bukharin that capitalism considered as a productive process had managed to invert itself in its final, state monopoly capitalism phase, and the recipe is well-nigh complete. Capitalist monopoly retarded instead of accelerating technological innovation, thereby betraying the promise bequeathed it by capitalism in its earlier, heroic phase, that of being able constantly to "revolutionize" the forces of production—which meant that the time had finally come when an overripe capitalism and its perfected state mechanism had become not just redundant and supernumerary but also malignant, cancerous. Only its excision could restore to society its lost vitality.

The startlingly obvious parallelism was in short order to suggest itself to Lenin. It was the "parasitic excrescence" Marx had identified in the *Eighteenth Brumaire* as the Bonapartist regime, the Second Empire, which had been replaced, of course, by the Paris Commune and the "communal constitution" of 1871. Marx's *The Civil War in France* was accordingly made the practical program of the Bolsheviks from April 1917 to April 1918. Lenin's insistence that they change their names to "communist"—which is why we still speak of communist regimes today—was explicitly intended as a signal that the now renamed Bolsheviks were proponents of a "state of which the Paris Commune was the prototype."[35] The Commune as blueprint yields what is still an almost stunning simplicity. All, literally *all*, the population were to be drawn into the administration of the common affairs of society. Through their Soviets, their factory councils, their regimental committees, their cooperative societies and their militia, the people were to resume their collective self-administration and to build up "[d]emocracy from below, democracy without an officialdom, without a police, without a standing army."[36]

It was a heroic moment, whatever one thinks of its regrettable aftermath. But at the same time it was based on an assumption of Saint-Simonian provenance, mediated not through Marx but through Engels, that "the government of persons" admitted of being replaced and countermanded by "the administration of things," and also on a fatal misreading of what state monopoly capitalism comported. Lenin, Bukharin and others thought, at least for a while, that it had simplified matters political and administrative out of all recognition. Only a minimum of the functions of the capitalist state are strictly necessary. Its main function is the repression of the working class, a task that will by definition be rendered redundant in future society.[37] (That there is some sort of intrinsic connection between bureaucracy and underdevelopment, which Lenin's writings of this period do more than imply,[38] would have stuck in the craw of Hegel). But beneath this, we have a more deep-rooted assumption: "Once we have overthrown the capitalists . . . and smashed the bureaucratic machine of the modern state, we shall have a splendidly equipped mechanism . . . which can very well be set going by the workers themselves, who will hire technicians, foremen, and accountants, and pay them all workmen's wages."[39] The "new means of control," in Lenin's rather ominous words, "have been created not by us, but by capitalism in its military-imperialist stage." "Capitalism simplifies the functions of 'state' administration; it makes it possible to cast 'bossing' aside."[40]

These assumptions are as instrumentalist as they are providential. They entail that socialism was simply a matter of remanning existing institutions created by state monopoly capitalism and perfected during the war, making them accessible to public control and obliging them to serve public need, not private greed. It is state monopoly capitalism not abolished, but simply turned to good account. Lenin himself guilelessly admitted as much. State monopoly capitalism, he said, had created "a complete material preparation for socialism, the threshold of socialism."[41] Those of us who are uncomfortably aware that it turns out to have provided a threshold for something very different from socialism in any worthwhile sense of the term have only to remember Marx's admonition, which Lenin, along with so many others in the course of this sorry century, appears conveniently to have forgotten, that "the working class cannot simply take hold of the state machinery and wield it for its own purposes," because the state machinery as such is contaminated. If Lenin learned this after the first flush of victory, he, and many others besides him, must have learned it the hard way, for what he had done was to pave the way for a redefinition of socialism as "that system of social ownership that best conduced to maximum economic efficiency and productivity," socialism, that is to say, "modelled in the mirror image of the imperialist state."[42] To compress a series of future developments, it is at one level unsurprising that a "principal task of the dictatorship of the proletariat" was to become "the creation of a proletariat in the place and in the proportion needed by the state, imbued with attitudes favorable to the maximization of productivity and free from defensive autonomous organizations that might have frustrated these goals."[43] In this sense Polan, his exaggerations notwithstanding, is quite right when he denies the "innocence" of *The State and Revolution* vis-à-vis what later came to be known as Leninism. His point is well taken that "the regrettable features of the Bolshevik party" ("its intolerance, it exclusivity, its hierarchical structure, its concentration of effective power at the top") "came to define the lineaments of the Russian state . . . [and that this] is due to Lenin's concept of state form, not his concept of party."[44]

Gramsci, at first glance, could not be more different from Lenin in this respect. Lenin's idea of state monopoly capitalism as the "antechamber of socialism" is conspicuously absent from Gramsci,[45] who returns to a Hegelian notion of the state as the highest expression of civil society, rather than as a mere tool of class domination. While Lenin had constantly stressed the state's class character, as well as its repressive nature, Gramsci deemphasized these, concentrating instead on the cultural-hegemonic function of the state: "its aim," he perhaps surprisingly claimed, "is always that of creating a new and higher form of civilization."[46] We are not going to find much in Lenin, even at his most visionary, about qualitative change resulting from the revolutionary process. Revolution in Lenin's hands is, rather, a mechanical transition, a set of purely external and objective changes.

In Lenin, the focus is always on power and the best organizational means to seize and conquer it. Socialism is seen in the first instance as a solution to capitalist problems (production, organization, efficiency) rather than as a rise of a new humanity, a new civilization, and the supercession of domination. These superstructural epiphenomena would automatically be taken care of with the establishment of the workers' state. No such assumption pervades Gramsci's thought, which again, quite to the contrary, stresses the latter, more positive set of concerns, with the former being seen as but the means to its attainment.

This said, we should not overdraw the differences between Lenin and Gramsci. Gramsci admired Lenin immensely as a political leader who had taken Marx's eleventh thesis on Feuerbach and put it into effect. The leader of a revolution that failed (to use Martin Clark's formulation[47]), could not but look up to the leader of a revolution that had worked. There is little direct criticism of Lenin, Leninism or the Soviet state in Gramsci's writings. Gramsci's famous formulation of the differences between Russia and the West deserves quoting at length at this juncture, with this point in mind.

> In Russia the state was everything, civil society was primordial and gelatinous; in the West, there was a proper relationship between the state and civil society, and when the state trembled, a sturdy structure of civil society was at once revealed. The state was only an outer ditch, behind which there stood a powerful system of fortresses—and earthworks: more or less numerous from one state to the next, it goes without saying—but this precisely necessitated an accurate reconnaissance of each individual country.[48]

Nothing in the foregoing, oft-cited passage suggests that Lenin had not succeeded in his "accurate reconnaissance" of his country at his own chosen time. It simply suggests that Lenin's mode of seizing power would not have worked anywhere else. This is not the place for a detailed examination of Lenin and Gramsci, which would lead us too far afield, and would also be redundant, since this rather intriguing task has been ably accomplished elsewhere. Suffice it to say that, for the purposes of the present argument, the differences between the two should not be overdawn. In particular, Gramsci's theoretical predicament was in essence similar to Lenin's. Both asked the same question—where in contemporary capitalist civilization does entrenched power lie?—and answered it differently. Gramsci's answer improves upon Lenin's, but does so disarmingly, by agreeing with it. Certainly entrenched power lies in the state, where it takes the particular form of domination. Power resides also, and more fundamentally, at least in the West, in a network of social institutions that may owe little or nothing to the state in any direct sense—the professions, the educational system, the Church, a whole network of public and private institutions that, taken together, constitute civil society.[49] It is from these institutions that people imbibe, often unwittingly, a great many beliefs, attitudes and values, values that ordinarily eventuate in an often tacit consent to the *status quo*. This, in turn, helps shore up and consolidate each separate institution, and through these, the system of civil society and the state taken as a whole. Society's institutions transmit its values from generation to generation, values that can have the effect, other things being equal, of stifling revolutionary ardor. For this reason alone, other things should not be left equal by practicing revolutionaries.

The axis of hegemony has partly to do with consent and belief, and partly with what people leave unquestioned. Either way, their cognitive and affective structures are involved in its operation. The institutions by which and through which hegemony is transmitted cannot be left unchallenged. Left to their own devices, they would feed on each other and reinforce popular passivity, and Gramsci even believed that "materialist superstition" comes naturally to the working class. But these same institutions cannot be destroyed outright. By their very nature they do not lend themselves to a singular, dramatic act of root-and-branch extirpation. In this respect they are conspicuously different from the state as Lenin had regarded it. The state can be regarded topographically, as a site that can be besieged from without, and in some respects is so regarded by Gramsci every bit as much as by Lenin. The point remains that institutions constituting civil society cannot be so regarded, since the force they exert is often invisible and intangible. But what this means, in its turn, is that Marxist theoreticians and stalwarts would ignore these institutions at their peril, since the institutions in question are the transmission belts for bourgeois values and bourgeois culture.

These institutions must then be transformed from within, such internal transformation being a vital part of, or preparation for revolutionary transformation in the West. In Russia, taking over the state was sufficient. The very act of doing so transformed society, because civil society was insufficiently "robust" and preformed to begin with, and because the Russian state virtually coincided with the Russian nation in any case.[50] But in the West, the state is but one of many elements in a long political tradition the Russians had perforce lacked. In Italy the only thing the state was even supposed to monopolize was armed might, which Gramsci, perhaps remarkably, chose to regard as its least important feature. If hegemony is strong enough, states resort to violence rarely enough,[51] and hegemony cannot be created by violence.[52] The bourgeois state in particular has less potential for coercion than other known forms of the state. It is upheld, normally, not by brute force but by beliefs in or assumptions about its legitimacy, that is by the cultural and moral directive power society's institutions disseminate and germinate. All this eventuates in the message that, if the workers' movement is successfully to gain power, it must first, in prerevolutionary times, build up counterstandards of legitimacy, or a counterhegemony, since hegemony had been the essential background to and *sine qua non* of domination all along. The Jacobins in the French Revolution "did not rest content with making the bourgeoisie a dominant class (element of force, command function). They did more, they created the bourgeois state and made the bourgeoisie the leading, the hegemonic class of the nation; in other words they gave the new state a permanent base and created the compact unity of the modern French nation."[53] Disciplined political action under tight party leadership is no less essential as a result of the importance of hegemonic struggles, or of what was called "the long march through the institutions" of civil society. But it remains adjunct to these. It is different in principle from them, as well as irreducible to them, and because of this difference, party-political action should never dominate hegemonic struggle, must must instead be subordinate to it. Hegemony remains "the most important face of power."

Whereas Lukács could blithely claim that "the proletariat is forced to seize power when it still inwardly accepts the bourgeois order of society as the truly legal one,"[54] Gramsci's whole point was that the notion of seizure of power under such conditions, conditions that appear not to have pertained during the Bolshevik Revolution anyway, could only be a pipe dream. The truth of the matter, a truth that does seem to be borne out if we look at the Russian Revolution, not to mention the French one, is that "every revolution has been preceded by intense critical activity, cultural penetration and permeation of ideas among groups of men at first unwilling to accept them."[55] The emphasis in revolutionary organizing should be placed on the building up of counterinstitutions among the working class of the kind that will dislodge hegemonic structures by working on and moderating people's beliefs. To the extent that the party and even the trade unions are counterinstitutions of the required type, and to the extent that parties can be what Gramsci called "schools of State life," Gramsci approves of them in principle. But he was always aware of countervailing tendencies, those of bureaucratization and institutional ossification. Indeed, Gramsci's early enthusism for factory councils, an enthusiasm raising a host of interpretational problems that cannot be entered into here, can in large measure be accounted for because these, being small-scale, went against the grain of bureaucratization; this meant that councils are much less likely than unions to turn into mechanisms or symptoms of cultural integration of the working class into the prevailing system of rewards and expectations. It was in this sense that Gramsci could refer to the factory councils as embryonic states; they enabled a certain rehearsal of power in that they culturally prepared the working class to be the ruling class of the future. Which is to say that Gramsci on the council added an arguably needed ingredient to Lenin on the Soviets.

Gramsci's concern, we may surmise, was to flesh out, substantiate and make operative Marx's idea that "theory becomes a material form once it grips the masses." He is also rather more aware than Marx appears to have been that this injunction, as it were, works both ways; in other words, that hegemonic as well as counterhegemonic institutions can in principle provide this idea with a medium of existence. The point remains that ideas have to be filtered through counterhegemonic institutions, including the party insofar as this can be considered a counterhegemonic institution, if they are to exert the desired "material force." Gramsci wanted to preclude the "checkmating of revolutionary possibilities at a prepolitical level."[56] Political hegemony must precede the attainment of power at the level of the state, not because this latter is impossible in principle without hegemonic struggle, but precisely because it could turn out to be perfectly possible— but might make very little real difference. The question of the seizure of power exists in the shadow of another, more fundamental question to which Leninism provided at best an ambiguous answer: how do you retain power once it has been "seized"?

Any adequate apprisal of Gramsci's elaborate theoretical structure, one which is not about to be attempted here, would involve interrogation of his own questions about the status and credentials of the revolutionary intellectual, around the answers to which Gramsci built an entire, intricate and original vocabulary ("traditional" versus "organic" intellectuals, "absolute historicism," the "war of position" as opposed to the "war of maneuver," the "organic bloc," "passive revolution," *civiltà capitalista*, *civiltà comunista* and so forth). This is not the place to traverse these formulations. But it is the place to ask where their elaboration leaves our subject, the state. This Gramsci regards as an externally mediating agency over and above a civil society that retains its independence and autonomy. The entire thematic of hegemony would become meaningless without such separation of civil society from the state. Unless the latter is seen as independently conquerable, Gramsci's notion of the "war of position," in particular, would be meaningless. But what kind of separation are we speaking of? It is anything but simple. Gramsci was not, for instance, simplistically taking the classical political economists' notion of the "night-watchman state" more literally than they did, even if his society and economy seem to tick over regularly enough without much in the way of "outside" state "intervention." Gramsci was aware that too much had happened since the heyday of classical political economy for this relatively simple separation to retain much valency. ("Naturally, liberals ['economists'] are for the state as *veilleur de nuit*, and would like the historical initiative to be left to civil society and to the various forces that spring up there—with the state as the guardian of 'fair play' and the rules of the game.")[57] He was concerned to recast the notion of the state as an instrument of class rule largely because of what he considered the conditioning of the modern state by the organization of the masses, who were beginning to be able to influence the province of state action, for good or for ill, from below. Such pressure is anything but uniform from country to country, and official responses to these demands were no less diverse. This means that what needs to be understood is not the nature of "the" modern state, which Gramsci follows Marx's *Critique of the Gotha Program* in regarding as a useless abstraction, but the forms assumed by various modern *states*.

These, Gramsci believed, are by now singularly unlikely to resolve themselves into any general notion of the state as an instrument of the ruling class. Political power in the period of mass parties and pressure groups confronts an economy where the role of the individual entrepreneur, the captain of industry, tends to be undermined by the growth of banking and finance. Other developments in the same period, after about 1870, emanated from a different direction, from below. They took the forms of demands proceeding from the underlying population, claims for entitlement and protection, claims that with democratization had to be afforded some degree of acknowledgment if the state's claim to legitimacy was not to become altogether meaningless. Recognition of these claims involved the state in new ventures, new functions that had found no place in the script of classical political economy. The novelty of these functions did not consist in some newfound magnanimity; the "welfare state" in its twentieth-century form was a long time coming, and can be regarded as an instrument of control anyway. The strategy of the dominant classes, or of the more far-sighted among their leaders, was to keep mass demands within the kind of limits that did not fundamentally threaten the logic of the social system, or the maintenance of political and economic decision-making in their own hands. The strategy of the workers' movement should, according to Gramsci, involve counterhegemonic struggle of the kind that breaks through the traditional distinction between leaders and led at its very root. Socialist transformation of society now involved the vast majority of the population becoming masters of their own lives, the economic and political decision-makers.

We should appreciate at this juncture that hegemony as a distinctively Gramscian concept, as opposed to the cheapened and overused concept it became in lesser hands, is streets away from the kind of functionalism that casts its lines of argument around consensus, integration and "norms." A dominant class can also be said to be hegemonic only if it carries the whole of society forward; it has a universalist aim, not an arbitrary one.[58] Hegemony was more nearly designed to refer to a period within modernity in which the lines between the state and civil society, between politics and economics, between public and private, were becoming increasingly blurred and harder and harder to disentangle. The state is less a command structure, or an agency or instrument of class rule, than a hegemonic, as well as dominant, apparatus, because of its antennae, which stretch down into the web of human relationships that constitute civil society. The state's ability to reproduce its dominance depends upon a network of relations in society that may be only tangentially related to the structure of the state itself.

It is at this point that we notice, or recall, something rather startling, which pushes our own analysis to a new threshold. Gramsci was concerned to return to a Hegelian notion of the state seen as the highest expression of civil society, rather than as a mere tool or instrument of straightforward class domination. Gramsci announced a kind of prolegomenon to the argument(s) of his *Prison Notebooks* in a letter to a friend:

> This research will also concern the concept of the state, which is usually thought of as political society—i.e. dictatorship or some other coercive apparatus used to control the masses in conformity with a given type of production and economy—and not as a balance between political society and civil society, by which I mean the hegmony of one social group over the entire society, exercised through so-called private institutions like the Church, trade unions or schools.[59]

Nicola Auciello is quite right on this.

> Unlike most of the international communist movement around the 1930s, Gramsci succeeded in perceiving the general trends of a profound process of transformation at a world-wide level, of the relation between the state and the economy (as produced by the new requirements and the new phase of capitalist development) precisely because in the previous years, and with particular reference to the kinds of investigations and observations connected with the analysis of fascism, he had gradually come to develop within his theoretical arsenal a concept of the state and its relations to "civil society" that rejected all dichotomous schemes of a traditional type and sought, rather, to trace the "presence" of the state in that "private" and "prestate" mass reality that is civil society.[60]

Gramsci's depiction of state and civil society is subtle and articulated largely because Hegel had been received differently in Italy from elsewhere, and was identified with the philosophy of Italian unification. The character of the opponents of unification effectively "radicalized" Hegel, whose statism became *ipso facto* progressive, and not reactionary. That Hegelianism clashed with existing social and political "realities" was accordingly the source of his marked appeal to generations of Italian intellectuals leading up to Gramsci. The Hegelianism these adopted did not even need to be mediated through Marx, as it was mediated to English-speaking intellectuals of a later generation. Gramsci himself referred to Hegelianism as that "world-historical moment of philosophical enquiry of which Marxism was a first reading."[61] We should not be too surprised by this. In Paul Piccone's words, Gramsci's

> brand of Marxism is qualitatively different from Lenin's or any other version of Marxism-Leninism. It is an almost direct continuation of the Italian tradition of social and political thought, which, from Spaventa to Labriola to Croce, sought to develop a neo-Hegelianism whose goal of human emancipation focused on social individuality and a qualitatively new form of existence. This was and is irreconcilable with any form of economistic, deterministic, or generally objectivistic vision that sees progress as the further extension of the logic of the given by removing such obstacles as private property or bourgeois institutions[62]

—institutions, we might add, like the state. Even Piccone's reference to "human emancipation" turns out to be not wide of the mark: somewhere in between 1929 and 1931 Gramsci translated Marx's "On 'The Jewish Question' " into Italian,[63] and its influence tolls like a bell throughout the *Prison Notebooks* as a whole.[64] Within the intellectual history of Marxist state theory, Gramsci's thought marks a real advance, but his advance is an advance over Marxism-Leninism, and not just that of the 1930s: the long, sorry story of the suppression and distortion of Gramsci's writings after his death, as well as before it, is eerily parallel with what happened to Marx's earlier writings in the hands of party orthodoxies. I would not be alone in suspecting and suggesting that these dual suppressions and distortions, each of which has a complex history of its own, were undertaken for the same basic reason, and, once accomplished, were defended, effectively, by both sides in an ideologically polarized Cold-War environment. Marxism had to be made to appear as a cold, objectivist, determinist worldview by both sides for different reasons. Necessity makes strange bedfellows, who collude in presenting a distorted picture of what humanist Marxism is, or can be, and then in marshalling all the resources they can muster in defense of this distortion.

Gramsci's thinking reveals a welcome affinity with the Marx-Hegel confrontation with which the argument of this book commenced. There is one important respect in which Gramsci actually manages to go beyond the terms of this original confrontation. Far from seeing in the state the simple instrument in the hands of a bourgeois class that is already constituted elsewhere, Gramsci analyses the role of the state in the constitution of a class, in its unification and consolidation *as* a class.

The bourgeois class "is not a unified entity outside the state. As a result of the working of free competition, new groups of capitalist producers are constantly forming to fulfill the state's economic capacity. . . . The state's function is to find a juridical settlement to internal class disputes, to clashes between opposed interests; thereby it unifies different groupings and gives the class a solid, united, external appearance."[65] Rather than being the mere instrument of the bourgeoisie, the state facilitates the juridico-political unification of the bourgeoisie, helping the class as a whole to overcome its internal divisions and realize its political hegemony. The state emerges now as the mediator of a class, and not as a mere epiphenomenon of some mysteriously pre-given class structure or as a mere site of class struggle, as with Lenin. What lurks in the background, but not too far back, is the idea to which Marx had given classic expression in the *Eighteenth Brumaire*, that because the bourgeoisie is divided into strata with conflicting interests, it needs a state to constitute its unity by juridical and political means.

5

SUBJECT-STATE, OBJECT-STATE: FROM GRAMSCI TO POULANTZAS

Today, as I write, it is clear that state intervention plays an indispensible role in maintaining whatever stability capitalist societies enjoy. It is no less clear that the theoretical response to this development among Marxist scholars and stalwarts has been sporadic and uneven. In general, it has proceeded by fits and starts, prompted by periods of revolutionary opportunity: 1917 to the early 1920s, the 1930s, and the 1960s and seventies (when Eurocommunist state theory briefly surfaced). Unsurprisingly enough, all these were periods when "the state" itself came to the surface, and presented itself as a, or *the*, problem that needed to be addressed. How well it was addressed on these successive occasions is, of course, another question. It is certainly arguable that, in general, an inadequate grasp of political economy, in the more modern understanding of the term, and of the influence of ideology has impeded comprehension of the historically changing role of capitalist states, and that this inadequacy applies in particular to those analyses that continue to treat the state as Lenin had treated it, as a separate problem pertaining only to the political realm of strategic, revolutionary action, only, that is, to the question of how to take or seize (rather than hold on to) power.

With respect to the state, the argument was all too frequently proffered that the capitalist state still performs the same role and functions as it always has, only more so, because capital is larger in scope and scale, more complex, and more demanding than it ever managed to be at earlier periods. This argument, which I think is a false one, did nothing to prevent theorists invoking Marx's specific observations (for instance, about the character of the Bonapartist state in *The Eighteenth Brumaire*), or his gross and notorious generalizations (for example, that the state is "the executive committee of the ruling class"). These would get wrenched out of their context and applied out of their element, onto what are quite different and quite specific social realities of present-day state-capital configurations.

Invocations of the Leninist model, which were not infrequent, may have been particularly unfortunate. Lenin, as we have already seen, regarded the state instrumentally and strategically, as a "machine for the oppression of one class by another." His characterization duly emphasized the state's repressive aspects (army, police, courts of law) and how they helped maintain the bourgeoisie in power. Lenin, throughout *The State and Revolution*, was just as concerned as Marx had been to dispel naïve, ideological illusions that the state acted as a free agent in the interests of all of those over whom it was set. What Lenin added to this was the injunction that the state considered as a *topos* (or as what I am calling the "object-state") had imperatively to be "smashed," and that anarchists were deluded in their belief that the state could "wither away" without the need for an organized proletarian state in the form of the dictatorship of the proletariat. Lenin argued in the same breath, against the parliamentary-road Social Democrats, that socialism could be achieved in no other way, and in particular could not be won through parliamentary legislation (which is certainly not what Marx had believed), because the bourgeoisie would be quick to employ the state's repressive apparatus against any truly radical threat. *The State and Revolution*, which pays no attention to the question of cultural hegemony, or even to the role of the state in the accumulation of capital, does not apply to forms of capitalist society more advanced than Russia in 1917, where its prescriptions never "applied" anyway. It is if anything a manual for those periods when capitalist state structures collapse, and not at all for periods of state expansion. *The State and Revolution* is, in essence, premodern, based on early capitalist state-forms of the kind that were as yet uninvolved in Keynesian or post-Keynesian intervention within society. *The State and Revolution* may have made Lenin more palatable; but as a theory of the modern state it is in large measure irrelevant.

If Lenin emphasized, well-nigh exclusively, the state's repressive apparatus, Gramsci, as we have seen, has put us in his debt for having illuminated the cultural hegemony of modern state-forms, for his astute, creative characterization of the state/civil society couplet, and for identifing the state not just as spoils for the victor, nor as a mere epiphenomenon of society, but as an arena within which class-formation as well as class conflict can in principle take place. It remains arguable, however, that this last-named point, which is of vital importance to the argument of this book, awaited its further specification outside the pages of the *Prison Notebooks*. This task was finally attempted only by the later Poulantzas. It is also arguable that the *Prison Notebooks* themselves provide pointers, not so much to the analysis of modern state sectors, as to that of the institutions and values of civil society that help uphold the modern state.

For all these reasons it is safe to say that while the relationship between particular states and their no less particular civil societies was changing, sometimes gradually and sometimes dramatically, throughout the twentieth century, Marxist state theory lagged behind it in its comprehension of how the two spheres were related or could relate in specific instances. Partly because of the permanent fallback or alibi provided by the ever-present vulgar economic-determinist position, which regarded the state as a mere superstructure reflecting changes in society's economic base, it proved impossible in the event for Marxists to develop a more adequate theory of capitalist states. Concepts of the state, which came to the fore only during periods of more or less intense politicization and turbulence like the late 1960s, were even then derived, to an overwhelming extent, from other concepts. Small wonder, perhaps, that such analyses of the state as were proffered, even at the best of times, were, in Boris Frankel's harsh but fair words, characterized by "exaggeration, ahistorical abstraction and general superficiality."[1] Under the impact of fascism and Stalinism, notions like the "authoritarian state," "state capitalism," and the "totalitarian state" came to pepper the writings of Frankfurt School stalwarts like Max Horkheimer, Friedrich Pollock, Theodor Adorno and Herbert Marcuse, but almost always for the sake of supporting a belief, already arrived at for other reasons, that in the "epoch of monopoly capitalism," or in that of the "totally administered society," the contradiction between the state and civil society no longer applies in the twentieth century, and was purely a product of the now long-surpassed heroic period of nineteenth-century capitalist industrialization. Frankel's verdict, again, is harsh but scarcely undeserved:

> The failure of the Frankfurt School to distinguish between forms of state apparatus and specific social forces was due to their over-preoccupation with cultural questions [which were usually not approached in the spirit of Gramsci] and their limited application of historically specific political economy.

Another school of writers (Baran and Sweezy, Mattick, Mandel, Dobb and Braverman) all analyzed the nature of the capitalist state by looking at the productive process that was going on in civil society rather than looking at the internal structures of state apparatuses. "They make the major error of assuming that if one understands capital/labor relations then one simultaneously understands capitalist states as well."[2]

This, not to put too fine a point on it, is an unwarrantedly reductionist argument that cannot be sustained, and which was, in the event, deservedly eclipsed, to the detriment of Marxism's intellectual standing in the academy, by other approaches. By the time Ralph Miliband wrote *The State in Capitalist Society*, as late as 1969, the ideological high ground had long been staked out and occupied with no small tenacity by Weberian, pluralist and managerial theorists of modern industrial society. Poulantzas was quick to notice the resulting defensive, "last ditch" tone of Miliband's argument in this book. This is not the place to rehearse the once-celebrated Miliband-Poulantzas debate of the 1970s, tiresome, contentious and sometimes absurd as it was. It has been covered adequately enough, and has been shown to have generated more heat than light, elsewhere. But we cannot ignore it altogether, because the Miliband-Poulantzas donnybrook led into what may be the most important contribution to twentieth-century Marxist state theory since Gramsci's *Prison Notebooks*, Poulantzas's final book, *State, Power, Socialism*, which awaits its treatment below.

For Miliband, Marx's slogan that the state is an instrument of class rule is not an embarrassment but an axiom to be taken with the utmost seriousness, and one that admits of empirical demonstration into the bargain. His largely descriptive account fails to specify the nature of the mechanisms of class domination. Empirical research, or the idea of it, dislodges theoretical specification of what the underlying determinants of class power, as exercised through the state, actually are. Miliband's instrumentalism commits him to the proposition that the character of the state is determined by the struggles among classes, which according to Poulantzas, who is here following Gramsci explicitly, is to misprise the state, which has to it a *sui generis* reality in its own right. By extension, the state according to Poulantzas is not an outcome or resultant of class struggle but a cause of class struggle or, in Gramscian terms, an agency of struggle or a site where this can take place.

The weakness of Poulantzas's position is suggested by this very comparison with Gramsci. It is not, as Miliband charged at the time, that of a "structural superdeterminism" that fails to distinguish structure from agency, wearisome though Poulantzas's structuralist jargon may at one stage have been. It is Poulantzas's tendency, which is in no way restricted to this particular debate, to produce "class struggle" like a rabbit from a hat, as a way of clinching the argument. Class struggle to Poulantzas is quite simply the analytical bottom line, something that is always going on by definition, a kind of theoretical demiurge or *deus ex machina*. Gramsci, by contrast, made and could afford to make no such easy assumption. The absence of class struggle is precisely one of the things his concept of hegmony is designed to explain, and might still explain. Poulantzian class struggle, by contrast, is the kind of intellectual trump card that, by being played too often, may end up explaining exactly nothing. Even so, Poulantzas's point against Miliband, that he does not satisfactorily theorize the capitalist state as a structure in its own right with its own logic, effectively provides Poulantzas with his own agenda. The state, he was to insist, in *State, Power, Socialism*, "does not constitute a mere assembly of detachable parts; it exhibits an *apparatus unity* which is normally designated by the term centralization or *centralism*, and which is related to the fissiparous *unity of state power.*" This formulation is cryptic. Poulantzas often had to struggle in print to make his meaning clear. His overall intention is, however, unambiguous enough. It is to theorize what he called the "specific internal unity" of the state, a state that "obeys its own logic" and which, as Gramsci had recognized, is constitutive of class relations, not just an outcome of their play in civil society. The state is a site, a "strategic field" for the exercise of power. Political struggles are "inscribed in its framework."[3]

This means that the prerogatives of class domination as such are *absent* from the institutions of the capitalist state. Poulantzas's troublesome notion of "relative autonomy," one which, in fairness, he shares with Miliband, who simply defines it differently, entails that the theory of the state can in no way be reduced to an analysis of the economic or the social. The state is not the simple reflection or expression of anything outside its own purview. Poulantzas's thinking on "relative autonomy" has been ably paraphrased by Jeffrey Isaac:

> The economy and the state differ not only in their personnel, but in their principles of existence and constitutive rationalities. The economy is constituted by a multitude of private institutions (enterprises, corporations, banks) whose rationality is particularism and private profit. The

state is constituted by a set of public institutions (executive, parliaments, courts, police armies, administrative bureaucracies) whose rationality is the provision of internal and external order and "security" and the "general interest." The concept of relative autonomy denotes the structural relation between class relations and the state. Each is a condition of the other's existence, and each is in this sense implicated in the other, while at the same time maintaining its own respective autonomy. Because of this essential and necessary relation between state and class, because the state is what it is in virtue of its relationship to class relations, and vice versa, they are only *relatively* autonomous. The concept of relative autonomy thus designates the causal determinations between two social structures, state and relations of production, each of which is characterized by institutional specificity and causal effectivity.[4]

As in Hegel's original formulation, as interrogated but finally accepted by the younger Marx as well as by Gramsci, the two spheres, state and civil society, are not hermetically sealed, one from the other, but are conceptually distinct and, in practice, mutually determining and interpenetrating. The concept of relative autonomy, which has itself been interrogated and criticized, nevertheless helps bring our wheel of argument full circle, back to the kind of state/civil society relationship that had been, as Gramsci recognized, Marx's starting point and Hegel's political legacy. Relative autonomy in Poulantzas's formulation, accordingly, is not meant to suggest the liberal, noninterventionist state of competitive capitalism, even though this idea could serve and has served as an ideological justification for the relatively autonomous state. It is meant to denote the more general structural separation of economic from political concerns, and the specificity of the political realm. Interventions of welfare states or those of a Keynesian character can accordingly be seen as what Poulantzas calls "transformed forms" of the relative autonomy of the capitalist state. The state can thus be viewed as a causal determinant even when it does not intervene overtly within civil society. When it does intervene, it does not do so in a zero-sum way, at the cost, in other words, of its own specific autonomy.[5]

The striking thing about Poulantzas's formulation of the state's relative autonomy is that in significant respects it recalls Marx's foundational argument in "On 'The Jewish Question'." As early as *Political Power and Social Classes*, Poulantzas could say of the capitalist state:

> Its fundamental distinctive feature seems to be the fact that it contains no determination of subjects (fixed in the state as "individuals," "citizens," "political persons") as agents of production; and this was not the case in other types of state. At the same time this class state presents another specific feature: namely, that political class domination is constantly absent from its institutions. It presents itself as a popular class state. Its institutions are organized around the principles of the liberty and equality of "individuals" or "political persons." Its legitimacy is no longer founded on the divine will implied by the monarchical principle, but on the ensemble of formally free and equal citizens and on the popular sovereignty and secular responsibility of the state towards the people. . . . The modern state thus presents itself as embodying the general interest of the whole society, i.e., as substantiating the will of that "body politic" which is the nation.[6]

How close we are here to the language of "political emancipation" and "alien politics"! The political sphere in Poulantzas's view appears and presents itself as a realm of human equality and the common good. Discussing bourgeois law in *Political Power and Social Classes*, Poulantzas admits that "all trace of class domination is systematically absent from its language."[7] This is true in one sense of private law, where persons are classified as equal bearers of private rights, and in another sense of public law, where persons are classified as equal citizens subject to the state. Hence Poulantzas's original formulation of the "isolation effect"[8]: bourgeois law conceals from workers the class nature and class-boundedness of their placement by "interpellating" them in a new way, by officially constituting them as individual citizens making up the ensemble of a "national community." This interpellation need not in principle involve outright deception, for it is the measure of something that really exists, the separation of political, universal roles from particular economic functions, this very separation serving to enable the system to operate continuously. It is, after all, a matter of lived experience for workers and capitalists that they are bearers of legal property rights, even if all the workers have to sell is their labor power; that they engage in formally free contracts, however unsubstantiated this formal freedom necessarily is in specific cases; that they compete with each other on the basis of legal equality or "equality before the law," however formal such equality may be in its turn; that there are no traditional or familial bonds between them; and that they possess equal political rights. All these are the decisive achievements of the modern state, not just ideological smoke screens or devices to pull the wool over people's eyes. Marx's original distinction between "political" and "human" emancipation was not designed simply to disparage the former but to reveal its character as presentiment, or mockery-in-advance, of the promise of the latter. Poulantzas, altogether similarly, regards the achievements of the modern state, which are precisely those of "political emancipation" as Marx had outlined it so presciently in 1843, as the measure of something that, however incomplete or unsubstantiated it may be in specific cases, is nonetheless real and valuable in principle. Poulantzas's "isolation effect" cannot avoid leading us back into Marx's carefully calibrated notion of "political emancipation."

The directionality of Poulantzas's argument is, then, almost eerily reminiscent of that of Marx's "Jewish Question," which resurfaces, after its long immersion in "state monopoly capitalism" and its instrumentalist kin, rather like the return of the repressed. The "isolation effect" is not an outcome of some pre-given division of society into classes. It is constitutive of the reality of classes. "It is thus not legal equality in abstraction that is highlighted by the theory of the isolation effect, but the effects of this equality within the capitalist mode of production."[9] As Poulantzas elaborates the "isolation effect," he effectively reelaborates and even refines "alien politics" into the bargain. It involves, he says, three separate processes or moments. First, there is the isolation of individuals through private law, which "interpellates" people as the bearers of private rights and legal entitlements. Second, we have the isolation of individuals through public law, which interpellates them as formally and juridically free and equal citizens subject equally to the state. And third, we are presented with the need to reconstitute the unity of individuals who have been dispersed and isolated or, as Marx would have it, fragmented and "atomized." This reconstitution necessarily takes the form of *re*presentation, as for instance in "representative democracy." Even though the upshot of the isolation effect, in all three of its moments, is according to Poulantzas the demoralization and disorganization of the working class, and even though I have no quarrel with this insight, there is no reason to suppose that the social outcome of the isolation effect, fragmentation, begins or ends with the proletariat. As Marx was aware in 1843, fragmentation is likely to affect the consciousness of everyone who comes under the purview of the alien state. Poulantzas, indeed, makes much the same point. "This ideology of individualization not only serves to mask and obscure class relations (the capitalist state never presents itself as a class state) but also plays an active part in the divisions and isolation [individualization] of the popular masses."[10] Here, we cannot but recall "alien politics" and "political emancipation," whether or not it was Poulantzas's intention to rouse these concepts from their long slumber. Class, conspicuous by its absence from the official vocabulary of the state, becomes demoted to the realm of the private and particularistic, civil society, and workers at the same time assume the public identity of free, equal citizens confronting the state. There is no congruence between these separate but mutually sustaining roles. Each makes demands on the worker, or on the individual at large, that are in a real sense absolute as well as exclusive. The organization of a working-class "public sphere," as Habermas was calling it at much the same time that Poulantzas was writing *State, Power, Socialism*, is going to be acutely difficult under these circumstances, but much the same could be said about the organization of those "new social movements" selected by Chantal Mouffe and Ernesto Laclau[11] to displace or replace the proletariat as an agency of emancipation. Indeed, the fissiparous, jagged character of what is currently being called "postmodernity" can, in the view Poulantzas is outlining, though not on that of Mouffe and Laclau, only make matters worse, not better. As workers pursue their "corporate" interests, they cannot but reproduce the separation of private and public that shapes their very identity, thereby constantly weakening their capacity to constitute themselves as a "class-for-it-self," capable of emancipating itself and with itself society at large. These constraints are not to be understood as the result of physical repression or legal prohibition. They are inscribed within the logic, within the very definition of the modern state, which can, of course, supplement these constraints with physical coercion and legal prohibition. The really frightening thing, to take one's cue from Gramsci, may be precisely that physical coercion and legal prohibition are not normally necessary.

Poulantzas, at this point in his argument, appears to be dousing with cold water any prospect we may realistically expect these days for hegemonic struggle as Gramsci had understood the term. Even so, Poulantzas does regard the democratic state as the characteristic form of the capitalist epoch. His discussion calls to mind Marx's characterization of "the political republic" as "the most developed form of the abstract state" and as "the negation of this estrangement within its own sphere."[12] Poulantzas's linkage of capitalism and democracy at the level of the state has nothing of Engels or Lenin about it. Its register is, rather, that already staked out by the young Marx. The democratic state embodies, expresses and represents the most complete institutional separation of the economic from the political. All people under the purview of the modern, democratic state are considered doubly, both as the bearers of determinate private rights, and as citizens having public and publicly recognized rights, too. This double register is precisely what enables the capitalist state to pose as the embodiment or representative of the general interest of society. Its claim to be able to do this is by no means utterly fictitious or mendacious. But it is nevertheless bounded. Democracy as the characteristic form of the modern capitalist state dispenses to the working classes the right to vote, and opens up the possibility of socialist politics through its relatively open and peaceful institutionalization of conflict, much as its outright defenders assert. Once citizenship and vocation are no longer linked organically, and indeed are no longer linked at all, the state can manifest its universality only in contradistinction to the asymmetries of private life—just as Marx had pointed out in 1843. Poulantzas, for his part, concludes *State, Power, Socialism* with the motto: "One thing is certain; socialism will be democratic, or it will not be at all"; but by "democratic" he has in mind not just the formal, attenuated notion that applies today, but also a more substantiated, more expansive concept: "human" as opposed to "political" emancipation.

How then are we to understand the credentials Poulantzas awarded the capitalist state as it then existed? It is to be understood as a relatively autonomous structure, in the sense already outlined, of centralized political power, which, far from standing in a mechanical relation of exteriority to its civil society, "has always, in different forms, been present in the constitution and reproduction of the relations of production."[13] It is a political structure concerned with territorial rule and with the maintenance of law and order, but unlike earlier states, which were also concerned with these, the modern state is not at the same time an economic structure in its own right. The state, that is to say, may secure the conditions of existence of economic practices, and it may even indulge in activities having economic effects, in its own right. Such practices are nonetheless conceptually and institutionally distinct from the province of state action, properly so-called. The relations of production in society and the domination of capital impose crucial limitations on the state, limitations that are acutely experienced by social democratic or socialist state forms that attempt to reform or challenge the prerogatives of capital. "Capital flight" is much more than a distant theoretical prospect. But short of so drastic and dramatic a threat, capitalism normally limits the province of state action in fairly obvious ways. To begin with, to the extent that the state does not indulge in economically productive actions in its own right, and this extent, I take it, is normally considerable, the state, like the Crown in King Charles I's England, cannot be expected to "live off its own." Its purse strings will be tightened and slackened from without. Since it does not directly produce its own sources of revenue, it is limited by the private accumulation process, and depends for its tax revenues on the circulation of commodities and the accumulation and reinvestment of capital. In Claus Offe and Volker Ronge's words, ". . . the state depends on a process of accumulation which is beyond its power to organize . . . the state is denied the power to control the flow of those resources which are indispensible for the use of state power"; this is the case regardless of the state's additional affinities and alliances with classes or class fractions in societies whose own interest in accumulation of capital is direct.[14] What follows is what Charles Lindblom has termed the "privileged position of business,"[15] a special relation between business and the state, which is a structural constraint upon the latter. Successful capital accumulation is bound to be an essential policy consideration, thanks to the state's dependence on capital for revenue and stability alike. What is of particular interest here is the state's ability, under these circumstances, to present itself as the guardian of society's general interest, the interest of all classes.[16] Adam Przeworski has put the point well:

> Since profit is the necessary condition of universal expansion, capitalists appear within capitalist societies as bearers of [a] universal interest. Their present interest happens to coincide with the future interests of anyone in the society; the larger the profits they appropriate, the greater the capacity of the entire society to improve the future conditions of material life. Demands on the part of any other group to improve their current conditions of life appear as inimical to the interests of the entire society in the future. Under capitalism disputes over wages and profits appear as a tradeoff between the present and the future. Capitalists are in a unique position by virtue of the organization of the capitalist system of production; their interests appear as universal, while the interests of all other groups appear as parasitic.[17]

Elsewhere:

> The emphasis on the distinct interests of the working class was necessary to prevent the integration of workers as individuals into bourgeois society. Under capitalism, capitalists naturally appear to be the bearers of future universal interests, while the interests of other groups seem inimical to future development and hence particularistic. Capitalists are the investors, the employers, and the innovators. The part of societal product they appropriate is necessary for investment and that means necessary for continued production, employment and consumption by anyone. Their particularistic interest in profit is a necessary condition for future improvement in the material condition of anyone else. Universalism becomes the natural ideology of the bourgeoisie, since as long as people are thought to have some general common or public interest, capitalists as a class are the embodiment of this interest. Hence it is in the interests of capitalists as a class—although obviously not in the interests of each individual capitalist or firm—that society be pervaded by an ideology that portrays it as composed of individuals endowed with common economic interests. A classless vision of society is in the class interest of capitalists.[18]

One is tempted to observe that the Gramscian formulation of "hegemony" could scarcely be better put, particularly if we consider the "basic structural asymmetry" Przeworski and Sprague's formulation in short order entails.

> The organization of politics in terms of class can be attempted at most by one specific class, workers. . . . The claims of workers are particularistic, and when workers organize as a class they seek to impose upon the entire society the image of classes, each endowed with particular interests. Capitalists, in turn, only in moments of folly represent themselves as a class under democratic conditions. The response to the particularistic claims of the working class is not a particularization of the bourgeoisie but [the elaboration of] ideologies that deny altogether the salience of class interests, either by posing a universalistic model of society composed of individuals—citizens whose interests are in harmony—or by evoking alternative particularisms of religion, language, ethnicity, etc. Hence, ideological conflicts rarely, if ever, concern the legitimacy or justice of the claims made by various classes. Instead, they juxtapose the class ideology put forth by the spokesmen for workers to nonclass alternatives.[19]

Marx's words, written as long ago as 1843, can still serve to supplement what is ominous about Przeworski and Sprague's observation:

> Civil society and state are separated. Hence the citizen of the state is also separated from the citizen as the member of civil society. He must therefore effect a fundamental division within himself . . . in order to behave as an actual citizen of the state and to attain political significance and effectiveness, he must step out of his civil reality, disregard it and withdraw from this whole organization [of civil society] into his individuality; for the sole existence which he finds for his citizenship of the state is his sheer, blank individuality, since the existence of the state . . . is complete without him and his existence in civil society is complete without the state. . . . The separation of civil society and political state necessarily appears as the separation of the political citizen, the life of the state, from civil society, from his own, actual empirical reality.[20]

Marx proceeded to argue, in *Capital*, that the sphere of exchange, modern civil society, has created the possibility of the liberal garden of "Eden for the innate Rights of Man," the "exclusive realm of Freedom, Equality, Property and Bentham." This is "the realm of free wills, free persons, equality before the law, equality in the exchange of equivalent values, and calculation of advantage; the selfishness, the gain, and the private interest of each."[21] All these, it goes without saying, are the presumptions of liberal individualism, particularly in its economic mode.

"Sheer, blank individuality" finds its political counterpart in the modern state. Individualism, to which individuality of any stripe is irreducible, as Hegel had recognized, is by contrast that principle that animates civil society. Its counterpart is the mock-"universality" involved in the state's pretensions about its own character, fortified by the very mock-"universality" the capitalist class, in Przeworski and Sprague's formulation, claims. The conceptual congruence between these mutually supportive claims was clear to Marx in his early writings, and had arguably been clear enough to Hegel too. It renders reductionist and crudely instrumentalist theories redundant and beside the point.

We should at this point recall Marx's words in "On 'The Jewish Question' ": "In moments of special concern for itself political life seeks to constitute itself as the actual, harmonious life of man. But it can do this only in violent contradiction with its own conditions of existence. . . ." Any attempt, be it Jacobin or Leninist, to use the state against the principle of private interest which, as the basis of social life, called forth the need for an autonomous, "universal" political realm in the first place, is bound to end badly because it is incoherent in principle. The state, because of its character as counterpart to the fragmentation rending civil society, is not about to provide a site of reconciliation, because it is itself an agency of this same fragmentation. It is the state, after all, that articulates the labor market and other forms of exchange, and defines them as "private." And it was the state, as Marx first pointed out in *The German Ideology*, that played a crucial part in the creation of a class of people who had nothing but their labor to sell on this market. Both what the state *does*, when it issues uniform paper currency, when it taxes us, and so forth, and what the state *is*, a monopolizer of the legitimate means of violence, guarantee the sanctity of the private. If we look at the modern state at the time of its emergence, we can see that it was delineating the boundaries of the private realm just as this very realm was arraying itself against the grain of traditional, premodern, property relations. And today we can see that, in significant senses, both the nation and the individuals that comprise it are products of the modern state. As Poulantzas so ably points out, the state constitutes the individual in his or her modern form, and attempts to homogenize this individual as part and parcel of this same individualization, both through disciplinary apparatuses like the military and the prison, and through the very articulation of "private" versus "public" that provides the modern state with its medium of existence. Secular legitimacy involves a:

> dual movement whereby the modern state creates individualizations and privatizations by consituting itself as their unity and homogenization— a movement . . . both of creating modes of isolation (of which the people-nation is composed) and of representing their unity (in the modern national-popular state). . . . In this dual movement, for the first time in history, there can be no limit *de jure* or in principle to the state's activity and encroachment in the realm of the individual-private. [This latter] is created by the state concomitantly with its relative separation from the public space of society, Therefore, not only is the separation but one specific form of the state's presence in socio-economic relations, it also involves an unprecedented presence in those relations.[22]

"Privatization" may appear to have to it a "ring" or meaning that is different these days from what Poulantzas had in mind in the 1970s. But even this change in the specificity of the term does not invalidate Poulantzas's point. If the Reagan and Thatcher years taught us anything, they taught us that state-forms can be very *dirigiste* indeed in their attempts to reprivatize civil society. It is no accident that one of the most thorough and successful examples of such "privatization" of an economy was carried through under the explicitly authoritarian auspices of Pinochet's Chile. Even elsewhere, the paradox of intervening for the sake of not intervening in the economy is by no means uncommon. What the state grants, the state can also take away.

The subject of representative democracy and individual rights is the citizen, whose perquisites Marx had outlined in 1843. But the citizen is shaped and determined by the state, which possesses and wields the power to determine who is, and who is not, a citizen capable of exercising the rights in question. Those who straightforwardly promote representative democracy as the "rule of law, not of men" fail as a rule to grasp the Weberian point that law and violence are intrinsically connected in the modern state. Poulantzas, for his part, never loses sight of it. Law, in his words,

> is an integral part of the repressive order and violence [monopolized by the state]. By issuing rules and passing laws the state establishes an initial field of injunctions, prohibitions, and censorship, and thus institutes the practical terrain and object of violence. Furthermore, law organizes the conditions for physical repression, designating its physical modalities and structuring the devices by which it is exercised. In this sense law is the code of organized public violence.[23]

Codified systems of law are intelligible in the main only to agents of the state and its disciplinary apparatuses. Knowledge of the law is taught to no one except professionals. Law becomes a "state secret." Poulantzas, who was trained as a lawyer, here as elsewhere calls to mind Gramsci, who had similarly observed that the state:

> seeks to create and maintain a certain type of civilization and of citizen (and hence of collective life and of individual relations) and to eliminate certain customs and attitudes and to disseminate others . . . the law will be its instrument for this purpose (together with the school system and other institutions and activities).[24]

But in general coercion plays a much more prominent role in Poulantzas's thought than in Gramsci's—surprisingly, perhaps, in that these are two of the few twentieth-century Marxist state theorists to have thoroughly analysed not just capitalist democracy but also fascism and authoritarianism, thereby serving to remind us of something that is often overlooked, that even Marx was much more likely to encounter at first hand authoritarian than democratic forms of the state.

Overall, Poulantzas's debt to Gramsci was considerable, and it emerges more clearly if we take into consideration the biographical fact that Poulantzas's theories developed in such a way that we can almost read in his successive writings the history of Marxist state theory in miniature. Poulantzas, that is to say, provides us with an inescapable opportunity to recapitulate much of my own argument. Poulantzas initially advocated a Leninist strategy in which the working-class movement was to be be mobilized in a counterstate organization external to the capitalist state, and subject to the leadership of a revolutionary, vanguard, political party. The capitalist state itself was viewed as what I am terming the "object-state," as the unambiguous and unequivocal institutional expression of bourgeois political domination. As such, it would be impossible for the working class to utilize the capitalist state, even in its liberal parliamentary-representative form. The state must rather be "smashed" as a precondition of the exercise of proletarian power. Poulantzas's thinking at the stage of development represented by *Political Power and Social Classes* was explicitly hostile to Gramsci. He believed that the working class cannot attain hegmony before it has seized power and transformed the structure of the state, which had been the official party line against Gramsci all along.[25] Then Poulantzas experienced his own Brumaire, the Greek *coup d'état* of 1967, and his own epiphany, *la jolie fête de mai* of 1968. In a theoretically interesting, and long overdue move, Poulantzas began to consider not so much states as *régimes*, which Marxism, with its obsessions about "the" state, had long overlooked, and as a matter of fact still does. The Greek dictatorship was misidentified by others as fascist, whereas to Poulantzas the point was to prevent the coup from consolidating its mass base in the manner of (real) fascist regimes. In this way the study of Greece and Portugal led Poulantzas back to the study of Italy, Germany and Spain in the 1930s, along with the strategy of the Comintern toward them. Throughout even this latter, sorry and distasteful task Poulantzas was concerned less to describe "the" state than to clarify the nature and character of exceptional regimes, and how best to combat these before and after the seizure of power by the far right, which is something the Comintern had never succeeded in explaining. In criticizing the tragic errors of the Comintern, Poulantzas concluded that a successful revolution, or even the successful defense of working-class gains within capitalist society as presently constituted, required the primacy of political class struggle over economic class struggle, as in Lenin; the consistent pursuit of a mass line; and a commitment to proletarian internationalism. At first glance this does not seem so very different from the official theories of a French Communist Party that was to prove the slowest in the West to adopt Eurocommunist initiatives. Even the other elements in Poulantzas's agenda (development of workers' councils as the site of mass struggle, development of a united front of the working class at the rank-and-file level, the development of a popular front with the poor peasantry and the petty bourgeoisie) seem to have a shopworn air about them. But Poulantzas weighted these elements in a way very different from party orthodoxy, and concluded that the errors of the Comintern were still in evidence in contemporary communist theories of state monopoly capitalism and the antimonopoly alliance. What further reinforced Poulantzas's status as a maverick was his denial of the continuing validity of the Leninist "dual power" strategy of building up a counterstate outside the capitalist state, on the grounds that the dual power strategy had done no one any good in Greece or Portugal and that, in any case, the capitalist state had undergone significant shifts since Lenin.

This, in a sense, is where we came in. The modern state according to Poulantzas is no longer a mere night watchman state; nor can it be considered a mere organ of open political repression. It has expanded in scope and scale in such a way that the state now penetrates every crevice of social life.[26] Poulantzas is more original if no less forceful in making his next claim, which is that there is a condensation of class contradictions inside the state of the kind that makes possible class struggle within the official state apparatus as well as class struggle at a distance from this apparatus. This insight has to do with Poulantzas's perception that the military dictatorships he had examined had collapsed because of internal contradictions within their power blocs, contradictions that were intensified through popular struggles at a distance from the core of the state; and that the failure of a revolutionary mass party to coordinate and centralize such popular struggles under working-class hegemony was the main reason why the dictatorships in question were replaced not by democratic socialist régimes but by bourgeois democratic ones.[27] This is not the place to enter into the niceties of what Poulantzas meant by his original notion of the "power bloc," for these would take us too far afield. For purposes of the present discussion, "power bloc" admits of the following characterization: the dominant classes or dominant fractions of classes of a given "social formation." Since a "social formation" is in turn irreducible to the more traditional notion of "mode of production" and is intended to explain the coexistence of elements of different modes of production, feudal, capitalist or what have you, within a given social formation, it follows that a "power bloc" is not going to be unitary or monolithic, or univocal. It is rather going to be contradictory, or what Poulantzas terms a "contradictory unity."

The state is not a mere instrument to be captured by the working class in a frontal assault, or through the tactics of infiltration or encirclement. Different states have different institutional forms that circumscribe changes in the balance of forces and enable the bourgeoisie to recuperate state power if the working class does not establish the institutional preconditions for the exercise of its own class power. Class struggle should consequently aim not at capturing but at *transforming* the official state apparatus. Poulantzas is most uncommon among Marxist theoreticians in that he pays due heed to Marx's warning that "the working class cannot simply take hold of the existing [capitalist] state machinery and wield it for its own purposes." A successful democratic transition to socialism would have to be more flexible than a straightforwardly Leninist coup would have been. More particularly, it would have to be three-pronged, and involve coordination of action within the state, action to transform the state, and action at a distance from the state.[28]

State, Power, Socialism is no less welcome for introducing other elements of flexibility into what was to emerge as a classic formulation of what was termed the "left-Eurocommunist" position on the state. Poulantzas indicates his concern with the problems of what was called "actually existing socialism" in the Eastern Bloc, problems which he thought a left-Eurocommunist standpoint in the West might be able to alleviate. At the same time Poulantzas indicates his no less heartfelt concern about the erosion of democratic sentiment and spirit within the emergent "authoritarian statist" system of bourgeois political domination, wherever there was such a system. In assessing this, we should recall that *State, Power, Socialism* was completed before the years of Reagan and Thatcher, who between them intensified the authoritarian tendencies in question. And Poulantzas was no less prescient in pinpointing the problems posed by the troubled relationship between class struggle and nonclass movements on the left, these problems being posed by the question of left unity in France and elsewhere. For all these reasons, Poulantzas, in his final book, which is in effect his testament, came to privilege the need to preserve and extend the institutions and values of representative democracy alongside, though not at the expense of, the development of direct rank-and-file democracy in the transition to socialism. To abolish parliamentary democracy on the grounds that its institutions and values were, at the end of the day, "bourgeois" ones would be to throw out the baby with the bath water. Without a parliamentary, representative forum within which issues could be raised, discussed and decided upon, there would and could be no guarantee that the emergent organs of direct, rank-and-file democracy would not be crushed by a self-appointed vanguard party. The liberties of a plural party system are, then, not a smoke screen for the maneuverings of a predatory bourgeoisie seen as the personification of capital, but are in principle the measure of something that is real and valuable. To take them as ends in themselves, or as forces capable of developing their own momentum, would be a first-order mistake. But to dismiss them out of hand, on the grounds that they are purely "formal," thus meaningless, valueless and a distraction, would be no less mistaken and myopic. Very much in the spirit of Marx's original formulation of "political emancipation," Poulantzas is concerned not to excoriate or to dismiss parliamentariansm, nor to take the claims it advances on its own behalf at face value, but to treat them as the mark or hint of an unsubstantiated liberty, as a part mistaking itself for the whole by virtue of the "purely political" perspective these claims would induce, unless, of course, their operation were supplemented by other perspectives. These alternatives by no means necessarily contradict or preclude parliamentariansm, but might well supplement it. Without such a parliamentary supplement, more-over, there is a specific danger that direct democracy might degenerate into a disunified, economic-corporative structure that could only be made systematic from outside and from above, by the conjuring up, that is to say, of the very authoritarian-statist forces the revolutionary struggle was designed to uproot and extirpate in the first place.

Poulantzas, who was an active member of the Greek Communist Party of the Interior, and not a party member in France, nevertheless at this point clearly risked marginalization, if not outright exclusion, for entering the lists against a Leninism that was far from dormant among the upper echelons of the French Communist Party at the time. Yet he entered these lists in almost every respect. He denied the need for a single, mass revolutionary party that would act as *the* vanguard in the transition to socialism. He argued that communist parties in the West were, and had long been, in crisis because of their principled and unquestioned commitments to the primacy of the working class as vanguard, and to the *a priori* primacy of working-class struggles even at a local, shop-floor level. These largely unquestioned priorities underestimated the importance of "new social movements"—femi-nism, nationalism, movements for greater regional or ethnic auton-omy, the Greens and other ecologically defined movements, student movements, consumer movements, squatters' movements, and the like. These movements are by their very nature *pluriclassiste*, located, that is, outside the site of production. But they are not to be dismissed out of hand for this or any other reason. They had not arisen and flourished for no reason at all. They were, and for that matter still are today, the register of social shifts taking place within and as part of advanced capitalist society. The workers' movement accordingly should build bridges to these movements, not dismiss them out of hand or in principle. Workers' parties worthy of the name should make themselves actively present within these new social movements, though they should do this in such a way that they do not stoop to mere populism. Conversely, these movements themselves should find a home within the party, but not the kind of home that would sop them up like a sponge and deny them their own, *pluriclassiste* specificity.[29] If there is to be tension between working class parties and social movements, so be it; this may be a healthy precondition for democratic socialism. And at the same time, if these tensions, like the movements that produce and profit from them, differ from country to country, this too is only to be expected. There is no point in denying the reality of different national roads to socialism, in the name of a Leninist organizational straitjacket or of anything else.[30]

The observation is prompted at this point in our elaboration of Poulantzas's contribution to Marxist state theory, a contribution which, I take it, is considerable, that, just as Marx had needed the experience of Bonapartism and its antithesis, the Paris Commune, to sharpen his understanding of the nature of "the political form, at last discovered, beneath which to work out the economic emancipation of labor," and just as Gramsci, in his turn, had had to undergo the rigors of theoretical work in a fascist jail, so Poulantzas too was stimulated in his turn to complete his trajectory from Leninist vanguardism to a distinctively "left-Eurocommunist" position under the impulse and impetus provided by his analysis of authoritarian regimes. These, Poulantzas came to believe, demonstrate the brittleness, fragility and frailty of what are to all appearances "strong" states; they also led him to understand that state power is best understood not as a derivative epiphenomenon of something categorically different and more fundamental, existing in civil society, but as a specific condensation of, or form taken by, class struggles, which are themselves going to vary from time to time and from place to place. This means that the state, in principle, can be either the factor of cohesion and equilibrium, or the nodal point of the contradictions, of a social formation. It all depends on what kind of social formation we are talking about. The left's failure adequately to oppose authoritarianism goes along with its failure to understand what a democratic alternative to authoritarianism might comport. It is too often overlooked that in the instances of Marx, Gramsci and Poulantzas, authoritarian forms of government were often more present and immediate than nonauthoritarian ones, although it is but rarely overlooked that Lenin too was faced with a particular, virulent form of Tsarist authoritarianism. The difference is that authoritarianism as lived experience warped Lenin's judgment, together with that of all too many of his later followers. It is no accident, either, that Marx, Gramsci and Poulantzas all, in their different ways, took a rather more balanced view, or that Gramsci and Poulantzas, for their part, developed in a resolutely non-Leninist as well as post-Leninist direction.

6

THE STATE OF THE STATE: KAUTSKY, EUROCOMMUNISM AND BEYOND

My argument thus far has proceeded on the assumption that the most significant twentieth-century Marxist state theorists were Gramsci and Poulantzas. The latter, under the increasing influence of the former, effected a shift away from the Leninism that has bedevilled Marxist state theory from Lenin's day down to our own. This shift can, as we saw, even be characterized as the rerunning of the history of Marxist state theory in microcosm. Its register, that is to say, is theoretical in the first instance. Historically, it remained subdominant and highly "unofficial," unsanctioned, that is, by any major Communist Party orthodoxy. Other, more obvious shifts away from Leninism were however so sanctioned, though not without difficulty. The most obvious among these was the brief fluorescence of Eurocommunism during the 1970s. But to acknowledge this is to encounter a paradox. My assignment of "left-Eurocommunist" credentials to Poulantzas was predicated on the character of Eurocommunism, which was a spectrum or constellation of beliefs, and not a univocal rejection of Leninism. At one extreme the spectrum of Eurocommunism was hospitable, for a while, to Poulantzas and other left-Eurocommunists (Ingrao, Claudin, Buci-Glucksmannn). But at another extreme, Eurocommunism was no less hospitable to others of a very different stripe. In assessing these modes of hospitality, what needs to be borne in mind is that Leninism, which almost all Eurocommunist theoreticians regarded as dispensable, remained as fundamentally narrow as it had always been. That its dispensability could in principle be advocated on any number of grounds gives us a vital clue to the character of Eurocommunism.

Now that the dust has settled we can see that Eurocommunism was an attempted amalgam of two distinct theoretical strands in the history of Marxism in general, and of Marxist state theory in particular. In a real sense, these two strands could not be more distinct, and their juxtaposition could not be more ironical. For if we ask ourselves whose agenda Eurocommunism at large was bent upon implementing, it is the figure of Karl Kautsky that most immediately snaps into focus. That the other strand appears to stretch from Gramsci through Poulantzas, and that in reality it was deliberately stretched backwards to incorporate Gramsci, is if anything more surprising than my invocation of Kautsky, an "official" figure if ever there was one. While the Gramsci-Poulantzas strand testifies to the theoretical strength of "unofficial" or "Western" Marxism, it does not at the same time testify to the theoretical coherence of Eurocommunist discourse, which can be seen in hindsight as a vain, doomed attempt to make extremes meet.

Few today would argue that Kautsky's theoretical weight, as opposed to his historical importance as a Marxist dignitary, measures up to that of Poulantzas and Gramsci. Kautsky's theory of the state is in a significant sense the *reductio ad absurdum* of Marxist state theory.

Even so, it was the other, the Gramsci-Poulantzas tendency that labored under a distinct disadvantage during the Eurocommunist decade. Gramsci, for one thing, far from being immediately available for Eurocommunist consumption, had to be retrieved, if not from oblivion, then certainly from the comparative obscurity in which Togliatti and others had lodged him as a way of preserving his iconic status. Gramsci's writings finally appeared in a more or less comprehensive edition only under the influence exerted on the Italian Communist Party by Eurocommunism. It could be argued, if we were concerned with causation, not that Gramsci's theoretical acumen "caused" the fluorescence of Eurocommunism, but that the fluorescence of Eurocommunism invoked Gramsci by creating an atmosphere where his views, or, more accurately, a particular version of them, could find acceptance.

Gramsci was dredged up and laid alongside a Kautsky who was anything but a kindred spirit, and who is hardly mentioned by name in any of Gramsci's writings. The two extremes signally failed to meet. Philosophically, Kautsky was the most illustrious representative of the kind of "mechanical determinism" against which Gramsci formulated his own, countervailing conception of Marxism as the "philosophy of praxis." Politically, Kautsky stands out as the most coherent and consistent proponent of the "parliamentary road" to socialism, which is at root why Eurcommunist theoreticians could not have ignored him even if they had wished to do so. On the other hand, Gramsci's most original formulations of the problem of the transition to socialism from advanced capitalism, structured as these are around his conception of the struggle for hegemony or the "war of position," are ambiguous, and do not have to be bent out of shape to lend themselves to interpretation of the kind that is consistent with a Kautskian strategy of gradual, peaceful and parliamentary transition to socialism. And this was how the join was effected, however clearly the seams showed. Kautsky and Gramsci were both conscious of the importance of democracy for socialism. Even so, they arrived at conclusions which had "exemplary" significance within the spectrum of Eurocommunism precisely because they were "political opposites."[1]

This is not to argue that Kautsky figured by name as a doctrinal reference point in Eurocommunist discourse. That he did not have to is one of many ironies that must at this point be savored. Kautsky's presence in Eurocommunist discourse was concealed, yet utterly obvious and much more straightforward than that of Gramsci, which was both latent and flaunted. Some of the reasons for this paradox have little enough to do with Gramsci, and much to do with Lenin. Kautsky, right up to his death in 1938, had to endure the Leninist sobriquet "renegade." This sobriquet, which became Kautsky's shroud, was at the time of its utterance anything but an innocent characterization on Lenin's part, being all too patent an attempt on Lenin's part to deflect attention away from the question of why he never broke with Kautsky before 1914. Kautsky's designation as "renegade," in any event, did much to make him the quintessential "loser," the King John of Marxism. And then, posthumously, in the 1970s, "the final snub." Just as Kautsky's ideas resurfaced after their long immersion, the Eurocommunists who dredged them up looked for "legitimation and inspiration . . . not in his abundant texts, but to Gramsci, who rejected everything for which Kautsky stood."[2] The point remains that:

> after the parenthesis of the cold war, and especially after the twentieth Party Congress of the CPSU, Kautskyism—the parliamentary-democratic and peaceful road to socialism—became *de facto* (without being recognized openly) the general line of the communist movement in the developed capitalist countries.[3]

Under these circumstances, there was no need to cite the renegade directly.[4]

Briefly put, Kautsky's pre-1914 political writings attempted to develop a strategic conception of socialist transition on the basis of themes outlined by Engels, not Marx, in his 1895 Preface to Marx's *The Class Struggles in France.* We have already noted the fact that this is the text that fatefully misidentified Marx's memorial to the martyred *fédérés* as an articulation of the idea of the "dictatorship of the proletariat"; Engels, and following Engels, Kautsky, specifically identified this "dictatorship" with a parliamentary majority in the hands of a workers' political party like the German SPD. The reason this amounts to confusion worse confounded is that it flies in the face of Marx's insistence that the working class "cannot lay hold of the ready-made state machinery and wield it for its own purposes," not, that is, if it wishes to avoid contamination by parliamentarism.[5] This is an admonition Kautsky signally failed to heed, and Eurocommunist theoreticians, once their turn rolled around, were largely deaf to Marx's warning for much the same reason. They, too, were concerned with the problem of socialist transition in the conditions of advanced capitalism, and they, too, defined this problem in terms of what is, conceptually speaking, *another* problem: that of the relationship between democracy and socialism. What is distinctive about Eurocommunism is not its reaffirmation of a linkage between socialism and democracy, a linkage which has deep roots in the Marxist tradition, but rather its identification of "democracy" with the institutional framework of Western parliamentary democracy, which necessarily made of Eurocommunism a variant of reformism.[6]

Democracy and socialism, so conceptualized, do not relate as ends to means. Democracy is not the path to socialism and socialism is not the path to democracy. Each is simply unthinkable without the other.[7] Moreover, both Kautsky and Eurocommunist theoreticians take their cue, once again, from Engels in categorically rejecting any distinction between "bourgeois" and "proletarian" democracy. Democracy, that is to say, has nothing of class about it; it is neither class-defined nor even necessarily class-influenced, but it *is* fatefully identified with the parliamentary institutional framework that was developing in Kautsky's day and had developed much more fully by the Eurocommunist decade.[8] Kautsky believed that the rights of citizenship and suffrage *sans phrase* are essential if the working class is to be transformed from what Marx, in *The Poverty of Philosophy*, had termed a "class in itself" into a self-conscious "class for itself." While under certain circumstances this may be true, it does not follow, except to Kautsky, that it is true unconditionally. Nor does it follow, except to Kautsky, that citizenship is the *only* significant way of effecting the transformation in question. Kautsky derives from this proposition the further proposition that the struggle to increase the power of parliament, and the struggle to increase the influence or representation of the working class within parliament, are the same struggle. The conquest of a parliamentary majority for Social Democracy, and the use of parliamentary legislation for socialist purposes, together constitute the "dictatorship of the proletariat" for Kautsky as early as the 1890s.[9] Parliament all along had provided not only an accurate reflection of the balance of class forces in society, but also an arena perfectly suitable for the mobilization of the working class. It is noteworthy that even when, under the influence of the Russian Revolution of 1905, Kautsky, apparently remembering that Marx had written *The Civil War in France*, argued that "the conquest of state power by the proletariat" could not occur without the "dissolution" of the "instruments of power" of the old state, he specifically does not include parliament with "the state church, the bureaucracy, the corps of officials" and the rest as an "instrument of power" of the old state.[10]

The possibility that working-class politicians or parties could be "co-opted" into the system of bourgeois class rule by parliamentarism seems never to have crossed Kautsky's mind. To Kautsky democracy meant "the rule of the majority," and parliament is a mirror that perfectly reflects the balance of class forces in society. "A genuine parliamentary regime can be *as much* an instrument of the dictatorship of the proletariat as an instrument of the dictatorship of the bourgeoisie."[11] The problem with Kautsky's view of parliamentary democracy as the more or less perfect reflection of the state of the class struggle, or of the balance of class forces, outside the parliamentary arena becomes obvious in the light of more recent Marxist theories of the state, which tend to see the state not as an epiphenomenon or as a mirroring device, but as an integral part of the system of class domination in its own right. It is to Gramsci that we owe the insights, which were adopted by Poulantzas and the left-Eurocommunists, that capitalism in its twentieth-century forms generates an enlargement of the state and a gradual displacement of civil society as a separate realm, and that the state is at once a mechanism of ideological-cultural hegemony and of physical repression. This effects in its own right a decisive break with instrumentalist views of the state. The state is now seen as a complex of structures through which subordinate groups are organically tied to the structure of power.[12] References in Kautsky's voluminous writings to the administrative, repressive and ideological apparatuses of the state are by contrast few and far between. Just *how* class rule is perpetuated through political mechanisms is a problem that eluded Kautsky, as Lenin quite fairly pointed out in *State and Revolution*.[13]

Kautsky's argument is as bald as they come. To understand the state, and what the state or anybody in the state can do, all you have to know is the condition of the balance of class forces in civil society. Such knowledge will then dictate strategy. On the assumption of increasing proletarianization and immiseration, an assumption cast into an artificial prominence in the course of Kautsky's anti-"revisionist" debates with Bernstein, there comes to be no need for any kind of confrontation with the state. Parliamentary gains are, after all, assured. The transition to socialism had, in his view, to be as smooth and free from rupture as possible, so that the working class would act cohesively and constructively once it had become the ruling class. The working class is to inherit, and to inherit legally, a highly productive apparatus that can be used directly, and no less legally, for the sake of eliminating the realm of necessity once and for all.

Not all of Kautsky's Eurocommunist heirs were party to anything like the same degree of fatal simplicity. But they too identified the "seizure of power" by the working class with the attainment of a parliamentary majority, and they too regarded the parliamentary road as implying and involving respect for preexisting legality. At this point "the bourgeois horizon of right" that must, according to the *Critique of the Gotha Program*, "be crossed in its entirety" recedes into the status quo and fades to black. Kautsky and his Eurocommunist legatees settled for "political emancipation" in an apparent belief that "political" and "human" emancipation now collapse into one, singular entity.

Kautsky insisted that modern society needs democracy because it depends upon an accurate representation of social forces, which alone could ensure the maximum development of productive forces. This determinist view led Kautsky to regard fascism as but a temporary aberration. He regarded gradual transformation of the economy and socialization of the means of production to consist of the ability of the working class to do what Marx had insisted it *cannot* do; that is, to use and wield the *existing* machinery of the state for its own purposes.

Prior to this shift, the gradual buildup of the strength of the working class within the framework of parliamentary democracy results in a final "showdown," which takes the form of a straightforward confrontation of government and opposition. The indivisibility of state power in this schema is not a result of the character of the state. Kautsky seems determined never to award the state any specificity at all. Indivisibility is a result of the character of the class forces represented as in a mirror in and by the state. The rupture involved in the transition to socialism does not take the form of an institutional transformation, but simply that of a reallocation of power within the existing institutional framework.

Even so, Lenin's well-known criticism, that Kautsky ignored the repressive side of "bourgeois democracy," or, in other words, that he underestimated the role of organized violence in perpetuating bourgeois class rule, is only partially correct.[14] Kautsky certainly thought the working class must avoid provoking a repressive response by needlessly resorting to violence and entering the favored terrain of the enemy. The trouble here is not what Lenin thought it was. It is that Kautsky never extended this notion of the favored terrain occupied by the class enemy to incorporate the political and ideological as well as the repressive aspects of state power.

Kautsky lacked a recognizable theory of the state. He repeatedly asserts both the class character of the state, and the neutrality of the state apparatus, without ever seeming to notice that these could in principle run up against each other. He leaves us with the absurd and dangerously complacent notion, which Enrico Berlinguer took care to deny, that if 51 percent of the votes cast in an election were working-class votes, the seizure of power would *ipso facto* have been effected, even if private property and the capitalist state still persisted.[15] Kautsky paints himself into a corner, but unwittingly provides a picture of how thin and attenuated Marxism would be without an adequate theory of the state.

Much Eurocommunist theory enjoined a specifically instrumentalist theory of the state, according to which the state can be more or less unproblematically placed in the service of the working class. This position is of distinctly Kautskian provenance. Any tension between a view of the state as becoming increasingly undemocratic, on the one hand, and the affirmation of a democratic road to socialism, on the other, could be relieved by regarding the machinery of the state as essentially neutral. Gradual transformation of society without any real institutional rupture, a specifically reformist outlook, was thus enjoined.

But where does this leave Gramsci's and Poulantzas's notion of class struggle within the state? Santiago Carillo's once-celebrated *Eurocommunism and the State* appears to subscribe to this notion, but interprets it as meaning the winning over of those who man the existing state apparatus, not changing what this machinery does.[16] Since this view entails that there is no class or social bias inherent in the structure of the state and within the unity of state power, we must observe at this point that the use made by orthodox Eurocommunism of Gramsci was highly selective. Gramsci, after all, had followed Marx's belief that the working class "cannot simply lay hold of the ready-made state machinery and wield it for its own purposes,"[17] this being precisely the danger represented in Gramsci's lexicon by "passive revolution" and "statolatry."[18] "The socialist state cannot be embodied in the institution of the capitalist state," Gramsci insisted,

> (but) must be a fundamentally new creation. The institutions of the capitalist state are organized in such a way as to facilitate free competition; merely to to change the personnel in these institutions is hardly going to change the direction of their activity. . . . So the formula "conquest of the state" should be understood in the following sense: replacement of the democratic-parliamentary state by a new type of state, one that is generated by the associative experiences of the proletarian class.[19]

The Marxian echoes here are unmistakable. But this critique-in-advance of Carillo's position carries other resonances too. Gramsci agreed with Lenin rather than Marx in maintaining that parliamentary democracy is by its very nature institutionally biased in favor of bourgeois rule. This point, which overreaches Eurocommunist debates, needs to be adjudicated with some care. Lenin and Gramsci would have agreed that elections are easily manipulated, thanks to the material and ideological resources of the ruling class, and serve only to ratify an already existing relationship of social forces. They would have agreed that the electorate has little to no control of its representatives, and that the electoral system serves only to perpetuate the passivity of the subordinate classes. They would have agreed that since only the legislative branch of government is elected, the power wielded by the state apparatus is well-nigh completely outside popular control.[20] Another marked area of overlap was indicated, deftly if in passing, by Georg Lukács in his book on Lenin, in a way that calls to mind what Marx had said in "On 'The Jewish Question' ":

> Many workers suffer from the illusion that a purely formal democracy, in which the voice of every citizen is equally valid, is the most suitable instrument for expressing and representing the interests of society taken as a whole. But this fails to take into account the simple—simple!— detail that men are not just abstract individuals, abstract citizens or isolated atoms within the totality of the state, but are always concrete human beings who occupy specific positions within social production, whose social being (and mediated through this whose thinking) is determined by this position. The pure democracy of bourgeois society excludes this mediation. It connects the naked and abstract individual directly with the totality of the state, which in this context appears equally abstract. The fundamentally formal character of pure democracy . . . is not merely an advantage for the bourgeoisie but is precisely the decisive condition of its class rule.[21]

This raises a point of some considerable importance, since Lukács, at moments like this, runs the risk of throwing out the baby with the bath water. Words like these could readily enough be put in the mouth of a fascist corporatist. Universal suffrage is not inherently bourgeois by nature. What is inherently bourgeois by nature is liberalism, which by no means admits of being equated with universal suffrage. Far from having run in tandem, far from having entailed each other, the two often existed at cross-purposes in nineteenth-century society, and came into frequent conflict even in the course of our own century. The links between democracy and socialism, links of which Marx was well aware, were anything but adventitious ones. It is hard to see how the "immense majority" Marx regarded as a necessary precondition for the socialist revolution could fail to translate into an electoral majority if universal suffrage were to be achieved, and as it was not achieved in most societies prior to Marx's death in 1883. It is in this sense that Marx's various observations on the possibility of a peaceful transition to socialism are to be understood.[22] Above all else, they are to be confused neither with a Leninist, nor yet with a Kautskian-Eurocommunist characterization of the hospitality of the existing state apparatus to the prospects of socialist transformation. Lenin reduces democratic freedoms and principles to their institutionalized class context. Eurocommunists effected the opposite reduction by treating democratic freedoms and principles as coterminous with parliamentary democracy, which is to deny the class character of the latter. Either way, as Jonas Pontusson points out, the distinction between democratic principles and the institutional framework of democracy gets lost.[23] It is likely that the influence of Gramsci, to whom this very distinction was perfectly clear, was fatefully downplayed during the Eurocommunist decade, as his iconic status was overplayed at the same time. It is certainly the case that the articulation of organs of direct democracy was deemphasized both by Carillo and by Georges Marchais in *Le défi démocratique*. In general, the "conciliar" theme that was so important to Gramsci was regarded as secondary or nugatory by orthodox Eurocommunists, who tended to treat organs of direct democracy as strictly local and auxiliary to parliamentary institutions. They also signally failed to heed Poulantzas's distinction between the state as the terrain of political conflict and the state as an institutional apparatus. Only if Gramsci's distinction between "political society" and "civil society" within the state, to which Poulantzas's distinction was meant to correspond, is respected will it make sense to speak about class struggle within the state without denying the class bias inherent in the structure of the state and within the unity of state power. This is the very bias that orthodox Eurocommunists took their cue from Kautsky in ignoring.

In the last analysis, Kautsky's much-heralded alternative to Leninism reveals a hidden, paradoxical parallel with Leninism, and one that a more nuanced, more open reading of Marx's state theory could have prevented. *State and Revolution*, as we have seen, ropes in a theory of the state, derived in its entirety from some of Marx's more extreme utterances, to do the work of a theory of transition, which is a different kind of theory, and was in any case left fatally untheorized by Marx. The incoherence of this maneuver can be seen not just in its practical outcome but also in its theoretical coordinates. It awards too little and too much to the state at the same time. Too little, because the specificity or relative autonomy of the state received inadequate attention. Too much, because this same state, an epiphenomenon that somehow becomes a demiurge, is then expected to sweep everything in society before it.

Kautsky, for his part, may be guilty of omission rather than commission. But in the end his guilt turns out to be not too dissimilar to Lenin's. Because he has no theory of the state—democracy understood in purely parliamentary terms takes us no further than "political emancipation"—Kautsky has no theory of transition either. This double lack enabled him to shift registers between the state and transition almost imperceptibly, or at least in a way that official Eurocommunist theoreticians, who were, ironically enough, obsessed with the state, signally failed to perceive. They failed to perceive it, to pile irony upon irony, because they had no desire to acknowledge their considerable debt to Kautsky in the first place. Lenin's assignment of "renegade" status evidently cast a long shadow, a longer shadow in a way than that cast by Eurocommunism itself. The Eurocommunists missed their chance. It is arguable, though this cannot be entered into here, that adequate theories of transition were readily available in the writings of Gramsci and Poulantzas, writings to which official Eurocommunists turned a blind eye or wilfully misrepresented.

State intervention in civil society, to a degree Marx himself probably never dreamed of, is today a fact of life. But this is no simple matter to analyze. On the one hand, the nature and structure of capitalist production necessitates state intervention. On the other hand capitalism, which is now well and truly international as well as national, can limit the scope and direction of such intervention. Here Marx can offer some help, since he recognized that capital accumulation is not a stable, regular, unproblematic process of linear growth, but a haphazard, contradictory hybrid, the successes of which produce what social scientists call dysfunctions, and what Marx preferred to call crises. Even defects in the market that are not the products of crisis tendencies—maldistribution, pollution—are going to confront the state as social problems demanding some form of solution. The solutions in question are singularly unlikely to proceed from the market or from civil society. They can only be the province of state action or public policy. The state as actor is constrained to respect the privileged position of capital as the source of investment, accumulation and wealth, wealth on which the state itself perforce depends. The state is at the same time constrained to remedy the problems of the capitalist market that are produced and reproduced as part of the accumulation process. Both Claus Offe and James O'Connor have pointed out the contradictions involved in these two strategies that "thwart and paralyze each other"; "the state must try to maintain or create the conditions in which profitable capital accumulation is possible. However, the state must also try to maintain or create the conditions for social harmony."[24] States these days must necessarily sustain a contradictory role. They must maintain the logic of capital accumulation, and at the same time they must legitimate themselves. These imperatives work at cross-purposes. The state depends on and sets the limits of capital accumulation. The latter task can be undertaken if and only if the underlying population accepts the prevailing form of legitimation. The state can succeed in facing in three directions at once only if private exchange-values, its own presupposition, are at least intermittently suspended in favor of public use-values. The state, for instance, must be prepared to pay the social costs of capital accumulation—pollution, ecocide, unemployment, workers' compensation for work-related industries, unemployment, homelessness, other forms of social and human degradation—whatever the capitalist classes may think about the matter. Habermas, Offe and O'Connor have all in their different ways indicated that capitalist states reproduce *as they offend against* exchange relations and the presuppositions of capital accumulation. States, that is, are in the nature of things contradictory unities.

Instrumentalist views of the state are of no use whatsoever in explaining or even in characterizing this inbuilt tension. The consequence of contradictory imperatives towards intervention is that, as Poulantzas foresaw, the state itself beomes the site of struggle over economic as well as distributional questions, questions for which there exist, and probably can exist, no formulaic answers. The state has to assume both a responsibility for those conditions of capitalism that cannot be secured through the operation of the market, and a responsibility to the electorate, or particular sections of the electorate, that may be adversely affected by the privileged position any capitalist state is perforce going to award the capital accumulation process. These are the elements involved in what is today commonly referred to, in a burgeoning literature about the state, as the state's "legitimation crisis," if we are to use Jürgen Habermas's formulation, or "governability crisis," if we are to use Offe's.

In the meantime, further attention needs to be paid to the setting in which these "crises" tend periodically to occur. The melancholy reflection is prompted by Marx's *Eighteenth Brumaire* that the "appalling parasitic body," the French "imperial" state in the middle of the last century, "with a host of officials numbering half a million," would amount to pretty small beer these days, and not just in France. It scarcely needs saying that one of the decisive contributions of our own century has been the attempt at well-nigh total expropriation of social functions by state-forms that are very bloated indeed, some of these being the very socialist states erected in Marx's name. It is no less obvious that such expropriation turned out to have limits, mainly because those state-forms that did the lion's share of it, and these include the socialist states, turned out to be failures simply on economic grounds, not to mention libertarian and humanitarian ones. Calls for reform in China and in the erstwhile Soviet Union can be read as admissions that the "socialist" program of utter expropriation had led to unexpected and disreputable consequences that needed urgently to be mitigated, even at the cost, as in Russia, of regime collapse. The question remains of how we are to interpret these developments. Not so very long ago, they would have been interpreted by some as the more or less straightforward triumph of a Weberian characterization of society over a Marxist or Marxian one. But I very much doubt whether so sanguine a defense of Weberianism could be mounted today. Harry Redner has recently suggested that these and other twentieth-century developments have had the effect of casting doubt on the continued validity of the Marx-Weber confrontation so beloved of social scientists, and that the coordinates of this confrontation no longer apply. "Weber's expectation that a vigorous entrepreneurial capitalism would keep itself independent of the state and would preserve opportunities for individual initiative and personal freedoms has . . . been falsified" every bit as much as some of Marx's expectations were. Capitalism can no longer sensibly be regarded in nineteenth-century terms as a "private" sphere, if what is understood by "private" is simply freedom from state control and supervision. States have expanded their functions and, whether they are democratic or not, reach further into their various civil societies these days. Capitalists are much more likely to cooperate and interact with specialist state agencies, or to infiltrate them, at any number of different levels than to seek to evade these agencies. In Redner's words, "a symbiotic relationship has grown up in many spheres of the economy between state agencies and business organizations and large corporations. . . . All this interaction is far from either extreme of wholesale expropriation or unfettered free enterprise."[25] But to conclude on this basis that Marx's theory of a different kind of state no longer has any application under present-day conditions would be peremptory and misleading. No matter how much the province of state action expands or contracts, private ownership of the means of production and private control of allocative resources are going to be maintained. In this more fundamental sense, capitalist civil society is just as "private" as ever it was, internationalization notwithstanding. And, in this fundamental sense, the coordinates of political emancipation apply just as much today as they did at earlier stages of capitalism. Far from having been overtaken by events and rendered inoperative, Marx's theory of the state, seen from the angle of alien politics, still has much to tell us. One can, of course, berate Marx for not having forseen the future lineaments of capitalist development, but to do so would be idle and, in a real sense, beside the point. Marx did forsee that relations of political authority are going to be kept separate, institutionally and conceptually, from productive relations, this separation being foundational and constitutive of capitalism. This, his main point, has lost none of its bite. The capitalist state has undergone several transformations in various directions—liberal, autocratic, democratic, Keynesian, post-Keynesian, welfare, antiwelfare—and bids fair to continue to do so. But its central defining feature has never been offended against and has remained sacrosanct throughout, so much so that in a significant sense it even managed to survive what once was considered the transition to communism.

The state today interacts with civil society, but only up to a point, a point Marx quite rightly regarded as foundational. It is for this reason, in large measure, that an older, and very non-Weberian notion of "corporatism," which can be detected *in nuce* in the very pages of Hegel's *Philosohy of Right* that gave the present book its starting point, revived itself for a while in social science scholarship. Here, as Roger King puts it, "the state is neither directive nor coupled to an autonomous private sphere, but is intermeshed with it in a complex way which undermines the traditional distinction between public and private."[26] This is true only of one sense of the word "private." It should therefore not be interpreted as meaning that the distinction between state and civil society no longer applies. It may no longer apply in the same way, but there is nothing surprising about this. Seen from the vantage point of alien politics, and not from the vantage point of ruling-class theories of the state, Hegel's original depiction of the state and civil society seems, if anything, to have stood the test of time remarkably well. It remains pointedly relevant to present day developments—which is at root why what went into the original Hegel-Marx confrontation on the state and civil society still deserves our attention.

The question remains: where would a specifically Marxist theorization of the state in its present form proceed? And what would a Marxist characterization of the modern state look like? The answer in large measure should already be apparent. One should proceed through the notions of "legitimation crisis" as adumbrated by Habermas, Offe and others, back to such notions as "hegmony" as "the most important face of power," as Gramsci so presciently termed it, and to Poulantzas's notion of the state as the relatively autonomous condensation of social forces, and to his idea of the "isolation effect." None of these notions relies in any substantive sense on outmoded or historically *dépassé* views of private and public realms as hermetically sealed compartmentalizations that do not involve or interact with each other. To the contrary, they come into their own as attempts to upgrade these distinctions and to bring them into line with changed, twentieth-century conditions. They help us see that the state is by no means above and beyond the realm of human practice and production, and that instead it is, these days, irretrievably imbricated within this realm; and they also help us see that the state is both the medium and the effect of political struggles, that it is "simultaneously a product, an object, and a determinant of class conflict."[27]

To take these in reverse order, the state is not an epiphenomenon of class conflict, the outcome or resultant of a geometrical play of social forces taking place outside its own boundaries and mysteriously ceasing to operate once these boundaries are traversed. Kautsky is an admittedly extreme touchstone indicating where this position can lead. The state's specificity as the *determinant*, not just of law and public policy but also, following Gramsci and Althusser, of social and national identity, has instead to be acknowledged. The state must also be characterized as the *object* of conflicts in civil society for these same reasons. We do not need to fetishize either class struggle, as Poulantzas sometimes did, or what I am terming the state as "object-state," to see that political and social organizations are going to seek to influence the state's processes and proceedings, or even to control or exercise some veto power over some of these. It would be simply unreal to suppose otherwise. It follows that the state should be seen as a process rather than as a thing, or as an object in the different, pejorative and reified sense of the term. It is in some sense a *product* of conflicts in society, but these conflicts are not about to cease at its gates. Instead, they are going to find a particular form of expression within its walls. Poulantzas, as we have seen, regarded the state as a "specific material condensation of a relationship of forces among classes and class fractions."[28] He sees the state not as a thing or as a *topos*, but as a series or system of institutions that are likely to change over time in response to pressures, pressures that might proceed from inside as well as from outside its machinery, and which are likely in their turn to be influenced by the structure and practices of the state against which they are exerted. As Poulantzas put it, "the state sets the limits within which the class struggle affects it: the play of its institutions allows and makes possible [its] relative autonomy from . . . dominant classes and fractions,"[29] much as Marx had suggested in *The Eighteenth Brumaire*.

Yet the *Brumaire*, as we have seen, is itself much more congruent with what I have termed alien politics, that is with the perception of the modern state as adumbrated in Marx's early writings, than it is with ruling-class, instrumentalist or functionalist theories of the state. And this in its turn suggests that alien politics is very much alive at a time when Leninist theories of the state fail to find much purchase. That people in advanced Western democracies *regard* politics as being in some sense "alien" to their everyday lives seems to be beyond dispute. One does not necessarily have to subscribe to the notion of "legitimation crisis" as proposed by Habermas, Offe and others to see this. Many citizens no longer appear to believe in what the state claims to stand for, or in the fundamental principles by which it justifies its authority. Large numbers of citizens no longer even try to exercize their hard-won rights to cast their votes in elections. Many, even among those who do vote, have become cynical or, arguably, just realistic about their representatives, and no longer believe that they or their interests *are* represented in any meaningful sense. People suspect, often quite rightly, that the crucial decisions taken supposedly on their behalf are made outside elected representative bodies or despite them. Fewer and fewer people trust the state as the sole guarantor of their basic liberties and rights. Gramsci was quite right in maintaining that the state can exact obedience, not, *pace* Weber, because of its monopolization of the means of violence but because of a process of culturation or indoctrination by which it influences the minds of its subjects through schooling, nonovert propaganda and what Althusser was to identify as "ideological state apparatuses." Whether we like it or not, the modern state has insinuated itself into society and managed to control society in ways that no premodern state ever did. It has at the same time taken itself for granted, as the monopolizer of the political. The state, because of its imbrication within civil society and the economy, has become a kind of "second nature."

What this means, if I am right, is that the twentieth-century shift in the relation of state and civil society has done nothing to dislodge alien politics from the position Marx presciently assigned it in 1843. Alien politics has by now in significant respects recharged itself over and over again. The concept of alien politics does much, in particular, to explain the recent intrusion of blatantly post- and anti-Keynesian regimes in the evolution of contemporary capitalism. Even though Marx developed the concept of alien politics to characterize the emergence of a certain kind of relationship between state and society, and even though this relationship is today in some respects surpassed, the distinction of private and public, and the privileging of the former over the latter, has endured. It has even, in the years since Poulantzas's death, managed to redefine itself. For these reasons alien politics, in an important sense, has become more pointedly relevant than ever more than a century after Marx's death.

Since the Second World War liberal-capitalist states have had more to do than simply represent the interests of the capitalist class, ensure the accumulation of capital and the reproduction of capitalist relations of production, and keep the lid on whatever social turmoil might ensue as a result. States, as Marxist theorists, to their credit, all too frequently came to acknowledge, had also to legitimate themselves in the eyes of their citizens. This they could do, not through the inaction implied by laissez-faire theories, but only by acting positively on and in society. Besides being anxious not to offend the electorate at large, states had to incorporate and integrate powerfully placed social classes, including the working class, and had to see to it that their demands and interests attained some degree of recognition and satisfaction.

With varying degrees of success, states endeavored to balance these demands according to the precepts of a broadly Keynesian postwar settlement. State management of the level of aggregate demand in the economy was geared to the maintenance of full employment. Increased social and welfare expenditures were traded against the promise of relative social harmony and industrial peace. The demands of producer groups, trade unions and employers' associations, were channeled, to an extent that was exaggerated by academics of a "corporatist" persuasion, through nonmarket political institutions that were designed as attempts to integrate the working class into the governmental process and thereby to contain industrial unrest and, by extension, class conflict.

There was a time, within living memory, when we, as citizens as well as theorists, had come to expect capitalist states to observe certain identifiable protocols. We had come to expect them to prefer compromise to conflict among contending producer groups. We had come to expect them to fashion welfare policies that, besides aiding the state in its task of macroeconomic management, would integrate the dispossessed into the polity rather than alienate them from it. We expected that states would forsake damagingly monetarist policies if beset by mounting unemployment. We expected states to implement wages policies or, more rarely, price restraint to offset inflation. We believed that states would shape macroeconomic policy to fit the contours of the business cycle. That these policies were in no way the "neutral" initiatives of a state seen as a beneficent, impartial arbiter should by now be evident. But this fairly obvious point is the least of it. My main concern is with a set of expectations we had come to entertain about the state, and it is accordingly a much more ominous one. It has taken the radical-right regimes of Ronald Reagan and Margaret Thatcher, which were committed to flying in the face of all these expectations, to show us how complacent we were in taking them for granted in the first place. Did not Marx more than a century ago chide the classical economists for treating then-existing social and economic relationships as though they were eternal, when in fact they were historical, that is, transitory and changeable? Should we not have done the same in our own day to those who argued for the permanence, or, with Offe for a while, the evolutionary logic of welfarism and the Keynesian settlement? What we overlooked was not just the possibility of economic downturn, a failure in civil society's capacity to reproduce itself that created an opening that radical-right regimes could exploit. Largely because we were in large measure blinded to what Marxist state theory in its fullest sense really comported, we also overlooked the ever-present possibility of a recrudescence of alien politics.

Full employment, social security, adequate unemployment insurance, maintenance of the "social wage," guaranteed free collective bargaining, the provision of decent levels of health, education and welfare—can we really still say that these areas of state action, these political aspects of the postwar Keynesian settlement, these struts and props of the political economy of the welfare state, are ineradicably inscribed in the logic of modern democratic politics? Have not all of them, not just in Britain or the United States, proved their vulnerability and reversibility? Today, they read like antiquated science fiction.

The central paradox of what Teresa Amott and Joel Krieger so aptly termed the "hyper-capitalist" regimes of Reagan and Thatcher is that they intervened "powerfully to restructure capital, alter the balance of class relations, and actively promote particular outcomes in the economy, while simultaneously posing as the champion[s] of state withdrawal."[30] These were, that is to say, strong regimes masquerading as weak, *dirigiste* regimes that stridently proclaimed their desire for weakness vis-à-vis their respective economies. They acted, not out of concern for the needs of any particular fraction of capital—indeed, the fragmentation of industrial and finance capital may well have reinforced the conditions that sustained their rule—but on the basis of their own, narrow, doctrinal, anachronistic and above all dogmatic panegyric on the virtues, moral and otherwise, of the free market.

The paradoxes here run deep. According to supply-side economists, the state must intervene drastically within civil society if it is to find, or create, its mythical "free market." Only a thoroughgoing alteration of tax policies, which are to be weighted away from capital, can release the required, if elusive, torrent of economic activity in a magically revitalized "private sector," which only then will no less magically revitalize the rest of us. The alchemists these days, if I may purloin a phrase from Marx, are those of reaction, not revolution. In the event this revitalization signally and unsurprisingly failed to work. In large measure it failed to work because it was not the outcome of pressure from civil society on the state. It was the state's revenge on civil society—and more pointedly, on those of us who have to live there. It has not yet run its course.

The sheer vengefulness of the hypercapitalist regime expresses rather than conceals a contradiction between its political practice and its ideological represenation of itself. The regime in its own estimation appears perilously close to what Marx attacked in the *Critique of the Gotha Program*. It sees itself as "an independent entity possessed of its own intellectual, ethical and libertarian bases."[31] As Marx pointed out in the *Eighteenth Brumaire*, once a regime's power of initiative comes to seem largely unimpaired by the wishes or demands of any one class, or any fraction of a class, it can proceed to claim to represent all classes and fractions, to represent society or the nation at large. More pointedly still, the regime can purport to embody all social interests and transmute or project them into a higher, "general" interest counterposed to civil society, and can do so even though, or precisely because, it was called into being in order to maintain and strengthen the existing social order, one based on the domination of labor by capital.

This at root is why hypercapitalist regimes, in Amott and Krieger's words "parade[d] the values of social cohesion and national unity, while [constructing] anti-integrative strategies which exacerbate class, racial and sexual divisions in society."[32] The sheer revanchism involved in the Falklands/Malvinas war, to say nothing of the Gulf War, together with attempts on the part of both hypercapitalist regimes to drum up public support for a recharging of the nuclear arms race, should, in the view I am outlining, be considered alongside, and as counterparts to, these regimes' frontal attacks on trade union, working-class, and welfare constituencies amid mounting, state-induced unemployment and homelessness. The now-surpassed Keynesian era, itself no utopia, was nevertheless characterized by various strategies that at least purported to be integrative. The articulation of sectional, corporate and class interests was not only enjoined but also encouraged by the state, both as a way of legitimating itself and as a means of alleviating people's subjection to the fortunes and vagaries of the market. To the extent that hypercapitalist regimes uncritically celebrate, indeed flaunt, the vagaries of the market and repudiate integrative strategies, their efforts are in the direction of depoliticization and disaggregation. They no longer need to acknowledge, but can dispense with, the power of organized labor, whose hard-won positions of access are no longer of much account. They freely introduce stark public policies that are designed to discipline and demoralize the working class and underclasses. And they proceed consciously to erode the egalitarian, universalistic claims and entitlements involved in postwar welfarism in favor of appeals for support that are fundamentalist, nationalist, chauvinist, denominational and racist.

These developments could not be more unwelcome. But faced with them, how can we not think of alien politics, of the instances Marx provides of the state's disjuncture from society in such a way that "bourgeois society . . . attains a development unexpected even by itself,"[33] of the state as an "abstract totality,"[34] superimposed upon a realm of private, self-interested activity, a realm that today is not just validated but actually recreated by the state itself? An already alien politics, not to put too fine a point upon it, is being realienated, and not for the first time. If alien politics reminds us that the estrangement of the state from society proceeds apace under the political guise of a supposed reconciliation or resolution of the split; that at the level of individual existence our political significance becomes detached from our private condition; and that citizenship and private life become mutually exclusive, how can we avoid concluding that these lines of division are being redrawn, and that they urgently need further theorization? I say this not resignedly, because theoretical retrenchment has become the order of the day. I say it because of the existence of a burgeoning social science literature on the state, much of which pays scant attention to Marxist state theory. I say it also because of my conviction that it remains relevent to the project of democratization, which is a more urgent project today because of the depradations of the Reagan-Thatcher years.

But if an intellectually valid Marxism it is to emerge, it must combat impatient summary dismissals of the kind that would tell us that the overthrow of Stalinism in Russia and Eastern Europe has discredited Marxism of any stripe once and for all, even as a method of inquiry. This is obviously not my belief. What was overthrown in the course of *perestroika, glasnost,* the aborted Russian coup, the "velvet revolution," and the annexation of East by West Germany, was a particular, highly repressive and unappealing form of Marxism, one that could well be regarded as scarcely worthy of the name. But no one could seriously claim that in a world like the one we inhabit even these regimes therefore monopolized repressiveness, domination, surveillance, technocracy, top-down control and other forces that are inimical to democratization. There are all too evidently motes in our own eyes too.

We are in particular entitled to our suspicion, occasioned if not caused by Marx's notions of alien politics and political emancipation, that the common epithet, "capitalist democracy" is an oxymoron. It is so at least in the sense that none of the recent defenders of this portmanteau term seem able to withstand the objection that the more capitalist a state is, the less democratic it is likely to be. Any number of distinguished political and social theorists, including Veblen, Hobson, Macpherson and Hayek, could be invoked in various ways in support of this point, though to do so here would take us too far afield. Capitalism from all appearances pulls in the direction of elitism, the free market and minority power, just as we might expect. Democracy points in another direction, staked out by equality, regulation and reform. It is true, in John Hoffman's words, that "for some time now liberals and even conservatives have taken to calling themselves democrats. But . . . we should view the democratic credentials of enthusiastic capitalists with a wary skepticism."[35] In the greater scheme of things, that is to say, the ultimate compatibility of democracy and capitalism is as at least as open a question as that between democracy and socialism. Can political institutions survive with their democratic credentials intact unless citizens begin to exercise some control over these same institutions, along with and not instead of institutions which govern their lives in civil society? The question is at the very least an open one. Whether political democracy will turn out to be brittle and precarious unless social institutions also acquire a more democratic hue, strikes me as being another, no less open question, and as one which Marx's prescient juxtaposition of political and human emancipation can help us resolve. Whether the much-trumpeted triumph of capitalism over communism will, by the same token, turn out to be a victory for democracy remains to be seen. "If the autocratic systems of rule which some Marxists felt they had to justify have been swept away by the movement towards democracy, why should we assume that logically problematic 'capitalist democracies' . . . will necessarily be spared the same fate?"[36] In assessing this question, which I take to be a good one, we must adopt a broad view. Jürgen Habermas recently made a telling point about the fall of European communism that is of great help.

> The presence of large masses gathering in squares and mobilizing in the streets managed, astoundingly, to disempower a regime that was armed to the teeth. It was, in other words, precisely the sort of spontaneous mass action that once provided so many revolutionary theorists with a model, but which had recently been presumed to be dead.[37]

In making this presumption we were overlooking what Norberto Bobbio rightly insists upon as the subversive nature of democracy.[38] As Anthony Giddens reminds us,

> the emergence of the "public sphere" in the American and French Revolutions, predicated in principle upon universal rights and liberties of the whole societal community, is as fundamental a disjunction in history as the commodification of labor and property to which Marx showed it to be intimately related. However asymmetrical they may have been in regard of the emergent capitalist class system, citizenship rights opened up new vistas of freedom and equality that Marxism itself seeks to radicalize[39]

—seeks, that is, to extend, not to deny. "Political" awaits its consummation in "human" emancipation, and why should not the fall of European communism remind us of this? Arnold Toynbee, looking back on the French and American Revolutions, gives us one kind of broad view.

> [T]he masses have now come alive to the possibility that their traditional way of life might be changed for the better and that this change might be brought about by their own action. This awakening of hope and

purpose in the hearts and minds of the hitherto depressed three-quarters of the world's population will . . . stand in retrospect as the epoch-making element of our age.[40]

It has not yet run its course.

CONCLUSION

I have argued above that both Lenin and Kautsky, in different ways and for different reasons, misinterpreted Marx's phillipic on the Paris Commune of 1871, *The Civil War in France*. Since Lenin and Kautsky were so different as theorists and political leaders, the question arises at this juncture whether *The Civil War in France* lends itself to misinterpretation. It may not be hard to knit together passages from *The Eighteenth Brumaire, The Civil War in France* and *The Critique of the Gotha Program* to show how these texts raise to the surface what I have called alien politics, something very different from and irreducible to the ruling-class theory within which it was long immersed. But I am unwilling to rest content with doing this, because the texts in question differ not just from other texts by Marx but also among themselves. *The Civil War in France,* in particular, proffers a scenario of revolution that differs in crucial respects from that put forward a few years later in *The Critique of the Gotha Program.* The latter emphasizes social and economic preconditions of emancipation which are unmentioned in *The Civil War in France,* where the emphasis is on struggle at the political level, and where transformation is a purely political process.

These two different emphases, which Marx presumably did not regard as incompatible, coexist uneasily in his projections for the future, not least because Marx's projections were few and far between.

However well judged Marx's reluctance to indulge in utopian speculation about the future may have been, it posed an acute interpretational
problem for his followers. We are never told how the social and
economic preconditions for transformation, on the one hand, and the
process of political transformation, on the other, are related. Attempts
to turn preconditions and process into successive "phases" of a single
revolutionary transition simply isolated them from each other all over
again, since no guarantee was proffered that they would or could be
coordinated over time. We are entitled to our suspicion that they are
not historical "phases" or stages at all, but products of an unresolved
theoretical tension.

If we lay this tension alongside Marx's more economic writings,
we notice something quite striking. While the concept of a new subject
of production, based not on top-down surveillance and control from
above but on the voluntary self-organization of the "assembled producers" from below is implied throughout Marx's economic writings, it
finds no place in *The Civil War in France*. Socialist revolution here, as
Andrew Feenberg reminds us, has to do with disalienation, but with
disalienation of the *state*. It is a purely political process. *The Civil War
in France* does not so much as mention the disalienation of productive
relationships. Instead, it characterizes the political leadership of a social
movement as "the political form, at last discovered, beneath which
to work out the economic emancipation of labor," as we have seen.
But the implications of this "political form" *for* the emancipation of
labor are anything but clear. Marx, in Feenberg's words, "seems to
have concluded that socialism's 'organizing activity' is radical democratic politics, and so leaves us in suspense as to what form of economic
and labor organization should replace capitalist practice."[1] If this is so,
it is Karl Marx and not Alfred Hitchcock who is the "master of
suspense." We have remained in suspense about this basic question
for well over a century by now.

This shortcoming has had serious and arguably fatal consequences.
It consists not in the lack of a theory of the state—the problem here,
if I am right, is that of too many theories of the state jostling about
uncomfortably in Marx's writings—but in the lack of a theory of the
transition to communism. So marked is this lack that all manner of

Marxist stalwarts took it upon themselves to rope in Marx's theory of the state to do the work of a theory of transition. Lenin was one of them. Marx, at least in *The Civil War in France*, was another. It may even be that Lenin's misappropriation of Marx's 1871 "Address" was an instance of highly selective, thus misplaced and monocular textual fidelity, rather than one of mendacious theoretical opportunism. In any event, Lenin duly effected the fateful slippage from the disalienation of the state outlined in 1871 to an already familiar, already sanctified ruling-class theory of the state. This slippage appears to have been effected all too easily. It no doubt seemed appropriate to Lenin and the Bolsheviks under the impress of events to make use of this composite theory of the state to do the work of a theory of transition. This shift, like many an ideological shift, no doubt appeared to make sense and to fit the political bill at the time it was effected. If the state is seen as an apparatus, an instrument, a mechanism for social transformation that lends itself more or less directly to use by those who happen to be manning its ramparts, the problem of transition may seem to be solved. It is solved, of course, rather too easily and mechanically. And, in any case, this supposed solution flies in the face of Marx's warnings, particularly the one admonishing us that "the working class cannot simply lay hold of the existing state machinery and wield it for its own purposes."[2] But the overarching remonstrance to be levelled here is that theories of the state and theories of transition are different *kinds* of theory. They are designed to answer different questions. To fail to keep these apart is to bequeath a kind of theoretical deadweight to future generations. That these will have trouble scrambling up from under it can be seen most recently in the parlous fate of Eurocommunism, in "official" versions of which transition at the state level was once again made to stand in for, and do the work of, transition at large.

But even the lack of a theory of transition is symptomatic of a more serious absence. There is in Marx's writings no antiauthoritarian strategy of resistance to work or productive relationships. It could be argued—there are intriguing hints of this in Gramsci—that democratization of work relationships is in principle simpler as well as more basic than democratization outside the factory gates.[3] We are, after all, in a position to know what the more finite world of the factory is *for*, while our sense of the purpose or end of political authority is bound to be much less direct, even if we identify ourselves as Aristotelians.

Small wonder, perhaps, that Marxism was derailed. It came to develop a void at its core, though not one that cannot in principle be filled. Instead of basing itself on the labor process and the organization of production, Marxism betrayed its own promise by turning its attention to ownership of the means of production, even to the extent of making the state the owner of these. Ownership of the means of production is but a part of what Marx had meant by "relations of production." But if the part is taken for the whole, the remedy to capitalism will appear as it has appeared, as nationalization of capitalist property by a state run in the presumed interests of (rather than by) the "immense majority." Public ownership will be asserted in principle, despite Marx's basic insight that under capitalist conditions ownership does not mean control—unless indeed this is understood as control of those persons manning the immediate productive process. Marx, under the influence of the Paris Commune, even forgot his own warning in the *Economic and Philosophic Manuscripts* about the state as "universal capitalist," along with his own distinction in, "On 'The Jewish Question'," between purely political and real, human emancipation.

The path was thus opened to Russian revolutionaries who wished simply to operate a productive apparatus inherited directly from capitalism, along with a state apparatus which, in crucial respects, predated the hothouse growth of capitalism in Russia. Once these found that experiments in workers' control reduced efficiency, they scotched the idea. They no longer considered adapting the conditions of production to new social requirements. Instead they reversed these priorities and repeated all the old mistakes in a new register. Leninism realienated alien politics in a revolutionary register. It did so, admittedly, under emergency conditions. But such conditions are likely to carry momentum beyond their own boundaries. Even in the absence of such conditions, even after the "council communism" period, Eduard Heimann was capable of producing the astounding assertion that "the introduction of factory councils had conceptually nothing to do with social-ization."[4]

By this point the damage is well and truly done, the critical oppor-tunity missed. Communist leaders came to subscribe to the imperative requirements of existing technology, the existing division of labor, the existing state, with a self-appointed, revolutionary, ruling class, claiming to represent the proletariat and the underlying population at large, at the helm. They defined capitalism not as a mode of production encompassing (social) relations as well as (technical) forces of produc-tion, but as a form of ownership that was in principle alienable. Author-itarian social control came to appear just as necessary to most commu-nists as it had to most capitalists before them. We can say of 1917 what A. J. P. Taylor said of that other purported *annus mirabilis*, 1848: that it was a turning point when history obdurately failed to turn. Our own decade, the 1990s, might well turn out to be another one. As I write, the democratization of once-communist societies stops at the factory gates. When the idols and monoliths were toppled, Marx's factory sign, NO ADMISSION EXCEPT ON BUSINESS, stayed right where it was. It still awaits its own consignment to the mausoleum.

While not all these developments were Marx's responsibility in any direct sense, it should by now be clear why I have sought to rescue Marx from Marx himself. He is responsible, perhaps by default, for having made these developments possible. But Marx is also responsible for providing us with a critical yardstick by which these developments can be judged, found wanting and changed for the better. This dual register of responsibility may seem ironical to some, but such, perhaps, is the cunning of reason. It should also be clear by now why alien politics, which provides us with the needed criterion, has lost none of its poignancy or pointedness a full century and a half after Marx first formulated it. Alien politics provides an Archimedean point from which both capitalism and communism can be critically appraised, and can be shown to have had rather more in common than avatars of either system were comfortable believing.

Capitalism means at the level of definition the separation of control over allocative resources from the orbit of those authority relations that connect the citizen to the state. As my introduction was at pains to point out, only these latter relations constitute political relations as capitalism understands the political. The history of twentieth-century communism demonstrates that to make the subject of revolution a political subject in this crimped and restricted sense is to alter nothing fundamental about the terms of the original, foundational separation. To alter political relations while leaving control over allocative resources untouched simply makes confusion worse confounded. It leaves the state under the control of a singular, monolithic, party apparatus, the singular heir-apparent of the operational autonomy, domination, control and surveillance won by the capitalist class and turned against the working population. In communist regimes the state as universal capitalist used repressive means to extract surplus-value from a sometimes cowed, sometimes defiant, but always unwilling and alienated working class. This was no mere rerun, however. The original capitalist division of labor was reproduced, to be sure, but with an ominous difference. Under capitalism, surveillance of the labor process and surveillance by the state of its citizenry were formally separate. They generally differed in scope and used different means. But this was much less true of communist systems. The reason why we cannot complacently breathe a sigh of relief at the passing of Soviet communism is that it may yet turn out to have been in this respect a grim presentiment of what is in store for us in the capitalist West: an osmosis of these two types of surveillance resulting from the use of the same kind of technology. On the one hand, the fact that such surveillance can scarcely appear "neutral," that technology, too, can disenfranchise people, separating them from the possibilities of common action, might appear to provide grounds for hope. But on the other hand, there are real dangers. Alien politics has in the past proved proactive, capable, that is to say, of charging and recharging itself from one register to another. There is no real reason to suppose that it will be incapable of doing so again, this time under technocratic auspices. Marxism, if it is to combat this unwelcome prospect, must be understood as I have endeavored to understand it, not just as an economic explanation and exposé of exploitation and crisis, but also as a political critique of domination and alienation.

NOTES

PREFACE

1. Anthony Giddens, *A Contemporary Critique of Historical Materialism, Vol. 1, Power, Property and the State*, Berkeley and Los Angeles, University of California Press, 1981, pp. 210–11.
2. Marx and Engels, *Collected Works,* New York, International Publishers, vol iii, p. 168
3. Marx and Engels, *Selected Works*, Moscow 1962, Vol i, pp. 521–2.

INTRODUCTION:
WHAT PRICE THE STATE?

1. Cambridge, MA, M.I.T. Press, 1992.
2. Anthony Giddens, *A Contemporary Critique of Historical Materialism*, vol. 1, *Power, Property and the State*, Berkeley and Los Angeles University of California Press, 1981, p. 187.
3. William E. Connolly, *Political Theory and Modernity* (Oxford, Blackwell, 1988), p. 134.
4. Andrew Feenberg, *Critical Theory of Technology* (New York and Oxford, Oxford University Press), 1991, pp. 43–4.
5. David Easton, "Political Science" in *International Encyclopaedia of the Social Sciences* (IESS) New York, Macmillan, 1968, Vol 12, pp. 283–4.
6. Morton H. Friedman, "State: The Institution," in IESS, Vol 15, p. 143.
7. John A. Hall, "The State," in William Outhwaite and Tom Bottomore, eds., *The Blackwell Dictionary of Twentieth Century Social Thought*, Oxford, Blackwell, 1993

p. 643. *Cf.* Hal Draper, *Karl Marx's Theory of Revolution*, vol. 1, *State and Bureaucracy* New York (Monthly Review Press, 1977), pp. 253 *ff.* for a remarkably similar characterization.

8. Theda Skocpol, *States and Social Revolutions. A Comparative Analysis of France, Russia and China* (Cambridge & New York, Cambridge University Press, 1979), p. 28.

9. Kenneth Dyson, *The State Tradition in Western Europe*, New York and Oxford (Oxford University Press, 1980), p. 104.

10. Bertell Ollman, *Dialectical Investigations* New York & London (Routledge, 1993), p. 89.

11. See Paul Thomas, "Critical Reception: Marx Then and Now" in Terrell Carver, ed., *The Cambridge Companion to Marx,* Cambridge and New York (Cambridge University Press, 1991), pp. 23–54.

12. Marx and Engels, *The German Ideology,* tr. Salo Ryazanskaya (London: Lawrence and Wishart, 1965), p. 36.

13. Giddens, *A Contemporary Critique of Historical Materialism*, p. 207.

14. Marx, *Early Writings*, T.B. Bottomore, ed., New York (McGraw-Hill, 1964), p. 85.

15. C. B. Macpherson, *The Real World of Democracy,* Oxford, (Clarendon Press, 1966) p. 9.

16. Marx and Engels, *Collected Works*, [henceforward MECW], vol. 3, New York, International Publishers, 1975), p. 29.

17. Marx to Arnold Ruge, May 1843, MECW, vol. iii, p. 137.

18. Martin Jay, *The Dialectical Imagination,* (Boston Little Brown 1973), p. 55.

19. Giddens, p. 238.

20. Marx, *Grundrisse*, Martin Nicolaus, ed. Harmondsworth, (Pelican, 1973), p. 111. *Cf.* Draper, p. 241.

21. Giddens, p. 213.

22. See Paul Thomas, *Karl Marx and the Anarchists,* Boston and London, RKP, 1980, esp. ch. 2, pp. 56–122.

CHAPTER 1
"THE STATE AS A FINISHED THING"

1. See Paul Thomas, *Karl Marx and the Anarchists* (London and Boston, Routledge, 1980), esp. ch. 2.

2. *Ibid.*; see also my "Alien Politics: A Marxian Perspective on Citizenship and Democracy," in Terence Ball and James Farr, eds., *After Marx,* Cambridge and New York (Cambridge University Press, 1984), pp. 124–40.

3. Shlomo Avineri, *The Social and Political Thought of Karl Marx,* Cambridge and New York, Cambridge University Press, 1968.

4. Marx and Engels, *Collected Works,* New York (International Publishers, 1975), (hence forward MECW) iii, p. 51.

5. MECW iii, p. 127.

6. MECW iii, p. 97.

7. MECW iii, p. 77.

8. MECW iii, p. 51.

9. MECW iii, p. 72.

10. MECW iii, p. 51.

11. MECW iii, p. 121.

12. MECW iii, p. 117.

13. MECW iii, p. 127.

14. MECW iii, p. 90.

15. MECW iii, p. 115.

16. G. W. F. Hegel, *The Philosophy of Right,* Knox T. M., ed. and tran. [henceforward PR], (Oxford, Clarendon Press, 1962), §303, p. 198.

17. MECW iii, p. 79.

18. PR §258A, p. 279.

19. MECW iii, p. 50.

20. MECW iii, p. 46.

21. MECW iii, p. 47.

22. MECW iii, p. 22.

23. MECW iii, pp. 45, 46.

24. Erica Sherover-Marcuse, *Emancipation and Consciousness,* Oxford (Blackwell, 1986), p. 20.

25. PR, §250, p. 152.

26. Marx and Engels, *Selected Works* (Moscow, Foreign Language Publishing House, 1962), vol. i, p. 44.

27. Sherover-Marcuse, *Emancipation and Consciousness. passim.*

28. MECW i, p. 262.

29. PR, §241, pp. 148–9.

30. MECW iii, p. 186.

31. MECW iii, p. 186.

32. MECW iii, pp. 186–7: emphases mine.

33. Alan Gilbert, *Marx's Politics* New Brunswick, N.J., (Rutgers University Press, 1981), p. 44.

CHAPTER 2
MARX AND HEGEL:
MEMORIES OF UNDERDEVELOPMENT

1. Marx, "The Prussian Counterrevolution and the Prussian Judiciary" in Marx, *On Revolution*, Saul Padover, ed. (New York, McGraw-Hill, 1970), p. 482.

2. G. W. F. Hegel, *The Philosophy of Right*, T.M. Knox, ed. (Oxford, Clarendon Press, 1962), [henceforward PR] § 273, p. 178.

3. PR § 21, pp. 29–30. See Joachim Ritter, *Hegel and the French Revolution. Essays on 'The Philosophy of Right'*, Richard Dien Winfield, trans., Cambridge, MA, MIT Press, 1982, *passim*.

4. Harold Mah, "The French Revolution and the Problem of German Modernity: Hegel, Heine and Marx", *New German Critique,* No 50, Spring–Summer 1990, p. 4.

5. Mah, *ibid*. See also G. W. H. Hegel, *The Philosophy of History,* trans. J. Sibree, New York, Dover Publications, 1956, p. 456, and J. E. Toews, *Hegelianism. The Path Toward Dialectical Humanism,* Cambridge and New York, Cambridge University Press, 1980, esp. ch 1, pp. 13–29.

6. Hegel, *Philosophy of History,* p. 447.

7. Toews, *Hegelianism,* p. 32.

8. See Mah, "French Revolution", p. 9.

9. This point is tightly emphasized by Man, "French Revolution" pp. 8–10.

10. Toews, p. 64.

11. MECW, vol. 3, p. 78.

12. Mah, p. 16.

13. MECW, vol. 3, p. 176.

14. MECW, vol. 3, p. 180. See also Mah, "French Revolution" pp. 16–20.

15. MECW, vol. 3, p. 183.

16. MECW, vol. 3, p. 183.

17. MECW, vol. 3, p. 176.

18. MECW, vol. 3, p. 183. See also Mah, pp. 17–8.

19. See Avineri, *Hegel's Theory of the Modern State* Cambridge and New York, Cambridge University Press, 1972, *passim*.

20. See Harold Mah, *The End of Philosophy and the Origin of "Ideology". Karl Marx and the Crisis of the Young Hegelians.* Berkeley and Los Angeles, University of California Press, 1987, p. 188; Paul Thomas, *Karl Marx and the Anarchists,* Boston and London, Routledge, 1980, pp. 62–3.

21. MECW iii, p. 183.

22. MECW iii, p. 176.

23. MECW iii p. 32.

24. MECW iii, p. 32; *cf.* p. 165.

25. MECW iii, p. 165.

26. MECW iii, p. 168.

27. MECW III, p. 32.

28. MECW iv, p. 117.

29. MECW iv, p. 117.

30. Marx and Engels, *The German Ideology,* Salo Ryanaskaya, trans., London, Lawrence and Wishart, 1965, p. 93.

31. MECW iii, pp. 153–4.

32. MECW iii, p. 174.

33. MECW, iv, p. 159.

34. MECW iii, p. 164.

35. MECW iii, p. 163.

36. MECW iv, p. 162.

37. MECW iv, pp. 120–1.

38. MECW iii, p. 168.

CHAPTER 3
"THE SABER, THE COWL, THE MUSKET":
MARX'S *BRUMAIRE*

1. See Ralph Miliband, "Marx and the State," in Miliband and John Saville, eds., *The Socialist Register, 1965,* New York, Monthly Review Press, 1965 pp. 278–96. This position is developed further in Miliband's subsequent writings, which are listed in my appendix, below, pp. 211–4.

2. Marx, *The Poverty of Philosophy. Response to 'The Philosophy of Poverty' of M. Proudhon,* New York, International Publishers, 1963, p. 174; Marx and Engels, *The German Ideology,* London, Lawrence and Wishart, 1965, p. 78; MECW, v, p. 90; MESW, ii, pp. 43, 44.

3. Marx and Engels, *The German Ideology*, Salo Ryazanskaya, ed. (London, Lawrence and Wishart, 1965), p. 45.

4. MESW, i, p. 142.

5. MESW i, pp. 189–90.

6. MESW i, p. 312.

7. MESW, i, pp. 331–2, 518. My interpretation of Marx's *Eighteenth Brumaire* is indebted to, and inspired by, Jerrold Siegel, *Marx's Fate. The Shape of a Life*, Princeton, N.J., Princeton University Press, 1978, pp. 201–16.

8. MESW i, p. 284.

9. MESW, i, pp. 284–5. See Richard N. Hunt's well-documented *The Political Ideas of Marx and Engels*, Pittsburgh, University of Pittsburgh Press, 1974, *passim.*, for further references to the "parasite-state" as a theme in Marx's writings.

10. MESW, i, p. 288.

11. MESW, i, p. 313.

12. MESW, i, p. 333.

13. MESW, i, p. 334.

14. MESW, i, p. 334.

15. MESW, i, pp. 340–1.

16. MESW, i, pp. 340–1.

17. MESW, i, p. 518.

18. MESW, i, pp. 343–4.

19. See Marshall Berman, *All That is Solid Melts into Air. The Experience of Modernity* Harmondsworth, Penguin, 1988, pp. 87–129. See also Jerrold Siegel, *Marx's Fate*, pp. 201–15.

20. MESW, i, pp. 521–2.

21. Shlomo Avineri, *The Social and Political Thought of Karl Marx*, Cambridge and New York, Cambridge University Press, 1968, p. 23.

22. MESW, i, pp. 516–7.

23. MESW, i, p. 333.

24. MESW, i, p. 516.

25. MESW, i, p. 520.

26. MESW, i, pp. 521–2.

27. *Archiv Marska i Engelsa, Moscow*, 1934, iii (viii), p. 314.

28. MESW, i, pp. 516–20.

29. Marx to Friedrich Bolte, 23 November 1871, in MESW, ii, pp. 466–7.

CHAPTER 4
THE STATE AS *TOPOS*:
LENIN AND GRAMSCI

1. Hannah Arendt, *On Revolution* (New York, Viking, 1963), p. 57; "Tradition in the Modern Age," in *Between Past and Future* (New York, Viking, 1961), p. 19. See also Horst Mewes, "On the Concept of Politics in the Early Work of Karl Marx", *Social Research,* 43, 1976, pp. 227–8.

2. E. M. Butler, *The Tyranny of Greece Over Germany,* Boston, Beacon Press, 1958.

3. Marx to Arnold Ruge, May 1843, New York, MECW, iii, p. 137.

4. *Marx and Engels on the Paris Commune,* Hal Draper, ed. New York *Monthly Review Press,* 1971, pp. 130, 221.

5. Marx Letter to Kugelmann, April 1871 in Draper, p. 221. See also Mewes, "On the Concept of Politics in the Early Works of Karl Marx," p. 278.

6. Marx *Frühe Schriften* (Stuttgart, Cotta Verlag, 1971), p. 235, quoted by Mewes, p. 279.

7. Marx and Engels, *Selected Works in One Volume* (New York, International Publishers, 1986), p. 325.

8. MESW ii, p. 325.

9. See J. Glenn Gray, *Hegel and Greek Thought* (New York: Harper and Row, 1968), *passim.*

10. See MECW, iii, pp. 30–31.

11. *Ibid.*

12. Engels to Bernstein in Marx and Engels, *Selected Correspondence,* Moscow, Progress Publishers, 1975, p. 350. 24 March 1884.

13. Terrell Carver, *Friedrich Engels. His Life and Thought,* London, Macmillan, 1989, p. 260.

14. Otto Kirchheimer, *Politics, Law and Social Change* (New York, Columbia University Press, 1969), p. 33.

15. Kirchheimer, p. 27.

16. Shlomo Avineri, *The Social and Political Thought of Karl Marx* (Cambridge, Cambridge University Press 1968), p. 204.

17. For a full checklist of the references to the dictatorship of the proletariat in Marx and Engels's writings, see Hal Draper, "Marx and the Dictatorship of the Proletariat," Cahiers de l'Institut de Science Economique Appliquée, Serie S, *Etudes de Marxologie* (Paris 1962), no. 6, pp. 5–73. See also M. Johnstone, "The Paris Commune and Marx's Dictatorship of the Proletariat," *The Massachusetts Review* (Summer 1971),

no. 3, pp. 447–62; and more generally Neil Harding, *Lenin's Political Thought*, vol. 2 (London, Macmillan, 1981), ch. 5.

18. Avineri, p. 206.

19. Kirchheimer, p. 28.

20. *Ibid.*

21. Kirchheimer, p. 29: see also Rosa Luxemburg, *The Russian Revolution and Leninism or Marxism* B. D. Wolfe, ed. (Ann Arbor, University of Michigan Press 1961), pp. 88–9.

22. A. J. Polan *Lenin and the End of Politics*, (Berkeley and Los Angeles, University of California Press, 1984), p. 7.

23. Polan, p. 57.

24. Polan, p. 140.

25. Neil Harding, *The State in Socialist Society*, (London Macmillan, 1984), pp. 13–4.

26. Harding, p. 15.

27. V. I. Lenin, *Collected Works,* (Moscow, 1964) vol. 25 [henceforward CW 25], p. 383.

28. Harding, p. 16.

29. Polan, p. 161.

30. CW, vol. 23, p. 117.

31. Polan, p. 164.

32. Bukharin, *Economics of the Transformation Period* (New York, International Publishers 1971), p. 41.

33. Harding, p. 16.

34. Bukharin, quoted in Harding, p. 17.

35. CW, vol. 24, p. 24n

36. CW, vol. 24, p. 170.

37. Polan , p. 59.

38. Polan, p. 68.

39. CW, vol. 25, pp. 426–7.

40. CW, vol. 26, pp. 108; CW, vol. 25, p. 430.

41. CW, vol. 25, p. 363.

42. Harding, pp. 27, 28.

43. Harding, p. 30.

44. Polan, p. 125.

45. Christine Buci-Glucksmann, *Gramsci and the State* David Fernbach, trans. (London, Lawrence and Wishart, 1980), p. 424 (n 13).

46. Gramsci, *Selections from the Prison Notebooks,* Quintin Hoare and Geoffrey Nowell-Smith, eds. (New York, International Publishers 1971), (henceforth SPN), p. 424, n. 13.

47. See Martin Clark, *Antonio Gramsci and the Revolution That Failed,* New Haven, CT., Yale University Press, 1977.

48. SPN, pp. 236–8.

49. *Cf.* Louis Althusser, "Ideology and Ideological State Apparatuses," in *Lenin and Philosophy* (London, 1971), p. 135n., for an extension of Gramsci's argument.

50. SPN, p. 238.

51. SPN, pp. 260–1.

52. Buci-Glucksmann, *Gramsci and the State,* p. 56.

53. Gramsci, quoted in Buci-Glucksmann, p. 56.

54. *Geschichte und Klassenbewusstsein*, Berlin, Der Malik Verlag, 1923, p. 271.

55. Gramsci, quoted by Clark, *Antonio Gramsci and the Revolution that Failed* p. 52.

56. Paul Piccone, "Gramsci's Hegelian Marxism," *Political Theory* (February 1974), p. 35.

57. SPN, p. 262.

58. Buci-Glucksmann, pp. 57–8.

59. *Letters from Prison*, p. 79, quoted in Buci-Glucksmann, p. 20.

60. *Socialismo ed Egemonia in Gramsci e Togliatti*, Bari, 1974, p. 111, quoted in Paul Piccone, *Italian Marxism* (Berkeley and Los Angeles, University of California Press, 1984), p. 197.

61. Gramsci, quoted in Neil McInnes, *The Western Marxists*, New York, Library Press, 1972, p. 146.

62. Piccone, *Italian Marxism*, p. 166.

63. Buci-Glucksmann, p. 453, n 17.

64. See, e.g., Buci-Glucksmann, p. 288.

65. "Class Intransigence and Italian History," *Selected Political Writings 1910–20*, pp. 39–40, quoted in Buci-Glucksmann, pp. 130–1.

CHAPTER 5
SUBJECT-STATE, OBJECT-STATE:
FROM GRAMSCI TO POULANTZAS

1. Boris Frankel, "On the State of the State. Marxist Theories of the State after Leninism," *Theory and Society* 7 (1979), p. 202.

2. Frankel, p. 203.

3. Nicos Poulantzas, *State, Power Socialism,* London, Verso, 1980. For the Miliband-Poulantzas debate, see Robin Blackbum, ed., *Ideology and Social Science,* London, Fontana Books, 1972, pp. 238–62. (Verso, 1980), p.136.

4. Jeffrey C. Isaac, *Power and Marxist Theory. A Realist View,* (Ithaca, Cornell University Press, 1987), p. 166.

5. Poulantzas *State, Power, Socialism,* pp. 166–7.

6. Poulantzas, *Political Power and Social Classes,* (London, Verso, 1973), p. 123.

7. *Political Power . . .* p. 214.

8. *Political Power . . .* p. 130.

9. Poulantzas, *Political Power . . .* p. 173.

10. Poulantzas, *State, Power, Socialism,* p. 66.

11. Ernesto Laclau and Chantal Mouffe, *Hegemony and Socialist Strategy. Towards a Radical Democratic Politics,* London, Verso, 1985, *passim.*

12. MECW, iii, pp. 30–31; Isaacs, p. 174 (n 68).

13. Poulantzas, *State, Power, Socialism,* p. 17.

14. Claus Offe and Volker Ronge, "Theses on the Theory of the State," *New German Critique,* 6 (Fall 1975), pp. 137–47, quoted in Isaacs, p. 179.

15. Charles Lindblom *Politics and Markets,* (New York, Harper and Row, 1977), p. 172.

16. Offe and Ronge, p. 142.

17. Adam Przeworski, "Proletariat into a Class: the Process of Class Formation from Karl Kautsky's 'The Class Struggle' to Recent Controversies," *Politics and Society,* 7 (1977), p. 350.

18. Adam Przeworski and John Sprague, *Paper Stones. A History of Electoral Socialism* (Chicago, University of Chicago Press, 1986) p. 47.

19. Przeworski and Sprague, pp. 8–10.

20. Marx, *"Critique of Hegel's "Philosophy of Right","* Joseph O'Malley, ed. (Cambridge and New York, Cambridge University Press, 1970), pp. 77–8.

21. Marx, *Capital* vol. I, trans. by Ben Fowkes; Harmondsworth, (Pelican, 1976) p. 280.

22. Poulantzas, *State, Power, Socialism,* p. 70.

23. *Ibid.,* pp. 72–3.

24. Gramsci, *Selections from the Prison Notebooks,* p. 246.

25. See *Political Power and Social Classes* (1973), pp. 108, 204, 275, 287–8, 299.

26. Poulantzas *Classes in Contemporary Capitalism* (London, Verso, 1975), pp. 165–74; *State, Power, Socialism* pp. 163–94.

27. Poulantzas, *Crisis of the Dictatorships* (London, New Left Books, 1976), pp. 134–62.

28. *State, Power, Socialism,* pp. 251–65; *Repères: hier et aujourd'hui—textes sur l'état* (Paris: Maspero, 1980), pp. 174–6.

29. *State, Power, Socialism*, pp. 263–4; "Political Parties and the Crisis of Marxism," *Marxism Today* (July 1979); "La crise des partis," *Le Monde Diplomatique* (28 September 1979); *Repères: hier et aujourd'hui* (Paris: Maspero, 1980), pp. 181–3, 200–1.

30. *State, Power, Socialism*, pp. 97, 115, 118–9; for a similar point of view, according to which, while the simplistic equation between anticapitalism and socialism has broken down, what has not broken down with it is the linkage between socialism and radical democracy, see Erik Olin Wright, *Classes,* London, New Left Books, 1985, pp. 287–8.

CHAPTER 6
THE STATE OF THE STATE:
KAUTSKY, EUROCOMMUNISM AND BEYOND

1. Massimo Salvadori, *Karl Kautsky and the Socialist Revolution, 1880–1938,* (London, New Left Books, 1979), p. 13.

2. Jules Townshend, "Reassessing Kautsky's Marxism," *Political Studies* (1989), xxxvii, p. 659.

3. Fernando Claudin, "Democracy and Dictatorship in Lenin and Kautsky," *New Left Review*, 106 (November–December 1977), p. 65.

4. But see Santiago Carillo, *Eurocommunism and the State,* London, Lawrence and Wishart, 1977, *passim.* for an exception to the rule of ostracism.

5. *Cf.* Jean Fabre, Lucien Sève, François Hinckler, *Les communistes et l'Etat* (Paris: Editions Sociales, 1977), pp. 44–5; Lucio Colletti, *From Rousseau to Lenin* (New York Monthly Review Press, 1974), pp. 45–108.

6. Jonas Pontusson, "Gramsci and Eurocommunism: A Comparative Analysis of Conceptions of Class Rule and Socialist Transition," Berkeley, California, *Berkeley Journal of Sociology*, xxv (1980), pp. 186–7.

7. Kautsky, *The Dictatorship of the Proletariat*, H. J. Stenning, trans. (Ann Arbor University of Michigan Press, 1969), *passim.*

8. Salvadori, p. 253.

9. Salvadori, pp. 35–7, 253–4.

10. Quoted in Salvadori, p. 93.

11. Salvadori, p. 37; emphases mine.

12. Pontusson, pp. 195–6.

13. Lenin, *Collected Works,* vol. 25, pp. 127–30.

14. See Lenin, *The Proletarian Revolution and the Renegade Kautsky*, in *Collected Works,* vol 28, Progress Publishers, Moscow, 1965, pp. 244–6; Claudin, pp. 67–8; Salvadori, p. 131.

15. See Berlinguer, "Réflections sur l'Italie après les événements du Chili," in Mariangela Bosi and Hugues Portelli, *Les P.C. espagnol, français, italien face au pouvoir* (Paris: Christian Bourgeois, 1976), p. 157.

16. Santiago Carillo, *Eurocommunism and the State*, chs. 2, 3, *passim*.

17. MESW, i, p. 516.

18. Gramsci, SPN, pp. 267–9.

19. "The Conquest of the State," in *Selected Political Writings*, 1921–26, trans. and ed. Quintin Hoare, London, Lawrence and Wishart, 1978, p. 76; *cf.* SPN pp. 192–5.

20. SPN, pp. 192–4, and, more generally, pp. 206–76.

21. Georg Lukács, *Lenin: A Study in the Unity of his Thought*, Nicholas Jacobs, trans. (Cambridge, MA, MIT Press, 1970), p. 65.

22. Marx, Amsterdam speech, MESW, ii, pp. 594–5. See also Paul Thomas, *Karl Marx and the Anarchists* (Routledge, 1980), *passim*.

23. Jonas Pontusson, "Gramsci and Eurocommunism: A Comparative Analysis of Conceptions of Class Rule and Socialist Transition," Berkeley, CA, *Berkeley Journal of Sociology* xxv (1980), p. 214.

24. Offe, " 'Crisis of Crisis Management': Elements of a Political Crisis Theory," in *Contradictions of the Welfare State* (Cambridge, MA MIT Press, 1984), p. 61; O'Connor, *The Fiscal Crisis of the State* (New York St Martin's Press, 1973) p. 76.

25. Harry Redner, "Beyond Marx-Weber: A Diversified and International Approach to the State," *Political Studies* (1990), xxxviii, pp. 641–2.

26. Roger King, *The State in Modern Society* (New Jersey: Chatham House Publications, 1986), p. 125.

27. Gösta Esping Andersen, Roger Friedland, and Erik Olin Wright, "Modes of Class Struggle and the Capitalist State," *Kapitalistate*, 4–5 (1976); see also Isaac, p. 184.

28. Poulantzas, *State, Power, Socialism*, p. 129.

29. Poulantzas, *Political Power and Social Classes*, p. 289.

30. Teresa Amott and Joel Krieger, "Thatcher and Reagan: State Theory and the 'Hypercapitalist Regime'," *New Political Science*, 8, p. 14.

31. MESW, ii, 1962, p. 32.

32. Amott and Krieger, p. 14.

33. MESW, i, 518.

34. MECW, iii, 205.

35. John Hoffman, "Capitalist Democracies and Democratic States: Oxymorons and Coherent Concepts," *Political Studies,* vol. xxxix (1991), p. 345.

36. Hoffman, pp. 348–9.

37. Jürgen Habermas, "What Does Socialism Mean Today?" *New Left Review*, 183, (September–October 1990), p. 7.

38. Norberto Bobbio, *Which Socialism?* Richard Bellamy, ed. (Minneapolis, University of Minnesota Press, 1987), pp. 73–7.

39. Giddens, *A Contemporary Critique of Historical Materialism*, p. 213.

40. Toynbee, quoted in Giddens, p. 213.

CONCLUSION

1. Andrew Feenberg, *Critical Theory of Technology* (New York and Oxford Oxford University Press, 1991), p. 47.

2. Marx, "The Civil War in France," in MESW i, p. 516.

3. But see Norberto Bobbio, *Which Socialism? Marxism, Socialism and Democracy*, Richard Bellamy, ed. (University of Minnesota, 1987), for a very different view.

4. Feenberg, p. 49.

APPENDIX: SECONDARY LITERATURE
ON MARXIST STATE THEORY

First, a note of caution. This book does not claim to be a fully comprehensive survey of Marxist state theory from Marx's day to our own, but a critical intervention within a series of debates that, as I write, are proceeding outside its covers. A fuller account would have said more about Luxemburg, Trotsky, Bernstein and a host of lesser luminaries. These are not unimportant figures for Marxist state theory. They are simply less important than others to the interpretation of Marxist state theory I am putting forward. I have excluded them, with regret, in the interests of brevity.

This guide to what has become a burgeoning and almost bewildering secondary literature is correspondingly selective. For more thoroughgoing bibliographies the reader is referred to Bob Jessop's *The Capitalist State* (New York, New York University Press 1982) and *State Theory: Putting Capitalist States in their Place* (Philadelphia, Penn State University Press, 1990). Here, I simply list and characterize those books (not articles) among a galaxy of secondary sources that are available in English, and are accessible, relevant and useful. I have included no straw men or Aunt Sallies, and for the most part, have not relisted works referred to in the footnotes.

On Marx, Richard N. Hunt's very well documented *The Political Ideas of Marx and Engels* (Pittsburg, University of Pittsburgh Press 1974) outlines a notion of the "parasite state" that overlaps with part of my argument about alien politics. Hunt argues convincingly against J. L. Talmon's *The Origins of Totalitarian Democracy* (London, Minerva Books 1961) that Marx does not belong in what Hunt calls a "tradition" of "totalitarian democracy" stretching from Rousseau to Lenin. But in excising Marx Hunt leaves this "tradition" itself intact, more intact, one could argue, than it ought to be. (My own *Karl Marx and the Anarchists* (London and Boston Routledge, 1980) also disputes the notion of Marx's supposed "authoritarianism," but does so on different grounds.) The "political ideas" of Marx and Engels turn, in Hunt's account, within the compass of ideas about revolutionary tactics rather than ideas about the state. This is not true of Hal Draper's *Karl Marx's Theory of Revolution* (New York, Monthly Review Press, 1977), the first volume of which, *State and Bureaucracy*, is a thorough investigation of Marx's theory of the state (the state as Caliban to capitalism's Prospero) that, like Hunt's, is vitiated by a determination to use Marx and Engels interchangeably. This is to do each of them a disservice (see Terrell Carver, *Friedrich Engels, His Life and Thought* (London and New York Macmillan, 1989), p. 257). John Ehrenberg's *The Dictatorship of the Proletariat* (New York and London, Routledge, 1991) goes Hunt and Draper one better (or worse) by treating Marx, Engels and Lenin in tandem. This approach differs from the one adopted here, and for that matter, from the approach adopted by Shlomo Avineri in his fine, pioneering study *The Social and Political Thought of Karl Marx* (Cambridge University Press, 1968). Avineri emphasizes the importance of Marx's early writings on the state, as well as Hegel's influence on Marx, which he sees as primarily philosophical (see Draper, vol. 1, p. 12). I see it as political in the first instance.

On Lenin, Neil Harding's *Lenin's Political Thought*, 2 vols. (London and New York Macmillan, 1977) remains unsurpassed. On Gramsci, Quintin Hoare and Geoffrey Nowell-Smith's introduction to *Selections from the Prison Notebooks of Antonio Gramsci* (London: Lawrence and Wishart, 1971) remains indispensable. Carl Boggs, *Gramsci's Marxism* (London, Pluto Press, 1976), Paul Piccone, *Italian Marxism* (Berkeley and Los Angeles, Univ. of California Press, 1983), and Anne Show-stack Sassoon, *Gramsci's Politics* (Minneapolis, Univ. of Minnesota Press, 1987), are all valuable surveys. Sassoon's contains a full Gramsci bibliography.

Of the other two twentieth-century theorists this book deals with, Kautsky and Poulantzas, it is the former, ironically enough, who is better served in the secondary literature, thanks almost entirely to Massimo Salvadori's *Karl Kautsky* (London NLB, 1979).

Bob Jessop's critical account of Poulantzas in *The Capitalist State*, like much else in this book, is rather tough going. Even so, *The Capitalist State*, which is thorough (arguably too thorough) is best considered alongside a more accessible recent survey, Martin Carnoy's *The State and Political Theory* (Stanford, CA., Stanford University Press 1984). Both Carnoy and Jessop seek to avoid monocausal, reductionist "explanations" of the state. It is almost alarming to discover, mostly in Jessop, how many of these there have been, how many dense theoretical thickets Jessop has laboriously to hack through in order to establish the relational nature of a capitalist state that has multiple boundaries and no institutional fixity. Sadly, Jessop, unlike Carnoy, dismisses Marx's early writings on the state as being "cast in a philosophical framework" (p. 7). I argue in this book, as Avineri did in his, for their importance. Had they become better known earlier in the twentieth century, we might have been spared some of the tangents Jessop so painstakingly takes it on himself to traverse. Carnoy's *The State and Political Theory* has a slightly different optic. It surveys post-Leninist state theory, liberal as well as Marxist, asking how each theory reacts to changes in the scope of state action since the heyday of liberalism. Carnoy criticizes class-based theories of the state without finally repudiating them. In general terms, much the same could be said of Eric Olin Wright's books, particularly *Class, Crisis and the State*, London, Verso, 1979 as well as Ralph Miliband's. To Miliband, in *The State in Capitalist Society* (London Quartet Books, 1969) and *Marxism and Politics* (New York Oxford University Press, 1977), as to Carnoy, the state, whose class coordinates are in one way or another to be stressed, must be able to separate itself routinely from segments of the ruling class, and act independently. Claus Offe argues against Miliband and Poulantzas that the state is not a capitalist state of the kind said to be determined by class power. Nor yet is it a "state in capitalist society," as Miliband understands the term, one which preserves its political power free from class interests. Rather, the state has its own interest in capital accumulation, which may nevertheless contradict people's needs and entitlements in society, for which the state must also provide. Offe's *Contradictions in the Welfare State* (London, Hutchinson, 1981) thus overlaps, not just with Jürgen Habermas's *Legitimation Crisis* (London Heinemann, 1976) but also with James O'Connor's *The Fiscal Crisis of the State* (New York St Martin's Press, 1973), and John Keane's *Public Life and Late Capitalism: Towards a Socialist Theory of Democracy* (Cambridge University Press, 1984) along with the same author's investigation of the political difficulties of Keynesian welfare states, *Democracy and Civil Society* (London, Verso, 1988). All these are themes that are picked up in the present book. It seems clear that they will be developed further elsewhere.

INDEX

Adorno, Theodor, 144
alien politics: authoritarianism and theories of transition to socialism, xvi; definition of, x; hypercapitalist regimes of radical right, 187; Leninism and realienation of, 194; Marx's theory of in On The Jewish Question, 82–85; and Marx's theory of the state, 24–25; Poulantzas on formulation of isolation effect, 149–50; resuscitation of Marx's theory of, 117–18; as theory of the state, x–xii, xiii; twentieth-century shift in relation of state and civil society, 183
Althusser, Louis, 181, 182
Amott, Teresa, 185, 186
Arato, Andrew, 2
Arendt, Hannah, 111, 117
Aristotle, 27
Auciello, Nicola, 138
authoritarianism: communism and social control, 195; impact of on theorists of alien politics, xvi, 163–64; Lenin's theory of the state, 124, 126
Avineri, Shlomo: on Hegel's theory of modern state, 64; Marx on bureaucracy and state power, 95; Marx's characterization of the proletariat, 31, 47; Marx on democracy versus authoritarianism,

36; Marx and Leninism, 121–22; philosophical interpretation of Marx-Hegel confrontation, 29

Bauer, Bruno, 72, 77, 81
Berlinguer, Enrico, 172
Berman, Marshall, 101, 102
Bernstein, Eduard, 171
Bobbio, Norberto, 189
Bonapartism: ruling-class theory and, 99, 104–105
Bukharin, Nikolay Ivanovich, 127–28, 129
bureaucracy: Marx's critique of Hegel on, 33–35, 39–40, 47; Marx on state power and, 95
Butler, Eliza Marion, 112

capital flight, 152
capitalism: history of twentieth-century communism, 195–96; Lenin's theory of the state, 126–27, 128, 129; Marxist scholarship on role of state intervention in, 141–64, 176–78; promotion of by the state, 3–4; and public-private polarity, 68–69; relationship of to democracy, 13–15, 188–89, 207n; relationship between state and civil society, xii–xiii, 2–3;